EDWARD ATIYAH

THE ARABS

—

PENGUIN BOOKS

Penguin Books Ltd, Harmondsworth, Middlesex

U.S.A.: Penguin Books Inc., 3300 Clipper Mill Road, Baltimore 11, Md

CANADA: Penguin Books (Canada) Ltd, 47 Green Street,
Saint Lambert, Montreal, P.Q.

AUSTRALIA: Penguin Books Pty Ltd, 762 Whitehorse Road,
Mitcham, Victoria

SOUTH AFRICA: Penguin Books (S.A.) Pty Ltd, Gibraltar House,
Regent Road, Sea Point, Cape Town

—

First published 1955

Made and printed in Great Britain
by R. & R. Clark Ltd
Edinburgh

CONTENTS

To
ALBERT HOURANI

INTRODUCTION

THERE are several points to be cleared up before a survey of the Arab peoples and their place in the world, past and present, can be intelligibly attempted.

The first is the different meanings which the word 'Arab' carries, and which are often a source of confusion to the Western reader, apart from exposing to unfavourable prejudice or romantic adulation Arabs who do not deserve either.

Originally, in Biblical and pre-Biblical times, the Arabs were a nomadic people inhabiting the Arabian Peninsula – a branch of the ancestral linguistic group that gave birth also to the Jews. Nomad Arabs are still to be found to-day, not only in the Arabian Peninsula itself, but also in Jordan, Syria, Iraq, and North Africa. They are known as *Bedu* or *Bedouin*, and their life has changed little since they first entered the records of history. They still roam the pathless desert on their camels, while the planes of the jet age fly above them. They live in tents of camel hair. Often they have to travel a day or two from the pastures on which their camels live to the nearest wells for the water without which neither they nor their camels can live, and which they carry back to their encampment in animal skins. They live a tribal life in which the fierce independence of the individual is ever struggling against the fetters of social discipline. Their code both permits the raiding of other tribes and imposes strict obligations of hospitality and sanctuary towards strangers.

It is these primitive people whom the word 'Arab' designates in its original sense. Even in the cities of the Arab world of to-day – Cairo or Khartoum, Damascus or Baghdad – the sedentary and civilized Arab is still apt to refer to the nomads as, specifically, 'the Arabs'. The writer remembers how, during the last war, the city merchants of the northern Sudan

– Arabs themselves – began to talk of the danger of *the Arabs* rushing in from the desert to loot if the Government forces withdrew before an Italian attack from Eritrea. Small wonder, then, that to many people in the West the word has only this designation and suggests camels, deserts, tents – if not exactly the *sheiks* whom Hollywood has from time to time attempted to bring to the screen in the person of a Rudolph Valentino or a Douglas Fairbanks. This primary meaning of the word has also been fixed in the Western mind in a manner which tends to equate nomads with all Arabs, by the writings of a school of distinguished British scholars and travellers – Burton, Doughty, T. E. Lawrence, Wilfrid Scawen Blunt, and others – who were fascinated by the desert and its people, and made them a subject of ardent study, if not romantic interpretation.

In the second place the word 'Arab' means the people of the Arabian Peninsula, or as some writers would call them 'the Arabians' – nomads and town-dwellers – who are all, more or less, of pure Arab race. In this sense the word is used to denote an ethnic group – the present-day Saudis, Yemenis, Kuwaitis, and other descendants of the original inhabitants of the Arab homeland. Here, in the Peninsula, there has not been much racial mixing. Such dilution of the original Arab stock as has taken place is the result of the importation into Arabia – particularly during the period of the Arab conquests – of wives and concubines from outside.

But in its most significant and common use to-day the word 'Arab' designates a culture group. It means all the peoples of the Arab world – namely, all that part of the Middle East and North Africa (in addition, of course, to Arabia itself) which was permanently Arabized by the Muslim-Arab conquests of the seventh and eighth centuries A.D. The process of Arabization was accomplished in three principal ways: (i) racial mixing by inter-marriage between the Arab conquerors and the peoples of the lands they conquered and settled in, (ii) the establishment of Arabic as the universal language of all the conquered countries, and (iii) the conversion of the vast majority of the population to Islam.

Racial mixing was, naturally, at its strongest in the countries on the fringe of the Arabian Peninsula (Palestine and Jordan) where the largest proportion of Arab emigrants made their home; but to a lesser degree it occurred in Iraq and Syria, in Egypt and the Sudan, and all along the North African littoral as far as Morocco. It is impossible to-day to determine the proportion of Arab blood in the racial stock of each of these countries; in most cases it is impossible for any individual to say to what extent, if any, he is descended from Arab ancestry. In the northern Sudan, for instance, the invading Arab tribes intermarried with the indigenous black population and produced a progeny which includes every shade of complexion from African ebony to the light brown tan of the Nejdi Arab; and every cast of features from the thick-lipped, snub-nosed negroid to the sharp, aquiline Semitic. Among the Egyptians, the Syrians, and the Lebanese the range of variety runs from black eyes and dark skins to sky-blue eyes, fair hair, and European features that may be the legacy of Graeco-Roman or Saxon Crusader ancestry.

Despite this uncertainty of racial origins, however, the peoples of the Arab world – a *bloc* of Arabic-speaking communities stretching continuously from the Persian Gulf in the east to the Atlantic in the west, and from Aleppo in the north to beyond Khartoum in the south – regard themselves as Arabs. They include the inhabitants of the Persian Gulf principalities, the Iraqis, the Yemenis, the Saudi Arabians, the Syrians, the Lebanese, the Palestinians and Jordanians, the Egyptians, the northern Sudanese, the Libyans, the Tunisians, the Algerians, and the Moroccans. In this immense area the proportion of nomads to sedentary population is very small, reaching its peak of 25 or 30 per cent in Saudi Arabia and sinking almost to nil in Egypt and the Lebanon. The large majority of the people are *fellahin*, or cultivators inhabiting the countryside; but a fair proportion live in ancient and famous cities – Aleppo, Damascus, Beirut, Cairo, Alexandria, Baghdad, Jerusalem, Tunis, Fez – that were once the centres of civilization, and where commerce and the crafts have flourished since the Arab conquest thirteen hundred years ago, if not since the days of Rome and Byzantium and even earlier.

The second point to make clear is that though Arabism and Islam are very subtly inter-related, and were indeed at the beginning coterminous (save for the Ghassanid and Hira pre-Islamic Christian Arab kingdoms) they are not so to-day. *Arab* does not always mean *Muslim*, nor does *Muslim* always mean *Arab*. Though Persia, for instance, was part of the Arab Empire, and has remained Muslim to this day, it never became Arabized, either in the sense of permanently adopting Arabic as its language, or in that of becoming racially mixed with the Arabs. Also, Islam made millions of converts in India, China, and the East Indies, without bringing them within the orbit of the Arab world or imparting to them the Arabic language. Even the Turks, the ultimate conquerors of the Arabs, were converted to Islam without being Arabized. Hence, we have to-day a number of large and important Asian states that are Muslim but not Arab. Apart from Persia and Turkey, they include Afghanistan, Pakistan, and Indonesia.

On the other hand, there are substantial Christian communities in the Arab world. Long before the advent of Islam, Arab settlements in southern Syria and Iraq (such as the Ghassanids and the people of Hira already mentioned) adopted Christianity; and it is possible that some of the present-day Christians of Lebanon, Palestine, and Iraq are descended from those early Christian Arabs, i.e. that they are Arabs by race and that Arabic has always been their mother tongue. Other Christian communities in the Arab world, such as the Copts in Egypt and the Maronites in the Lebanon, are not Arabs by race. Like many of their Muslim fellow-countrymen they were Arabized by conquest; but whereas the former accepted Islam as well as the Arabic language, the latter became Arab only in speech and general culture in so far as this did not conflict with their Christian faith. Yet so strong is the influence and pressure of a ruling majority that many of the pseudo-religious customs of the Muslims were perforce adopted by the small Christian minorities that survived among them. Thus, until twenty years ago, and though the ruling power in the land had ceased to be Muslim and become Christian (France), the Christian women of the inland towns of Homs and Hama in Syria went about veiled, like their Muslim sisters.

The largest concentrations of native Christian communities in the Arab world are to be found in Egypt (where the Copts number about a million and a quarter of the country's total population of twenty-two million) and in the Lebanon, where the million inhabitants of the country are almost equally divided between Christians and Muslims, and where Mount Lebanon itself (as distinct from the coastal cities and the plains of the interior) is predominantly Christian in population and social complexion. In Syria about 10 per cent of the population (of about three and a half million) are Christians. In Iraq there are ninety thousand Christians in a population of nearly five million. The Palestine Arab population, before its dispersal in 1948 when the state of Israel came into being, consisted of about a million and a quarter, of which nearly one hundred and twenty thousand were Christians. Most of these Palestine Christians are to-day to be found in the state of Jordan.

In the Arabian Peninsula itself there are no native Christian communities, it having been decided in the reign of the second Caliph, Omar, that the cradle of Islam should be inhabited only by Muslims. The small Christian (and Jewish) communities that lived in the Peninsula at that time were required to leave, but they were given land in which to make a new home in southern Syria. Also, in the countries of the western Arab world (i.e. Libya, Tunisia, Algeria, and Morocco) there are no Christian elements among the native population, though their absence here is not the result of any deliberate policy of exclusion.

As for the Churches to which these Christian Arabs belong, they reflect, in the main, the great schism between Rome and

Byzantium as well as some of the earlier and later divisions that broke up the unity of Christendom. The Coptic Church, for instance, is an offshoot of the Monophysite heresy of the fifth and sixth centuries, and is an independent organization under its own Patriarch, not subject either to Rome or to the Eastern (Greek) Orthodox Church. This last has many adherents in Egypt, Palestine (now Jordan), Lebanon, and Syria, and three of its four ancient Patriarchates are located in the Arab cities of Alexandria, Jerusalem, and Antioch, the fourth being in Constantinople. Its flock, however, is not as large as that of the Catholic Churches, which include, apart from the Roman Church, the Maronite, Greek Catholic, and other so-called 'Uniate' Churches, which entered into communion with Rome at some time or other, preserving a certain autonomy in linguistic and other matters of form. In the last hundred years or so small Protestant Churches (mainly Evangelical or Presbyterian) have come into being as a result of the activities of American and British missionaries, recruiting their adherents almost entirely from among the Greek Orthodox sect.

The survival of these Christian minorities in the Arab world is a tribute partly to the tolerance, partly to the sagacity of the Muslim conquerors. It refutes, in a practical manner, a fairly common belief that the Muslim invaders offered to the peoples they conquered the choice of Islam or the sword. This, indeed, was the choice offered to the pagans of the Arabian Peninsula; but to the People of the Book (Christians and Jews) and to the Zoroastrians in Persia there was added the third alternative of retaining their faith and paying tribute to the Caliph. The Christians who declined conversion were even allowed to remain under the jurisdiction of their Churches, whose heads were therefore accorded a quasi-political status by the Muslim rulers under what came to be known as the Millet (Sect) System.

True that even where these Christian minorities were of Arab race, they were treated as second-class citizens of the Arab Empire – tolerated but never accepted as equals by the

Muslims. On the other hand, new Muslims in the early days of Islam were not accepted as equals by the Arab believers unless they were of Arab race, and this despite the theoretical equality of all the faithful insisted upon by the Prophet. One had to be an Arab as well as a Muslim to occupy the highest station of all. But status was determined solely by the race and religion of the father. The son of a Muslim Arab was an aristocrat regardless of the race or religion of his mother (for Muslims were allowed to marry unconverted Christian or Jewish women), regardless even of whether the mother was a wife or a concubine.

In the course of the centuries the Christian Arab communities acquired, in the memorable phrase of Albert Hourani, 'the sad wisdom of minorities – the knowledge of how to survive'. For survive they did, and their attitude and status in the Arab countries of to-day will be discussed later in this book. Here let it suffice to remember their existence as an element of the Arab world throughout its history.

Lastly, a word as to Islam itself and its relationship with Judaism and Christianity. The God of the Muslims is the same as the God of the Jews and the Christians, but without the racial exclusiveness attributed to him by the former, or the intricate metaphysical theology woven about him by the latter. The Prophet Mohammed not only learned his monotheism from Jewish and Christian sources, but he also accepted and venerated Moses and Jesus as his forerunners, merely claiming to complete their message and be the last of the prophets. Many of the familiar stories and names of the Bible are to be found in the Koran; and it is indeed a moot point at what moment in his career Mohammed realized that he was not merely preaching Judaeo-Christian monotheism to the idolaters of the Arabian Peninsula, nor calling back the icon-ridden Byzantines from their debased Christianity to what he considered a purer form of it, but launching a new, independent, and conquering religion upon the world.

This religion was a theocracy as well as a creed, for Mohammed became a conqueror and a ruler in the course of fulfilling his prophetic mission. In Islam the realms of God and Caesar become one, instead of having separate jurisdictions, as allowed by Christ. Here, by providing a complete system of social legislation based on divine sanctions, Islam comes much nearer to Judaism than to Christianity. On the other hand, by definitely and persistently offering rewards and threatening punishments in a future life rather than in this one, and by delivering a universal rather than a tribal message, it follows the Christian eschatology and appeal rather than the Jewish; and though for the mass of believers its promised paradise is not of as spiritual and intangible a quality as the Christian heaven, the austerity of early Muslim life on earth was in many cases (and particularly as typified by the lives of the first two Caliphs, Abu Bakr and Omar) similar to the asceticism of the early Christians, sharing with it the same simple grandeur of the spirit and the same contempt for wealth and pomp which are born of a belief in eternal values.

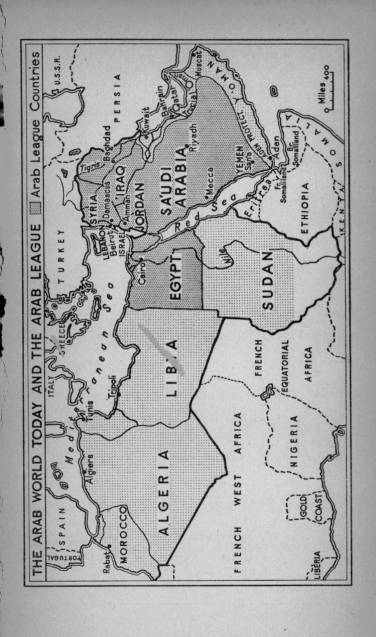

THE ARAB WORLD TODAY AND THE ARAB LEAGUE ░ Arab League Countries

U.S.S.R.

PERSIA

TURKEY

GREECE

ITALY

SPAIN

PORTUGAL

Mediterranean Sea

Tunis
Algiers

Tripoli

Rabat

MOROCCO

ALGERIA

LIBYA

FRENCH WEST AFRICA

GOLD COAST

LIBERIA

NIGERIA

FRENCH EQUATORIAL AFRICA

Baghdad
Tigris
IRAQ
SYRIA
Damascus
LEBANON
Beirut
ISRAEL
JORDAN
Amman
Cairo

EGYPT

Nile

SUDAN

Mecca
Riyadh

SAUDI ARABIA

Red Sea

YEMEN
Sana

ADEN PROTECT.
Aden
Br. Somaliland
Fr. Somaliland

ERITREA

ETHIOPIA

KENYA

Kuwait
Bahrain
Qatar
Trucial Oman
Muscat

OMAN

SOMALIA

0   400
Miles

The Arab Empire (c.80...

SPAIN
- Toledo
- Córdova

MOROCCO

Algiers

Mediterranean

Sardinia

Rome

Sicily
Syracuse

BYZANTINE

Constantinople

Crete

SAHARA

EGY...

N...

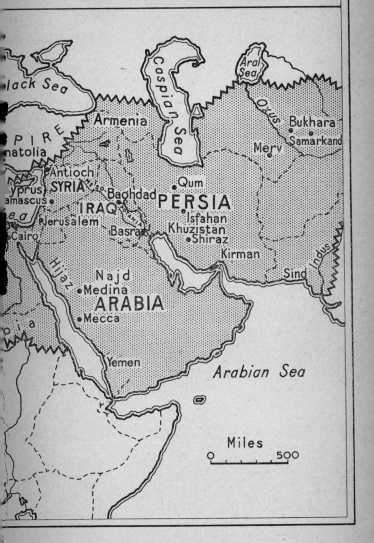

1,000 A.D) ⌇⌇⌇⌇ Limits of Conquests
                ----- Modern Frontiers

Black Sea

EMPIRE
Anatolia

Armenia

Caspian Sea

Aral Sea

Oxus

Bukhara
Samarkand

Merv

Antioch
SYRIA
Cyprus
Damascus

Baghdad
IRAQ

Jerusalem
ea
Cairo

Basra

Qum

PERSIA

Isfahan
Khuzistan
Shiraz

Kirman

Sind

Indus

Hijaz

Najd
Medina
ARABIA
Mecca

Yemen

Arabian Sea

bia

Miles
0   500

CHAPTER ONE

THE RISE AND FALL OF THE ARAB EMPIRE

I

THE forty-seventh chapter of Gibbon's *Decline and Fall of the Roman Empire* ends with the following paragraph :

While the emperor [Heraclius] triumphed at Constantinople or Jerusalem, an obscure town on the confines of Syria was pillaged by the Saracens, and they cut in pieces some troops who advanced to its relief: an ordinary and trifling occurrence, had it not been the prelude of a mighty revolution. These robbers were the apostles of Mahomet; their fanatic valour had emerged from the desert, and in the last eight years of his reign Heraclius lost to the Arabs the same provinces which he had rescued from the Persians.

This was how the Arabs entered history. They were projected into it, in an apparently casual manner through a back-door, by the genius of a man who had enthroned the One God where previously a number of pagan deities reigned, and who had compelled the turbulent and divided Bedouin tribes of the Peninsula to accept his rule as the prophet of that God.

Until this skirmish on the borders of the Byzantine Empire, the Arabs had made no deep or lasting impact on the world, nor had the world taken much notice of them. Early migrations into the countries now known as Jordan and Syria had resulted in the creation of the Nabatean kingdom with its capital at Petra, and of the kingdom of Palmyra. Both states, however, though of Arab origin, became to a large extent hellenized and adopted Aramaic as their language. The kingdom of the Nabateans was made a Roman province in the first century B.C., and Palmyra, under its famous queen, Zenobia (in Arabic, Zaynab), was also conquered by Rome some three centuries later. Later migrations established the border states of Ghassan in Syria and of Hira in Iraq, both of which adopted Christianity and survived, as vassals of Byzantium and Persia respectively, until the rise of Islam. From time to time the great powers of the world around Arabia – Egypt, Persia, Rome, Constantinople – claimed an unreal and passing suzerainty over the Peninsula. Only once did an expedition from outside (under a Roman consul) penetrate into the heart of the Arab homeland. On the other hand, an Arab from the border states sat on the throne of the Roman Empire in the third century A.D.

* * *

More than two thousand years before the rise of Islam another branch of the race from which the Arabs were descended had made an equally historic exit probably from the same Peninsula, thereby entering and shaping for ever after the course of human thought and action. The Christian realm itself which Mohammed's followers had now come out to raid was one of the creations resulting from that former Semitic incursion into the world outside Arabia.

While, however, the Hebrews endured their Egyptian and Babylonian captivities; while Moses led them through the desert and Solomon built the temple in Jerusalem; and even later while the Graeco-Roman world was being conquered by the message given to mankind by the offspring of the house of David that was born in Bethlehem, the Arabs had mainly remained in their homeland, pursuing their traditional life, outside the main stream of civilization. This life was polytheistic and, principally, nomadic. In the southern part of the Peninsula a substantial agricultural civilization had developed, but in the north only scanty agricultural populations subsisted here and there around the all too few wells and springs that softened the harshness of the land.

These settled communities lived in walled towns to protect themselves from the marauding Bedouins; and caravan routes developed between these towns and southern Syria. By the seventh century A.D. the foremost of these towns, Mecca and Medina, had attained a certain prosperity and a population of about fifteen or twenty thousand each, Mecca being slightly the larger of the two.

The chief significance of Mecca, however, was neither agricultural nor commercial but religious. The city was the centre of Arab polytheism – a place of pilgrimage, truce, and sanctuary amidst the warring tribes. The sanctuary was provided by the Kaaba, a small, square temple of black stones of great antiquity. A meteorite, connected by tradition with Abraham, formed its corner-stone and was regarded as the presiding deity that protected all the little tribal gods of the country around. There were months of truce during which tribal feuds were suspended and pilgrims flocked to Mecca to worship at the Kaaba and celebrate the holy armistice.

At a place called Okaz, some distance from Mecca, a market was held, and the chief form of celebration was the recitation of poetry – love-lyrics, elegies, poems in praise of some prince or patron, or of the poet's camel, tribe, and ancestors; or again, with extreme vainglorious licence, of the poet himself and his prowess. Rival masters competed for pre-eminence in what was becoming the Arabs' chief source of aesthetic and creative delight – the use of their language. The winning poets were acclaimed as laureates and their masterpieces were hung up on the walls of the Kaaba. Seven of these 'Suspended' poems, as they were called, have survived to the present day.

The importance of the development of the Arabic language to the stage it had reached by the time Mohammed appeared on the scene cannot be exaggerated. Arab civilization and the Arab Empire were the joint creation of the Muslim religion and the Arabic language. The double achievement could not have been realized but for the fact that the rough and primitive people of the Arabian desert were by the seventh century the possessors of one of the finest and most expressive forms of speech ever fashioned by the mind and tongue of man. Islam itself is unthinkable except in terms of the spoken Arabic word. For the Koran was delivered by Mohammed verbally, in verses which had the majestic rhythms and resonance of poetry and, sometimes, the imaginative beauty and power of its conceptions. Who shall say how successful the Arabian Prophet would have been in preaching his new faith if the instrument of its communication was not so accomplished, or if the minds and ears of the Arabs had not become, through their love and practice of poetry, so susceptible to the magic of language? Also, the Arabs' passion for poetry and recitation in an age when writing could not be widely practised led the desert people to rely prodigiously on their memories, learning long poems by heart and transmitting them orally from place to place and from generation to generation. This fact is quaintly illustrated in the story told of an Arab prince of the time who had a slave boy and a slave girl so gifted with memory that the boy could repeat any poem after hearing it once, and the girl after hearing it twice. The prince amused himself by proclaiming throughout the land that if any poet could recite before him a poem which neither his slave boy nor his slave girl had heard before, he would give him the weight of the parchment on which it was written in gold. Bard after bard responded to the challenge with an original composition, but no sooner would he finish reciting it than the slave boy would say, 'I have heard this poem before', and proceed to repeat it without a slip. To confound the poet still further the prince would then turn to the slave girl who, having heard the poem twice, would recite it as flawlessly as the boy. At last an astute poet presented himself and recited an endless poem consisting of meaningless tongue-twisters. When he finished, the prince turned to the boy, who shook his head with a despairing negative. The girl looked even more helpless. 'Well,' said the prince, 'it would seem that your poem is truly original. Therefore, bring forth the scroll that we may give you its weight in gold.' The poet answered, 'Your

Highness, I am a poor man and could not afford the price of parchment, so I inscribed my poem on a block of stone which is outside on my camel's back. Be so good as to order your servants to bring it in, for I alone could not carry it.'

It was this widespread practice of memorizing poetry that was largely responsible for the preservation of the Koran and its eventual commission to writing. For the Prophet would deliver the verses as the spirit moved him or occasion demanded, and his companions would memorize the words and not always write them down subsequently. Their assembling into a single book was not completed until the early years of the reign of the Caliph Omar (some four or five years after Mohammed's death), when every word that had ever emanated from the Prophet, in the way of revelation, was called for 'whether inscribed on date-leaves, shreds of leather, shoulder-blades, stony tablets, or *the hearts of men*'.

2

There were Jews in the Yemen and in Medina (mostly Arabs who had been converted to Judaism) as well as a number of Christian communities scattered about in polytheistic Arabia; and it was from these sources that the idea of Allah as the one God reached Mohammed while he was still a young man living with his grandfather (his father had died while he was a child), a member of the house of Hashem of the tribe of Qoraish in Mecca. It is also possible that he may have travelled in charge of the caravans of Khadija (the wealthy widow whom he subsequently married) to southern Syria. If he did go there and see Byzantine Christianity as it was practised, then he would seem, while accepting with increasing fervour and conviction the idea of the One God, to have been repelled by the excessive Mariolatry, Trinitarianism, and image worship which had come to be its chief features, and which to Mohammed seemed a retrogression towards paganism and polytheism.

Until he was forty years old the Prophet of Arabia lived a respectable but in no way distinguished life. Then commenced his astounding destiny with the preaching upon which he embarked among his relatives and friends. He soon made converts, and at first the ruling conservative aristocracy of Mecca did not object to his activities. It was only when the new faith began to threaten the position of Mecca as a centre of pilgrimage and the seat of a profitable cult for its citizens that the guardians of the Kaaba began to oppose the Prophet and his followers. The opposition was beginning to develop into persecution when Mohammed was invited by the Arabs of Medina to seek refuge with them and become their judge and lawgiver, they being divided into two factions that had exhausted themselves by mutual conflict and were glad to welcome a neutral arbitrator. The Prophet prepared the way for his own move by sending all his supporters to the new city in advance, with the exception of his father-in-law and closest adherent, Abu Bakr. With him he at last left Mecca on a night in A.D. 622. They were pursued, but by making a long detour and hiding for a while in some hills, where food and water had been stored for them in advance, they succeeded in making good their escape and reaching Medina. Thus began one of the great periods of human history – the Muslim era, dated from the year of the *Hijra*, meaning emigration.

In the following eleven years a large portion of the Arabian Peninsula, including Mecca, was converted to Islam and brought under the theocratic rule of the Prophet, whether by preaching, diplomacy, or the sword. With his own people and former enemies, the Meccans, the Prophet made a compromise. In return for their accepting Islam, he recognized the holiness of the Kaaba – taking his stand on the tradition that connected it with Abraham – and directed that all Muslims should turn their faces to it when praying, instead of to Jerusalem, as had been his rule till then.

The Koran, together with the precepts and practice of the Prophet, gave to Muslims the beliefs of their religion and the rules of the life it required them to lead. The beliefs were those of a simple, uncompromising monotheism, based on the Judaeo-Christian tradition but rejecting anything in it which tended, in Mohammed's view, towards paganism or polytheism, such as the divinity of Christ or the doctrine of the Trinity. Christ was accepted only as a prophet, and is, throughout the Koran, referred to as 'Jesus, son of Mary'. For the story of his Passion and crucifixion was substituted the belief that he was bodily raised to Heaven without dying, only 'seeming' to the spectators to have died on the Cross. The injustices of this world were to be redressed in the next. There was to be a resurrection and a Day of Judgement. Man, who had been given by God the power to choose between good and evil, would be called to account and treated according to the choice he had made. For the good – the true believers – there were the delights of Paradise; for the wicked, hell fire.

To become a Muslim all that one had to do was to 'testify', by reciting the words, 'I believe that there is no god but Allah, and that Mohammed is the Messenger of Allah.' This was the first of the so-called Five Pillars of Islam. The remaining four were the rules prescribing the religious duties to be performed by the Faithful: the five daily prayers; the annual fast – total abstinence from food and drink and sexual intercourse between dawn and sunset during the month of Ramadan; the pilgrimage to Mecca at least once in a lifetime, if within the means of the individual; the giving of alms to the poor.

In addition to these purely religious duties, Islamic law, or *Sharia*, as it developed out of the teachings and example of the Prophet, claimed to regulate all the aspects of life, ethical and social, and to embrace criminal as well as civil jurisdiction. Its origins are to be found in the judgements given by Mohammed himself when sitting as a judge in Medina, and which sometimes followed the usages of the Arab and Jewish tribes in the city, and sometimes expressed his own personal decisions. These decisions might be spontaneous or the application of principles and injunctions already enunciated in the Koran. Some examples of Sharia law may be given here, particularly from among those that indicate a connexion with the Mosaic law, or that came to have far-reaching social, economic, or artistic consequences in the development of Arab society. The eating of pork was prohibited, as were also gambling and the drinking of intoxicating liquors. Theft was punishable by the amputation of the thief's hand. A strict ban was imposed on the lending of money at interest, no matter at what rate, and on the representation of animals or the human figure in art, as a precaution against any lapse into idolatry.

After the Arabs' conquering exit from their Peninsula and the establishment of the Arab Empire in lands formerly under Byzantium or Persia, it was found increasingly impossible to enforce the rigid, theocratic Sharia as the universal civil and criminal law of the whole Muslim community. This community now included a diversity of sophisticated peoples with their own ancient laws and customs, many of which they were unwilling to relinquish despite their acceptance of Islam. The Muslim rulers found that Sharia was inadequate or unsuitable to the conditions of their new dominions. The view began to prevail that Sharia expressed an ideal which the imperfections of society often made it impossible to realize in all its purity. Later, under the Ottoman Empire and in the Arab states of to-day (with the exception of Saudi Arabia and Yemen) a system of secular law arose to replace Sharia in all criminal and civil jurisdiction save matters of marriage, divorce, and inheritance.

It was here, however, that the law of Mohammed produced some of its most enduring and in many ways damaging social consequences. Like the Jews and many Christian communities in ancient and medieval times, the Arabs had practised unrestricted polygamy before Islam, so that in allowing each man a maximum of four wives at any one time, the Prophet was bringing the practice under control and setting limits to it. Moreover, he made it a condition that the husband should treat his spouses equally, adding, 'And this ye cannot do' – a codicil which is interpreted by some progressive Muslims of to-day as meaning that, in fact, Mohammed pronounced against polygamy. However that may be, the Muslims accepted the permissive part of the law without unduly worrying about the qualifications with which it was hedged. Again, divorce was so easy for the man (being dependent only on his will and the payment of a certain sum of money) that though he might not have more than four wives simultaneously, he could, when his financial circumstances permitted, have any number in succession. Thus the Prophet's grandson al-Hassan, though he lived only forty-one years, had married and divorced one hundred wives by the time of his death. And besides legal wives a man could have any number of concubines. Of this legal liberality the Muslim Arabs were able to take the fullest advantage when they burst out of their Peninsula to conquer whole empires and capture thousands of women, who were distributed among the victors of the new faith as part of the spoils of war.

In these conditions, two of the most potent formative influences of Western civilization – the building up of the family as an equal partnership between the husband and the wife, in which the woman created a *home* for her men-folk, and the humanizing mixing of the sexes in social life – were excluded from Muslim society. Instead of the home there was the harem; instead of a balanced and complete social life in which women played a healthy active part (as indeed had been the case with the Arabs before Islam, and despite polygamy), there was the segregation of the sexes and the keeping of women in a degraded position, from which they did not begin to rise again till the present century. In defence of the Prophet and of Islam, it must be said that Mohammed never ordained the veiling or segregation of all women. He segregated his wives, but made it quite plain that this was on account of the special status of the wives of the Apostle of God, and was not to be taken as a precedent by other Muslims. His practice, nevertheless, came to be copied,

particularly in conjunction with the growth of concubin-
a e and conquest-swollen harems.

It is only just, however, to add that in some respects the
position of a married Muslim woman has always been
superi r to what the position of her English sister was before
the rece t legal emancipation of the latter. For the Muslim
wife was om the beginning allowed to hold property in
her own rig : and a fixed share of her husband's estate was
ensured to h in the event of his death. Indeed, in the
matter of inher ance, Sharia law tried to provide for every
member of the mily of a deceased person, by allotting
fixed shares not on to wives and children (a son had twice
the share of a daugh er), but also to fathers and mothers.
While the humanity o hese provisions must be admired, it
will be readily seen that they involved serious social and
economic dangers, since they led to the progressive fragmentation of inherited land into uneconomic units.

The injunctions against the representation of the animal or
human form in art exercised from time to time a restrictive
influence over Arab aesthetic expression and gave it a certain
orientation towards architecture and abstract design in
decoration. The restriction, however, was frequently evaded
from the earliest times, as witness Persian and Mogul art; and
in all the Arab and Muslim countries of to-day it has lapsed
completely. Even King Ibn Saud (who belonged to the puritanical Wahhabi sect that sought to restore the original purity
and theocracy of Islam) allowed himself to be photographed.
This relaxation of the original Sharia rule is due to the liberal
interpretation that the Prophet's injunction was only meant
to apply where idolatrous intention was present.

A liberal interpretation came also to be put on the pro-
nouncement against lending money at interest in order to
make possible the financial transactions necessary to the
commerce of a developing economy. According to this interpretation interest may be charged when the money loaned is
to be profitably employed and so increased. To this day,
however, devout Muslims still respect the command of the

Prophet in all its rigour, and one comes occasionally across the anomaly of a wealthy Egyptian or Syrian refusing to take any interest from the bank in which he has enormous deposits of money. The National Bank of Egypt had such a client not many years ago, to whom they used to present, at an annual tea-party, a silver tray worth a few pounds in token of their gratitude for the thousands he declined to accept.

3

When the Prophet died in the eleventh year of the Hijra he had become a temporal sovereign as well as the founder of a new religion. His religion, however, had no church and no priesthood. The only rock on which it was to stand, the only key to Heaven which its devotees were to have, was the Koran. It was a simple, practical religion, whose tenets did not involve the unattainable and were well within the grasp of the least tutored understanding. Mohammed's prophetic mission was strictly personal and must end with his life and the conclusion of the Koran. There had never, therefore, been any question of his nominating a spiritual successor. But it was different with the tremendous political powers he had acquired. The Arabs, as Muslims, had become a nation (though still only precariously held together) ruled by Mohammed, and would obviously need a new ruler to succeed him when he died. Mohammed had no male heirs, all his sons having died in childhood; and only one of his daughters – Fatima, wife of Ali who was one of his closest friends and earliest converts – was still alive when the Prophet lay sickening for death. In any case, kingship, or hereditary leadership, was unknown in Arabia. Among the tribes when a sheikh died, the most suitable of the elders was elected to succeed him. In the case of the Prophet it might have been expected that he would instruct his people whom they should select from among his companions to rule them when he was gone.

But he had not done so. He had, however, when he became too ill to lead the believers in prayer himself, asked his father-in-law, Abu Bakr, to take his place as Imam; and it was Abu Bakr who thus (after a moment of confusion, during which the people of Medina chose one of their own number to succeed Mohammed) was elected as first Caliph – or *Khalifa* in Arabic, meaning 'successor'. The fact that the Caliphs came to be known as 'Commanders of the Faithful' shows clearly the essentially temporal nature of the office; the Caliphs were rulers, not Popes, though as rulers of the Muslim state they were also the spritual heads of Islam.

Abu Bakr was an elderly man, but he combined an indomitable spirit with a saintly purity of faith; and it was due to his unfaltering resolve and ability to take great and risky decisions that Islam survived the shock of Mohammed's death and was firmly re-established and extended throughout the Peninsula after a moment of terrible danger during which it was rocked to its very foundations.

First, there was the stunning fact that Mohammed had died. Although the Prophet had scrupulously repudiated any supernatural qualities and always insisted that he was a man of mortal clay, his followers were dazed with incredulity when the news spread among them that Mohammed was no more. Omar, one of the pillars of the new faith (and later to become Caliph himself after Abu Bakr), would not accept the awful fact of his master's death, affirming, after he had seen the body, that the Prophet had merely swooned. It was then that Abu Bakr came out and addressed the people, saying: 'Whoso worshippeth Mohammed, let him know that Mohammed is dead; but whoso worshippeth God, let him know that God liveth and dieth not.'

On many of the Bedouin tribes converted and subjugated by Mohammed, Islam had sat lightly, in so far as their belief in it was concerned, and heavily, in regard to the discipline and duties it imposed upon them. Their impatience found an opportunity in the Prophet's death which, in their eyes, terminated the compact they had made with him. Apostasy and secession began therefore to spread among these volatile believers; while, encouraged by Mohammed's success, three rival prophets had appeared shortly before his death and were winning adherents in different parts of the Peninsula.

This was the situation that confronted Abu Bakr on his becoming Caliph. Yet his first action was to execute an order given by Mohammed shortly before he died, the effect of which was to deprive him of the services of a considerable body of reliable Muslim warriors. In an action fought three years before on the borders of Syria the Arabs had suffered heavy casualties, including Zeid, a close friend of the Prophet. In his last days Mohammed had ordered an expedition to proceed to the Syrian border, under Zeid's son, to avenge the martyrs of the former battle. The force was assembled ready to start when the Prophet died. Seeing the dangers that threatened the Faith on every side, many Muslims urged Abu Bakr to cancel the expedition. But the old man refused to countermand an order given by the Prophet, adding shrewdly that the apostates and the seceders would see in the dispatch of the expedition a sign of Muslim strength. So the expedition marched forth, and though it was no more than the raid mentioned by Gibbon it was significant in being the second thrust of the Muslim Arabs at the frontiers of the Byzantine realm, and a portent of things to come.

At home, Abu Bakr struck vigorously at the rival prophets and the seceders. In his hand he held *The Sword of God* – the name given later to the brilliant and conquering commander, Khaled ibn-al-Walid – so that his blows were swift and victorious. The new claimants to the prophetic office were destroyed, the apostates were beaten and reclaimed, the waverers remained on the side of the Faithful. Thus the second crisis of Islam was passed; in just one year after the Prophet's death the Muslims were finally and securely triumphant in the entire Arabian Peninsula, and the world lay before them to conquer.

This rapid recovery of Islam and the tremendous consequences that followed it have been interpreted as meaning

that Mohammed did not so much create a new movement as
stimulate and redirect the latent forces of an Arab national
revival and expansion already present when he appeared – an
urge among the Arabs towards unity and an aspiration to a
higher religious ideal than the primitive polytheism and
animism of the old order.

4

From times immemorial economic pressure had launched
upon the world one Semitic migration after another from the
deserts of the Arabian Peninsula. The Hebrews had gone out,
and the Canaanites and the Phoenicians, as well as the Arab
tribes that established the kingdoms of Palmyra and Petra, of
Ghassan and Hira and others still that occupied, as feudatories of Byzantium, the land between the desert and the
sown along the fringe of Arabia.

The Arab invasion of Persia and the Byzantine Empire
that began shortly after the death of Mohammed was fundamentally another of these outward surges of a population
that had become too numerous for the scanty resources of its
homeland. Islam provided the immediate occasion as well as
a new and powerful psychological equipment for making the
most of it: a sense of unity and common purpose, self-confidence and a *mystique* added to and transcending the
Bedouin's old love for war and loot. The pagan raider had
been willing to risk his life for purely earthly rewards; but
now Paradise awaited the believer if he fell in battle. There
was no risk, but only a greater prize to win! However, it has
been pointed out, in support of the theory that the invasion
was essentially an expansion of the Arab nation and not of
Islam, that the chief commanders of the conquering host –
Khaled ibn-al-Walid and Amr ibn-al-Aas – were first and
foremost worldly warriors whose faith was of a somewhat
formal and opportunist character, and that very few crusad-
ing believers took part in the early campaigns.

Nor were the conquests, for the most part, planned by the Caliphs and executed in pursuance of a deliberate policy. There was, in fact, little design behind them. They followed, in a haphazard way, from the subjugation of the seceding tribes by Khaled. It was not so much that the conquest of the Peninsula spilled over the northern borders to become a world conquest. It was rather that the Peninsula itself could not have been completely conquered and permanently won for Islam but for the unifying stimulus and attractions of foreign war. Instead of continuing to attack one another, the Arab tribes launched themselves, as a united force, against the great world outside the Peninsula.

This great world was dominated by the Sasanid Persian Empire in the east, and the Byzantine Empire, based on Constantinople, in the west. Both these giants suffered from serious internal weaknesses, in addition to having exhausted one another in mutual war over a period of three centuries. The Byzantine Empire was Greek in culture and Christian in religion, but the heresies of the fifth century which had flourished in Syria and Egypt (and been persecuted by the Greek Orthodox power in Constantinople) had left the Aramaic population of the former and the Coptic population of the latter bitterly resentful of the Imperial government. In both provinces heavy taxation added to the discontent of the people. Nor was Christianity itself, whether orthodox or heretical, the living force it had once been. Divisions, abstruse theological controversies, and the worship of images had drained away much of its spiritual vitality. Persia, too (whose official religion was Zoroastrianism), had its heresies and divisions. Its old feudal structure had been destroyed in a violent convulsion, and the empire that the Arabs were about to attack was ruled by a stern military despotism. In southern Iraq the Persians had a disaffected Semitic province, crushed by harsh taxation. Similarly, the Byzantine Arab feudatories in southern Syria were resentful at the discontinuance of a subsidy they had formerly received from the Byzantine Emperor.

These are some of the logical reasons that help to explain the amazing success of the Arabs when they flung themselves at these two apparently mighty empires. Yet, as in many of the great events of history, there is something that transcends logic in the victory of a primitive desert host against the established governments, the trained armies, the fortified cities of the two principal powers of the seventh-century world.

On the positive side, the assets of the Arabs included three major factors: (i) the high morale of a new nation inspired by a new faith, especially when after its first few victories it knew itself to be a David facing a vulnerable Goliath, (ii) the genius of their two chief commanders, Khaled and Amr, whose dazzling campaigns in Syria, Iraq, and Egypt are worthy to stand beside the greatest military achievements of Napoleon or Alexander, (iii) their use of new tactics and of a strategy admirably suited to the medium through which they moved to attack their enemies – the trackless desert. Their tactics included an effective use of cavalry, which the Romans and Byzantines had never learned, while in their strategy the camel played a very important part carrying troops across large distances in a comparatively short time, so that they could appear at some decisive point unexpectedly and completely transform a situation – as when Khaled, in response to an appeal from the Arabs attacking Damascus, struck across from Iraq and in a few days arrived outside the city with the needed reinforcements. Professor Bernard Lewis compares the use made by the Arabs of the desert to that made by the British of the sea. The desert was the Arabs' natural element; they knew their way about it, whereas their enemies did not. They could emerge suddenly from its wastes to deliver an attack; they could vanish into them as suddenly to elude pursuit. The towns in which they established their power in their conquered territories were often strategic settlements on the fringe of the desert – the equivalent of Gibraltar and Malta and Singapore in British history.

5

The triumphant exodus from the Peninsula received a great stimulus from the reports that soon began to arrive of the fabulous wealth that was to be found in Syria and Iraq. Here were the luxuries of old civilizations – conquests and spoils beyond anything the penurious Bedouins had ever dreamed of; and all the booty captured – women, money, jewellery, sumptuous clothes, and fabrics – was distributed among the warriors after each battle, except for the fifth that was sent to the Caliph in Medina. No wonder that, as these reports spread, more and more fighters flocked to join the forces of the Faithful. Whole tribes, including the women and children, left the Peninsula. Estimates of numbers must naturally be very tentative, but it is believed that within twelve years of the Prophet's death half a million Arabs had emigrated, and that before long this number must have doubled and trebled.

The great conquests outside the Peninsula began during the short reign of Abu Bakr (632–4), but it was during the ten years of Omar's Caliphate that they reached their apogee in the final defeat of the Persian Chosroes and the Byzantine Kaiser by the Commander of the Faithful. The Persian Empire was completely destroyed and, together with its feudatory province, Iraq, was occupied by the Arabs. The Byzantine Empire survived in Constantinople and Anatolia, but Syria and Egypt were (with the acquiescence of their Christian populations who found the Muslims more tolerant than the Greeks) wrested from its grasp. Such ancient and famous cities as Damascus, Jerusalem, and Alexandria fell into the hands of the desert warriors.

Omar ibn-al-Khattab, the Caliph whose armies accomplished these wonders, is one of the greatest figures in Muslim or Arab history. In his time, the Caliphate, apart from its temporal conquests, reached its spiritual zenith as a noble, concentrated, and universally accepted theocracy. His successor, Othman, was altogether a man of inferior clay, and under the fourth Caliph, Ali (the Prophet's son-in-law), began the great schism which has divided Islam ever since, while with the Umayyads the Caliphate became really a secular monarchy.

Despite his triumph over the two greatest rulers of the contemporary world, Omar retained the austerity and simplicity of his early life. When he came to Jerusalem to receive its official capitulation, he entered it riding on a camel, wearing a coarse woollen shirt, and accompanied by only one attendant. Awaiting him were the Arab commanders, who had already been sufficiently seduced by the civilization they had conquered as to array themselves in gorgeous silken garments. It is said that Omar was so angry at this display of worldliness that he picked up a handful of earth and threw it at the costly robes that confronted him. It is also told that when the Patriarch invited him to pray in the church of the Holy Sepulchre, Omar declined on the grounds that were he to do so, the Muslims might use the occasion as a precedent to dispossess the Christians of the church and convert it into a mosque. The glorifications of Muslim legend have made of Omar the hero of many incidents exemplifying, above all, his unbending sense of justice. Allowing, however, for all apocryphal exaggeration, it is impossible not to see in Mohammed's second successor a man of lofty moral stature as well as a great ruler.

Apart from the territorial expansion of the Muslim-Arab nation that took place under the rule of Omar – an expansion that made of the desert people and their religion a world power – the second Caliph is responsible for two events of special significance. It was he who, during the reign of Abu Bakr, had realized, as a result of the death in battle of many of its memorizers, the necessity of committing the Koran to writing and assembling it into a single book. The task was begun forthwith, and the first compilation was completed in the reign of Omar, though this was superseded by a later compilation, made in the reign of his successor, as the official text.

The other event was worldly, not religious; and though falling far short of the permanent recording of the Koran in importance, it had a great historical significance in establishing the character and status of the Arab conquerors in the early days of their empire. This was the registration of all Arabs and the allocation to each (in accordance with his or her claim as determined by certain criteria) of an annual pension from the spoils of conquest and imperial revenue. Thus the Arabs became a subsidized military caste, and remained so until the growth of the empire and the processes of procreation and racial mixing had gone so far as to make the continuance of this practice impossible.

A defamatory legend concerning the Arab capture of Alexandria gained credence in the Western world at a subsequent date but has, since the day of Gibbon, been exposed as a fabrication. This was to the effect that the priceless library of Alexandria was consigned to the flames by the Arab commander acting under the orders of the Caliph, who took the view that the books were either in accord with the teachings of the Koran, in which case they were superfluous, or were in conflict with the Koran, in which case they were wicked. The grounds on which modern scholarship has rejected this story are that the famous library of Alexandria had ceased to exist long before the Arabs conquered Egypt, having been destroyed by two accidental fires, the first of which occurred when Julius Caesar was fighting in the city. The ascription of its destruction to the Muslim Arabs by a deliberate act and on the bigoted grounds invented in the legend is an example of the prejudice which has often distorted the Christian view of Islam.

6

The pristine theocracy of Islam and the Arab Empire may be said to have come to an end when Ali (the last of the four so-called Orthodox Caliphs) left Medina in 656 for Iraq to join battle with a rival party of Muslims who disputed his title to the succession. With this move Medina ceased for ever to be the capital of the Arab Empire; for no Caliph ever again had his seat in the city that had given the Prophet refuge, fostered Islam as a community under his rule, and sent out the first conquering armies to attack Byzantium and Persia. Arab power had moved out of the Peninsula, which henceforth was relegated to a secondary position, politically and militarily, in relation to the empire that was being created outside it. In this expanding empire (and while Mecca and Medina retained their spiritual primacy) one city after another became the seat of government and the centre of civilization – al-Kufa, Damascus, Baghdad, Cordova, Tunis, and Cairo.

Ali's exit from Medina had another and a less happy significance. For it was the first time that Muslims went forth to fight Muslims. Out of this conflict arose that basic division of the Muslim world which has endured to this day between *Sunni* (meaning in a certain sense 'orthodox') and *Shia* (meaning 'partisans', i.e. of Ali).

The great majority are Sunni Muslims, though the Shia are preponderant in Iraq and are represented in the populations of most of the Arab countries. The Fatimid dynasty that established itself in Egypt in the eleventh century belonged to this sect.

It was in Damascus, under the Umayyad dynasty founded by the Caliph Muawiya in 659, that the Arabs established their first centralized, secular state, retaining the basic structure of government and administration bequeathed them by the Byzantine Empire, but superimposing on it the Arab settlers as a ruling caste, and binding the Arabs themselves in a common allegiance to the Caliph as their temporal lord, if not quite yet their monarch.

The Arabs, already subsidized by the decree of the Caliph Omar, lived apart at first, as a military aristocracy, holding aloof from trade, farming, or manual crafts. Far from pressing their faith on the Christians or Jews around them, they preferred to leave them outside the Muslim community so that they might get enough money from them, by way of tribute, to keep the state treasury well replenished and help to pay their own fixed stipends. The Muslims themselves had to pay certain taxes, but these were considerably lower than those required from non-Muslims. This fact, together with the prestige of belonging to the religion of the ruling caste, rather than any active proselytizing on the part of the Arabs, caused increasing numbers of Christians and Jews to embrace Islam. This, indeed, led to such serious financial consequences – since it is obvious that the productive, tribute-paying population cannot be allowed to fall below a certain level where there is a subsidized non-productive ruling class – that state action was taken to discourage conversion. The chief measure resorted to was the fiction that in the matter of land tax it was the land on which tax was levied and not its owner, so that all converts to Islam after a certain date were required to pay the higher non-Muslim rate of tax on their property.

Nor, as we have seen, did conversion to Islam at first place the non-Arab Muslim on a footing of equality with the Arabs. The blurring of the frontiers between Arab and non-Arab, the emergence of a community that was partly Arabized by racial mixing and completely Arabized in regard to language did not take place till some time later. The polygamy and extensive concubinage practised by the Arab conquerors, though it led to many social evils, was a powerful factor in the Arabizing of the conquered lands, particularly since Islam did not debar the Arabs from marrying even unconverted Christian and Jewish women, and the sons of an Arab father stood on a footing of equality regardless of the status or religion of the mother.

It was in Syria under the Umayyads, too, that that great flowering of culture, known as Arab or Muslim civilization, began – a culture which, for the next five hundred years, was to spread, in harvest after harvest, throughout western Asia, north Africa, and Spain, giving light to the Middle Ages, contributing to thirteenth-century scholasticism in Europe, and sowing some of the seeds of the Renaissance long before the Greek scholars fled westwards from Constantinople on its capture by the Ottoman Turks. This may therefore be a convenient moment to make clear the sense in which this mixed civilization of many sources may be legitimately called 'Arab'.

For mixed it certainly was in a very wide sense, both in regard to its materials and to the race, religion, and geographical environment of the thinkers, scientists, and artists who collaborated in creating it out of these materials. From their Peninsula the Arabs brought two great contributions: Islam and the Arabic language, together with their code of desert chivalry. They also brought the psychological stimulus of their impact, as a vigorous conquering people, on the stagnant, if more civilized inhabitants of the outside world. In this world there was Greek philosophy, Roman ideas of law and government, Byzantine and Persian art, Christian theology, and the Judaic tradition. Arab civilization was a product of all these factors. Among the men who fashioned it and produced its masterpieces in the various fields, many (often the majority) were not Arabs, but Byzantine Syrians, Persians, Jews, and men of other races. To those who see in Islam the unifying principle of this civilization, and therefore prefer to call it 'Muslim' rather than 'Arab', it may be pointed out that in one of its most fertile periods (the early Abbasid days in Baghdad) Christians and Jews played a prominent part in all the creative and communicative (by translation from the Greek or Syriac) activity that produced the learning and culture of the new universal society. These Christians and Jews had adopted Arabic as their language. They wrote in it; they translated into it. Arabic became the new language of the new civilization, the medium of thought in it, the instrument of law and administration.

This, then, is one sense in which the medieval civilization of western Asia, north Africa, and Spain may be called 'Arab'. Another sense is that it came into being as a result of Arab conquests, under Arab patronage, within a political and social system established by the Arabs. Thus the Arabs created the conditions for the new civilization and brought together the various sources out of which it developed. Of course, all the populations of the Arab Empire (with the exception of small Christian and Jewish minorities) were Muslim; and Islamic thought, whether expressed in law, theology, or mysticism, played a fundamental part in directing their thought and shaping their life. Yet Islam itself, it must not be forgotten, came from the Arabs and was propagated by Arab arms.

7

In 750 the rule of the Umayyads came to an end. They were supplanted by the Abbasids (descended from an uncle of the Prophet called al-Abbas); and the centre of the Arab Empire moved from Syria to Iraq, from Damascus to Baghdad, the legendary metropolis of the *Arabian Nights*, where Harun al-Rashid held his court. Unlike Damascus, Baghdad was not an old city with a pre-established life and culture of its own. The Abbasids themselves built it on the site of an old village, and the life and culture that sprang up in it were entirely its own, though their sources came from other places and older ages.

Several important changes occurred in Arab history as a result of this change of dynasty and capital. Just as the move of Ali out of Medina at an earlier time and the seizure of power by the Umayyads had brought to an end the period of Muslim theocracy, so the accession of the Abbasids destroyed for ever the political unity of the Arab Empire under one Caliph. A member of the House of Umayya, escaping the massacre of his kin by their supplanters, made his way to Spain (where Arab power had been established since 711) and there set up a new state that did not recognize the authority of the Caliphs of Baghdad, and whose own rulers came eventually to adopt for themselves the title of Caliph. That was the first step in the process of fragmentation to which the Arab Empire was to be subjected, even while it was still expanding and conquering – a process that was to lead in later centuries to a considerable shifting and division of the ruling power, as dynasty succeeded dynasty and capital capital, until once again unity was imposed on the Arab world, from above this time, by the Ottoman Turks in the sixteenth century; though by then, of course, the Arabs had lost Spain.

A second important result of the supersession of Damascus by Baghdad was the flowing into Arab life and thought of a rich stream of Persian cultural influence. Whereas in Damascus the main immediate impact on the Arabs had been Byzantine, in Baghdad it was Persian and even (via Persia) Indian. This was the case at least in regard to contemporary environment, social intercourse, and the enterprise of living thinkers and artists. It is necessary to bear this qualification in mind, for as regards past thought, a new and tremendous Western current began to flow into Arab thought side by side with Persian influence. This was Greek philosophy, science, and mathematics as translated into Arabic from the original or, more frequently, from the intermediate Syriac, under the enlightened and munificent patronage of the Abbasids in Baghdad.

It was in Baghdad, too, that the Arabs finally ceased to be a subsidized ruling caste, living apart from the population. Indeed the revolution that raised the Abbasids to power was essentially one against the racialism of the Arab aristocracy of the Umayyad regime. Among the elements that collaborated in bringing it about were not only the non-Arab converts to Islam, but also Arabs from the southern part of the Peninsula who were not accepted as full equals by the aristocracy from the north. Hence, there arose in Baghdad a mixed urban society presenting the features of a homogeneous culture-group. A fundamental change also took place in the very nature of the Caliphate and the government based on it. No longer depending on the support of a racial caste, the Caliph became now much more of a personal autocrat, surrounded by pomp, imposing his will through a salaried and cosmopolitan bureaucracy and a trained, professional army.

42

Even before the end of Umayyad rule the Arabs had reached India, but the move of their capital to Baghdad, which lay along the main trade routes to central Asia, made it easier for them to continue their expansion eastwards, both politically and commercially. Here, in central Asia, the Arabs first met the Turks, with whom their destiny was to link them, in one form or another, until 1918. These first Turks the Arabs came in contact with were the Seljuq branch of the Turkish race, as distinct from the Ottomans who in the sixteenth century conquered not only the whole Arab world (with the exception of Morocco and some parts of the Arabian Peninsula) but also Byzantium itself which had held out successfully against the Arabs.

At first the Seljuqs were imported into Baghdad as individuals either captured in war or purchased in the slave markets. It is this fact that led to their being later known as *Mamluks* (meaning 'owned'), even when as a military caste they seized power and founded a dynasty that ruled Egypt for many centuries. Their military qualities caused their Arab masters to make use of them in the army, where they soon became a sort of pretorian guard. It was not long, however, before whole tribes of them migrated into Iraq, nor much longer before they became the real rulers of the eastern Arab world centring on Baghdad, where the Abbasid Caliph was retained merely as a figurehead, the Seljuq monarchs taking the title of 'Sultan'.

Meanwhile, a third Caliphate, causing a further division of the Arab empire, rose to power in north Africa and Egypt in the tenth century; and, being of the Shia persuasion, became known as the Fatimids or Fatimites, after Fatima, the Prophet's daughter and wife of Ali, through whose descendants alone Mohammed's blood had survived. Their rule was ended by the famous Saladin (Salah-ad-Din al-Ayyubi), a Kurdish officer who, beginning his career under Seljuq rule in Mosul in the twelfth century, rose to prominence in Egypt and eventually founded a powerful state comprising Syria and Egypt, and a dynasty called, after him, the 'Ayyubids', which was later overthrown by the Mamluks.

The rise of Saladin to power was closely associated with the Crusades. It was, in fact, part of the vigorous Muslim reaction to this Western Christian challenge. The eleventh century saw the first serious reassertion of the will of the European Christians against the Arab-Muslim Empire that had stretched out to the gates of Constantinople in the east, and stood established a short way from the Pyrenees (which it had actually crossed for a while at the end of its expansionist phase) in the west. In 1085 Toledo fell to the Spanish Christians, while, ten years later, the first Crusade set out to recapture the holy places of Christendom in Palestine. As with the Arab conquests in the early days of Islam, other motives, in addition to religious fervour, impelled this Christian venture, namely the commercial hopes and enterprise of the Italian cities, the need to find an occupation for the younger sons of the feudal nobility, and the fact that a common effort against a foreign enemy was an effective way of putting an end to local baronial wars in Europe.

For two centuries Syria, Palestine, and even Egypt were subjected to sporadic invasions from Europe and, in parts, to a fairly lengthy occupation. Thus, the Latin kingdom of Jerusalem lasted nearly one hundred years, and even after its termination the Crusaders continued to hold a number of fortified coastal districts in Lebanon and Syria for a considerable time.

But the Crusades did not inflict any permanent damage on the structure of the Arab Empire, or cause any radical change in its character. A more devastating experience was the Mongol invasions which started under Jenghis Khan and culminated in the capture and destruction of Baghdad in 1258 by Hulagu, who had the nominal Abbasid Caliph executed. From that time until the advent of the Ottoman Turks in the sixteenth century, Iraq was incorporated in a Mongol empire centred on Persia. The Mongols, however, like the Seljuqs before them and the Ottomans after them, embraced Islam, just as the Goths had embraced the Christianity of Rome.

Syria and Egypt were saved from the fate that overtook Iraq by the Mamluk ruler, Baybars, who inflicted a decisive defeat on the Mongols in northern Syria. Subsequently, the Mamluks invited an Abbasid to assume the Caliphate in Cairo. The historic office was thus revived, but it had no more reality here than it had had under Seljuq rule in Baghdad.

Meanwhile the process of splintering continued in north Africa; but the greatest reverse that the Arabs suffered was in Spain. For here a whole country that had for many centuries been a part of the Arab Empire and a centre of Arab civilization was eventually won back by the European Christians. Cordova, the most fruitful and splendid source of this civilization in the west, was captured in 1236, and Granada in 1492. Not only did sovereign power pass out of the hands of the Arabs, but the country itself ceased to be Arab or Muslim. The Arab-Berber tide that had begun to overrun it in 709 was rolled back completely into its original source in north Africa eight centuries after its northward crossing of the straits of Gibraltar, and the farthest limit of the Arab world in the west was henceforth the Atlantic coast of Morocco. A similar reverse befell the Arabs in Sicily.

It was not, however, until the occupation of Cairo by the Ottoman Sultan, Selim I, in 1517, that the Arab community finally fell into slumber. All the Arab lands (except Morocco which remained a separate sultanate, and Nejd which retained a more or less continuous independence under its emirs in the heart of the Arabian Peninsula) were incorporated in the Ottoman Empire. Everywhere the Arabs and the Arabized peoples lost the position of rulers, the seat of power became Constantinople – or, as the Turks called it, Istanbul – and the title of Caliph was eventually assumed by the Ottoman Sultans. It was not till the nineteenth century that the Arab world began to stir with a new cultural life and with new political aspirations; it was not till the twentieth century that these aspirations began to receive satisfaction.

The swift decline and fall of Arab dominion and Arab

civilization have never yet been fully explained. Break-up
and stagnation followed advance and efflorescence with be-
wildering rapidity, and many of the explanations offered do
no more than beg the fundamental question. Among these
explanations are the early divisions that destroyed the unity
of the Arab Empire, such as the great schism between Sunni
and Shia Muslims and the subsequent fragmentation of the
Caliphate which began with the secession of Spain under the
Umayyads when the Abbasids overthrew the former in the
east. But one is inevitably tempted to go back still farther and
ask if there was, inherent in the Arab character and the Arab
tradition, any specific force that militated against sustained
unity. When the great Arab historian and sociologist, Ibn
Khaldun, retired to his native Tunis towards the end of the
fourteenth century to meditate upon the decay of Arab
society, he propounded the theory that 'generally speaking
the Arabs are incapable of founding an empire except on
a religious basis such as the Revelation of a Prophet or a
Saint ... because their fierce character, pride, roughness, and
jealousy of one another, especially in political matters, make
them the most difficult of peoples to lead, since their wishes
concord only rarely', and also because 'every Arab regards
himself as worthy to rule, and it is rare to find one of them
submitting willingly to another, be it his father or his brother
or the head of his clan, but only grudgingly.' Ibn Khaldun
here was using the word *Arab* to designate the Bedouin tribes
of the Arabian Peninsula, but it is certainly open to question
whether the extreme and turbulent individualism of the
desert inhabitants did not, despite the discipline of Islam,
impart strong centrifugal tendencies to the whole Arab Empire, and remain the basic social weakness of Arabs even after
centuries of settled life in fusion with other races. To this day
one finds a startling topical relevance in the words of Ibn
Khaldun. The stubborn individualism and unwillingness to
accept the leadership of another, which he described so elo-
quently six centuries ago, is still present in all Arab communities, sedentary as well as nomad, Christian as well as

Muslim. The faith of Mohammed and the rewards and exultation of early conquests helped for a time to hold these disruptive forces in check and made possible the establishment of the Umayyad Empire from the Pyrenees to the confines of China. But as the first fervour of the victorious faith cooled, the pre-Islamic weaknesses which the Arabs had brought with them from the desert began to assert themselves.

The Caliphate itself, at its principal seat in Baghdad, and the entire system of government based upon it were heavily undermined by the fabulous extravagance of the court. Wealth, resulting in luxury and self-indulgence, exercised its corrupting influence (as in the case of Rome) on the manly qualities of the Arabs. Polygamy and concubinage prevented the growth of unity or solidarity in the family, and often led to disputed succession and family feuds even among the Caliph's own progeny. The development of the Caliphate into an autocratic power depending on the support of a professional army resulted eventually in the reduction of the Caliph to a position of impotence under the domination of a military caste – the Turkish Mamluks who, through their resemblance to the Pretorian guard, suggest another analogy with Rome. Finally, the difficulty of communications was a great obstacle in the way of maintaining unified rule over such an immense territory as the Arabs had conquered and helped the process of division and the rise of local sultanates and dynasties. Here again one is reminded of Rome – of the splitting of the Roman world into an eastern and a western empire and the separate destruction of the two. But whereas the great Christian schism between the Roman Church and the Church of Constantinople occurred as a result of geography and political separation, in Arab history the Sunni-Shia split occurred in the early days of Islam, and, instead of resulting from, often caused, political divisions. All in all, the passing away of the Arab Empire recalls in many respects the passing away of the Empire of Rome.

It is important to bear in mind, however, that when the Arab Empire was finally destroyed, the Arab world was not partitioned among a number of different states but, as we have seen, was almost entirely incorporated in the Ottoman Empire, so that the fundamental unity of this world was preserved within a common political framework. Also, the Ottoman Turks occupied and ruled the Arab world without either absorbing or being absorbed by it. There was a certain amount of racial mixing between the two peoples, and as for culture, the Ottomans had already adopted Islam as their religion and, like the Persians, they evolved a new language for themselves, incorporating a large amount of Arabic and using Arabic script. Thus, though Ottoman rule was generally sterile in that it imparted no new cultural values or creative impulses to the Arab world, and though it was often harsh and destructive of the sources of wealth in it, it did not impinge on the Arabism of its people, so that when they began, three and a half centuries later, to awaken to a new life, it was as Arabs that they did so. But before we proceed to this later chapter of Arab history, it is necessary to pause for a moment to consider the cultural achievements of the Arabs and their contribution to world history.

CHAPTER TWO

THE PLACE OF THE ARABS IN HISTORY

I

JUST as the ancient world, from about 600 B.C., was dominated by the Greeks and the Romans, and the modern world has been dominated by the Western Europeans and their offshoots in the New World, so the Middle Ages were dominated by the Arabs.

The place of the Arabs in history or the influence they have exercised over its course may be assessed in reference to three separate criteria.

First, as we have seen, the Arabs have made part of the map of the world indelibly their own by permanently Arabizing most of the Middle East and the whole of north Africa. In these regions a total of some sixty million people speak Arabic to-day and call themselves Arab in one sense or another. Secondly, the Arabs spread the Muslim religion far beyond the frontiers of the Arab world. By conquest (when their empire stretched from Spain to China and was twice as large as the Roman Empire had ever been) or through trade and cultural expansion, they carried the faith preached by their Prophet into the heart of Asia, down into its southeastern tip of Malaya and across the sea into the islands of the East Indies. The number of Muslims in the world to-day is about three hundred and fifty million – a great monotheistic community spread throughout the eastern hemisphere and still living, in the main, a life largely determined by the dogmas and social legislation laid down in the Koran.

Although six-sevenths of this world society are not Arabs nor Arabic speaking, yet it is the product of Arab inspiration and enterprise – a contribution to history no less important than the creation of the smaller but more compact and homogeneous Arab world. Thirdly, the Arabs, at the peak of their creative effort, in Damascus and Baghdad, in Toledo and Cordova, led the world in civilization, and whether by what they originated themselves or what they learned and transmitted from ancient Greece, Persia, and India, played a vital role in the continuity of human progress. It was they who gave light to the Mediterranean world – the channel-bed of the main stream of civilization – between the great dawn illumination of classical antiquity and the noontide blaze of the Renaissance. It is this last contribution which we must now examine.

2

Alike in the heavens and on the face of the globe the Arabs have left in the words of their language a permanent mark of their culture and its penetration of Europe. *Betelgeuse*, *Rigel* (foot), *al-Kaid* (the leader), *al-Tair* (the bird or eagle), and others of the names of the fixed stars in the international scientific vocabulary are Arabic words, testifying both to the Arabs' work in astronomy and to its permanent place in the corpus of world knowledge.

A famous square in London and a great citadel of British sea power bear Arabic names that entered British history and the daily life of Londoners through Spain. Trafalgar comes from the two Arabic words *Taraf al-Ghar* (meaning 'the cape of the cave' or, alternatively, 'the cape of laurels'); and Gibraltar is in Arabic *Jebel Tariq*, or the mount of Tariq, Tariq being the commander of the first Arab armies to cross from north Africa to Spain.

Indeed the map of Spain is littered with Arabic names. Many Spanish rivers are called *Guada*, a corruption of the

Arabic word *wadi*, meaning valley and hence river. Guadal-quivir means 'the Great River'. Similarly the names of many historic Spanish buildings are still those originally given to them by their Arab builders. *Alcazar* means 'the palace', and *Alhambra* 'the red building'.

But it is not only in the names of stars and places that Arabic words have made their way into the European languages. They are to be found in the everyday vocabulary that describes objects, occupations, games, government functions. As is to be expected, Spanish and Portuguese have the highest proportion of such words. Thus the Spanish word for cupboard, *alacena*, comes from the Arabic *al-khizana*; *alcalde* (judge) comes from *al-qadi*; *aduana* (custom-house, and the equivalent of the French *douane* and the Italian *doagne*) comes from *al-diwan*; while the Portuguese *alcatifa* (carpet) is derived from the Arabic *al-qatifa*, meaning 'blanket' or 'velvet'; *alfandega* (custom-house) from *al-funduq* ('hotel' in contemporary Arabic); *safra* (waste place) from *sahra*. But even English has several hundred words of Arabic origin, many of them of a more or less international character, at least in the languages of Western Europe. What word could sound more embedded in English tradition or evoke more English associations than 'admiral'? Yet that comes from the Arabic words *amir al-bahr*, meaning 'commander of the sea'. It will be seen that the French version *amiral* is even closer to the Arabic original, consisting as it does of the first Arabic word and the definite article of the second, on the analogy of 'Abdul' in contemporary English usage. Also, the words 'arsenal', 'sloop', 'cable', 'traffic', 'tariff', and 'monsoon' are of Arabic origin – a further indication of the great part played by the Arabs in the navigation of the Middle Ages.

'Algebra', 'algorism', 'zero', 'alchemy', 'chess', 'check', 'checkmate' are other words of Arabic derivation, suggesting Arab influence in mathematics, chemistry, and the intellectual recreations of a civilized society. As was implied in the foregoing paragraph, *al* is the Arabic definite article; and a good many European words beginning with this combination of letters are descended from the Arabic. Another case of interesting borrowing is to be found in the French word *salamalec*, from the Arabic greeting *salam aleik*, meaning 'Peace be on you'.

The cipher, the so-called Arabic numerals, and the decimal system of notation were all invented by the Indians, but it was the Arabs who brought them into the service of world civilization and handed them on to Europe, thus making possible not only everyday arithmetic as we know it, but also far-reaching mathematical developments which the Greeks, for all their original genius and intellectual power, had not been able to embark upon without the cipher and the Arabic numerals.

Similarly, chess was invented by the Indians, and the Arabs first came across it in Persia. Its English (and still more its French) name as well as the expression which announces the end of the game, 'check-mate', came through the Arabs from the Persian *shah* and *shah mat*, meaning 'the king', and 'the king is dead'.

Yet other sets of English words derived from the Arabic indicate Arab influences in commerce, craftsmanship, and agriculture. The word 'cheque' comes from the Arabic *saqq*, suggesting an Arab origin for many trading and financial transactions. This Arabic word survives to this day in the sense of 'title-deed', or an 'i.o.u.', but so full a cycle has the wheel come that present-day Arabs use the word 'cheque' when referring to the payment orders they draw on their banks! The word 'sofa' – now as English as Jane Austen herself or Queen Victoria – comes from *suf*, the Arabic for 'wool'. Also, the word 'mattress' comes from the Arabic (*matrah* meaning the place where you lie down); and so do such words as 'atlas' and 'damask' and other names of fine material for clothing or furniture. 'Lemon', 'rice', and 'sugar', as well as 'syrup' and 'ginger' are also Arabic words, indicating either that the articles they stand for first came into Europe from the Arab countries, or that they were brought there by Arab enterprise from central Asia. It has even been suggested that 'tennis' comes not from the French word *tenez* (used before serving to warn the opponent) but from Tinnis, an Egyptian town famous for weaving certain kinds of material, and therefore the original source of tennis balls. If this theory is correct then Drobny, by winning the Wimbledon championship for Egypt in 1954, would seem to have paid an overdue debt!

Citing, *inter alia*, this etymological evidence, one of the authors of *The Legacy of Islam* concludes that 'though Europe owes much to its own force and initiative ... it has also largely profited by the knowledge and experience of those who were at one time the masters of the world', and 'ought to look upon them as its cultural ancestors in the domain of geographical knowledge, of discovery, and of world trade'.

3

In their turn, however, these 'cultural ancestors' of Europe were, in geography, as in so many other things, the pupils of the Greeks. The Arabs first came in contact with Hellenism in Damascus, and the translation of Greek works, either directly into Arabic or through the medium of Syriac, was begun in Syria, in a sporadic manner, under the Umayyads. But it was in Baghdad, under the Abbasids, that this labour of rendering Greek thought into Arabic became organized, sustained, and officially patronized.

The Caliph al-Mamun (813–33) established a school for translators with a library and paid scholars who travelled sometimes as far as Constantinople in search of manuscripts to translate. One of the great figures of this school and, indeed, of the entire ninth century and the civilization it brought to its peak, was the Christian doctor, Hunain ibn Ishaq (809–73), who translated the works of Galen and Hippocrates – preserving for posterity in Arabic the seven books of Galen's anatomy which perished in the original Greek – and is also credited with having translated Plato's *Republic* and many of the works of Aristotle.

It was as a result of the labours of the Baghdad translators that the Arabs learned of Ptolemy's work and began the scientific study of geography themselves. The Caliph al-Mamun founded two observatories at Baghdad, and had a geographical degree measured in the Syrian desert and 'an image of the earth' executed by seventy scholars, among whom was the famous astronomer and mathematician al-Khawarizmi, already the author of a book based on Ptolemy's work and giving latitudes and longitudes.

Many Arab astronomers and geographers followed al-Khawarizmi in the next few centuries, including a number of travellers who collected and published a vast amount of information about the countries they visited. The most famous of the geographers, and the one whose history is the most interesting to Europeans, is al-Idrisi who wrote his great work at the court of the Norman king of Sicily, Roger II (1130–54), after the passing away of Arab rule from the island, and called it in honour of his royal patron, *Kitab Rujjar* – the Book of Roger.

One of the greatest contributions of the Arabs to the science of geography and to the great geographical discoveries that ushered in the modern age was their keeping alive – during the Dark Ages of Europe when Christian men of learning held the opposite view – the idea put forward by the Greeks that the earth was a sphere. For it was this idea that inspired Columbus with his tremendous project and led to his discovery of the New World.

But directly and in practice, it was in the Old World that the Arabs expanded and exploited their knowledge of geography, becoming the chief navigators and merchants of the Middle Ages. Their ships sailed the whole length of the Mediterranean, and between the ports of the Persian Gulf and India. The great rivers of Iraq linked the Persian Gulf itself with Baghdad, whence caravans set out for the Mediterranean ports. Another route from the Indian Ocean led into the Red Sea and so to the ports of Jeddah and Suez. It is interesting to note that when Vasco da Gama reached the east coast

sheikh. 'Afflatun knew everything there was to be known. Aristo merely took his knowledge from Afflatun.'

This little story illustrates the survival to this day in Arab tradition of the fame of the two great thinkers. It was, however (contrary to the opinion of Huxley's Druse friend), to Aristotle rather than Plato that the Arabs accorded the place of pre-eminence, calling him 'al-Muallim al-awwal' – the First Teacher; and it is very much due to Arab translation, interpretation, and teaching in Spain that Aristotle came to be the supreme arbiter of thought in medieval Europe after profoundly influencing the whole intellectual complexion of Islam.

Ibn Rushd, known in medieval Europe by the corrupted Latinized version of his name, Averroes, was the greatest of the Arab Aristotelian commentators – as he was indeed, whether in philosophy, jurisprudence, medicine, or mathematics, one of the foremost figures of Arab civilization. He lived and taught in Cordova in the twelfth century, and from there his influence reached into the very heart of Europe and of Christian philosophy and theology. His commentaries on Aristotle were an obligatory subject of study at the University of Paris; and though some of his original teachings as a philosopher were misunderstood by European scholars and led to the development of a line of thought called, after him, Averroism, which St Thomas Aquinas refuted, and which Ibn Rushd himself would probably have repudiated, the similarities of outlook, method, and aim between him and the Angelic Doctor show that even St Thomas was influenced by the Arab philosopher's thought, particularly in his approach to Aristotle and on the paramount question of reconciling faith with reason, philosophy with revelation. It may, indeed, be claimed that it was Ibn Rushd who led the way alike for Mohammedans, Jews, and Christians in the great medieval venture of trying to show that the truths of philosophy, as expounded by Aristotle, did not conflict with the word of God. The harmony which Ibn Rushd tried to deduce between Aristotle and the Koran (though he was sometimes

57

bold enough to follow reason even to the point at which it might contradict religion), the Jewish Maimonides (under the influence of Ibn Rushd) tried to deduce between Aristotle and the Old Testament; and later, the Schoolmen, steeped in the Aristotelian expositions of Ibn Rushd, tried to do in regard to Christian dogma.

Until the era of Arab civilization in Spain there was only one inadequate Latin text of Aristotle (that of Boethius) available to the Europeans. The text that became the source of medieval Aristotelianism was a translation from the Arabic into Latin made by Michael the Scot in Toledo, after its recapture by the Christians in the eleventh century.

As Ibn Rushd was the greatest figure of Arab civilization in the West (particularly in regard to his influence over European thought) so Avicenna, or Ibn Sina (born at Bukhara towards the end of the tenth century) was the most influential figure of Arab civilization in the East. Like Ibn Rushd and many others of the leading thinkers of that age, he was an encyclopaedic figure, taking – in the phrase Francis Bacon applied to himself – 'all knowledge for his province'. It was, however, chiefly in medicine that his influence reached Europe and dominated European learning. As late as the seventeenth century, Latin translations of his medical Canon (of which the last years of the fifteenth century had seen fifteen editions) were still used at all European centres of medical study as the principal text-book. In the Arab countries one hears to this day some of the opinions of Ibn Sina quoted in oral tradition as the final authority on certain medical points!

A contemporary of Ibn Sina (and a more original and universal genius, though not so famous or influential in the history of European thought) was al-Biruni, whose learning embraced physics, chemistry, geography, history, mathematics, astronomy, and medicine. Al-Kindi (born 830) combined philosophy with mathematics, alchemy, optics, and musical theory. His work on optics, based on Euclid's, became known in Europe and influenced Roger Bacon. A century earlier Jabir ibn-Hayyan (Geber to the Europeans) had, as the father of Arab alchemy, stressed the importance of experiments and made significant discoveries in chemistry. In Arabic there are only twenty-two works to-day that bear his name. Those that have survived in Latin – though a good many of them are judged to be spurious – are far greater, and were at one time the most influential treatises in Europe. Rhazes (al-Razi) was a contemporary of Ibn Sina and, in medicine alone, his superior. He too influenced Roger Bacon.

The list of thinkers and scientists who, from Bukhara and Baghdad to Toledo and Cordova, created Arab civilization and passed a great deal of it on to Europe includes many names for which there is no space in this brief summary. Yet a few more must be mentioned. In Spain, beside the outstanding figure of Ibn Rushd there is one of almost equal stature – that of the philosopher Ibn Bajja (Avempace in the Latin version) who was a free-thinker and denied personal immortality. In the eastern Arab world, there lived about the same time (dying at Khurasan in A.D. 1111) al-Ghazali (Algazel), the greatest mystic thinker of Islam and a philosopher-theologian whose commentaries on Aristotle were, like those of Ibn Rushd and Ibn Sina, translated into Latin and exercised much influence over European thought. A century later another Arab mystic, Ibn al-Arabi, described heaven and hell in terms which are reproduced in Dante's *Divine Comedy* so closely as to suggest borrowing rather than coincidence.

Lastly, there is the unique figure of Ibn Khaldun (born in Tunis in 1332, though his ancestry is traced back to Hadhramaut in the Arabian Peninsula). Ibn Khaldun is unique because in his chosen field he was greater than any predecessor in the east or west, whether in medieval or ancient times and because, unlike Ibn Rushd, Ibn Sina, and al-Ghazali (all of whom surpassed him in metaphysical insight) he was a complete originator and owed nothing to previous thinkers. He wrote a history and an introduction to it. The history itself, though the most detailed of medieval times, is not a work of

supreme genius, but the introduction, the famous *Prolego-
menon*, is. For here Ibn Khaldun formulates a philosophy (
history and establishes himself as the first great systemat.
sociologist. Of this work Professor Toynbee says that it 'ı
undoubtedly the greatest work of its kind that has ever ye
been created by any mind in any time or place', while Robe
Flint, in his *History of the Philosophy of History*, says of th
author: 'Ibn Khaldun, considered simply as a histori.n, ha
superiors even among Arabic authors, but as a .ıeorist c ı
history he had no equal in any age or c: .ıry ... Plat/ ,
Aristotle, and Augustine were not his peers.'

It is an indication of the position held by the leadi g
figures of Arab civilization in medieval Europe that, as ıe
reader will have noticed, many of the names we have ı-
countered in our rapid sketch had a conventional La in
rendering – Algazel, Averroes, Avicenna, Avempace./ ıe
prefix 'Ave' in this Latinised form stood for the Arabic '. } ı',
meaning 'son of'.

5

The poetry and drama of the Greeks, unlike their philosc ɔhy
and science, did not attract the Arabs, so that they ne: her
absorbed them into their own civilization nor helpe l in
communicating them to Europe. Nor did Arabic poetry tself
– which is the most distinctive and intimate creation of ırab
aesthetic genius – become widely known to the Europe. ıs or
strike any creative response from them – if one exce s the
possibility that the early troubadours in southern Franc were
influenced by Arabic love poetry of the popular, lyrical kind.
The Arabs had not evolved any drama or epic poetry. Their
favourite poetic form was the *Qasida* or ode, having th same
rhyme throughout its forty or fifty (or maybe more) ve es. In
pre-Islamic poetry, the poetry of the *Jahiliya*, or time o ignorance, as the Muslims call it, the main themes, as me ioned
earlier in this book, were valour, love, war, praise of a ,atron,

abuse of an enemy, glorification of oneself or of one's tribe, camel, or horse.

The two greatest poets of the Islamic period of Arab history are al-Mutanabbi and al-Maarri, who lived in the tenth and eleventh centuries A.D. But it is a significant commentary on their failure to make any impact on Europe that their names are not mentioned in any of the books that deal with the place of the Arabs in history or their cultural influence on the West. One has to go to the specialized literary work of modern Arabists to meet these two figures. In the case of al-Mutanabbi the reason is not far to seek. There is little spiritual or philosophic content in his poetry, almost none of that profound concern about the significance of human experience and destiny without which poetry is mainly rhetoric. His sentiments, which the Arabs call 'the wise sayings of al-Mutanabbi' are largely platitudinous; and indeed the secret of the high position he occupies in Arabic literature is to be mainly found in the (to Arab ears) magic sound and imposing structure of his verses. But this is not the case with al-Maarri, who was a philosopher-poet, a sceptic, and a stoic – not unlike Lucretius – and addressed himself in his poetry to the universal themes of life and fate. Indeed, according to the Lebanese-American writer, Amin Rihani, who translated them into English in 1920, the *Luzumiyat* of al-Maarri closely foreshadow the *Rubaiyat* of Omar Khayyám, who came a century later, except that al-Maarri, being strictly abstemious, did not seek solace with the daughter of the vine. It may be that the Arabs themselves were responsible for keeping al-Maarri's light under a bushel, since the poet was, in religious matters, sceptical to the point of unbelief and therefore frowned upon by orthodox Muslim opinion.

However that may be, poetry is the most difficult thing to appreciate in a foreign tongue and the least amenable to translation. Arabic was never learned in Europe as Latin and Greek were, so that even if Arabic poetry had contained such universal masterpieces as the Homeric epics, the Athenian tragedies, or the *Aeneid* (which it did not), it still would not have penetrated into European thought with the vividness of the Greek and Latin classics. Yet, to the Arabs themselves, their poetry with its intoxicating verbal effect, with the hypnotic power of its monotonous rhyming, was and still is one of the chief sources of pleasure and inspiration.

But if in poetry the Arabs had little influence over the developing susceptibilities of Europe, it was not so with music. Both in theory and practice, and with regard to the actual instruments of the art, the Europeans learned much from the Arabs. The names of the Arab musicians at the courts of Castile and Aragon have been preserved; and the rhythms and melodies of Arabic music are still discernible in the music of Spain. The word 'lute' comes from the Arabic *al-'ud*, 'guitar' from the Arabic *qitara* (in its turn derived from the Greek) and 'rebeck' or 'ribible' (mentioned in Chaucer) from the Arabic *rabab*.

More important still, there is a distinct possibility, as J. B. Trend points out in *The Legacy of Islam*, that European musical theory was influenced both by the treatises which the Arabs translated from the Greek, and by their own original contribution to the subject. Al-Farabi (tenth century) was translated into Latin under the name of Alpharabius, and his theories, like those of al-Kindi, Ibn Bajja, and Ibn Sina, became widely known in Europe. The fact that a new principle – namely, that the notes have an exact time-value among themselves – appeared in European music about the same time as the Latin translations of the Arab musical theoreticians, suggests Arab parentage for a very important development in Western music; and we have the enthusiastic assurance of the greatest European musicians of the thirteenth century that their art owed much to the Arab masters.

The role played by the Arabs in architecture is unlike their roles in poetry and music; or rather it is a combination of the two. In poetry, they created an art which was and remained entirely their own, in that there was nothing in it which they owed to others or were able to communicate to others. In music, on the other hand, while creating little of lasting value themselves, they were able to teach Europe a substantial amount of both theory and practice. In architecture they did the two things: they created their own monuments which stand to this day, throughout the countries embraced once by the Arab Empire, as works of art in their own right; and through these monuments they influenced in no little measure the development of European architecture.

When one speaks of Arab or Muslim architecture, however, it is necessary to remember that like the rest of Arab civilization (except pre-Islamic poetry) it was not an original product of the Arabian Peninsula, but a synthesis of the forms and processes found by the Arabs in the more civilized countries they conquered – particularly the Byzantine provinces of Syria and Egypt and the Persian Empire with its dependency of Iraq. In their ancestral home the Arabs had known very little architecture. The majority of them were nomads living in tents; and even in the few cities that existed in the Peninsula before the rise of Islam, the buildings were of a simple and primitive type – despite a sixth-century cathedral as far south as San'a in Yemen. The first mosque built by Mohammed at Medina in 622 (which in essence became the prototype of all future mosques) was not a work of art raised to the glory of God, but an unadorned, utilitarian enclosure designed to accommodate his worshippers. It was a large, open square, surrounded by walls of brick and stone. Only part of the enclosure, where the Prophet led the congregation in prayers, was roofed, probably with mud and palm mats resting on palm trunks. Yet, before the century was out, the beautiful and magnificent Dome of the Rock was built in Jerusalem, and a few years later came the Umayyad Mosque in Damascus.

Greek, Syrian, and Armenian artisans were undoubtedly employed in building these monumental mosques, and ideas were borrowed from various schools of architecture, both Western and Eastern. But already, in both these noble buildings, and particularly in the Damascus mosque, we see emerging a style of architecture which, despite its mixed origins, was to become characteristic, whether in mosques or palaces, of the whole Arab Empire. It was Islam and the traditional development of the mosque pattern that produced this style by imposing a harmonizing unity on diverse material.

Apart from the two mosques just mentioned, the greatest monuments of Arab architecture are to be found at Samarra in Iraq and in Cairo, Tunis, and Spain. Cairo abounds in mosques, the most famous of which is the mosque of Ibn Tulun (ninth century). In Tunis, the Qayrawan mosque (eighth century) has the oldest surviving minaret. Spain, apart from mosques – of which the best known is the Great Mosque of Cordova – has the two beautiful and gracefully ornamented palaces of Alcazar and Alhambra.

Between the tenth and thirteenth centuries the building energy of the Arabs turned away from mosques to fortifications. In both spheres, Saracenic (from Arabic *Sharq*, meaning east) art, as it came to be called, made a substantial contribution to the development of European architecture. The mosque supplied features for the church; the citadel for the castle.

The most important and distinctive contribution of all was the pointed arch, without which Gothic architecture is unimaginable. This arch, it would seem, was first used in the mosques of Iraq, whence Ibn Tulun borrowed its shape for the Cairo mosque that bears his name and, possibly with other users in Syria, set it on the journey which ultimately produced the great French and English cathedrals. Similarly, the minaret seems to be the ancestor of the campanile of Italian churches, Italian architecture having been directly influenced by the Arab architecture of Sicily. If we turn from structure to decoration, we find that the ornamental battlements of Gothic architecture came to Europe from Cairo, as also did the decorative carved inscriptions of late Gothic; while the name *arabesque* describing low relief patterns used on English walls since Elizabethan times clearly indicates the origin of this form of decoration. It has even been suggested that stained-glass windows may have come to Europe from the Arab world.

Many features of Arab military architecture were introduced into Europe by the returning Crusaders. Chief among these was machicolation or the construction, at a certain height along castle walls, of parapets resting on brackets and having trap-doors through which arrows, boiling oil, or other forms of ancient ammunition could be discharged at the enemy. Specimens of this are to be found in England at Norwich and Winchester.

Saladin's citadel at Cairo and the citadel of Aleppo show another typical feature of Arab fortification (first introduced by the Abbasids in Baghdad) which was borrowed by the Europeans. This is the right-angled or crooked entrance to a fortress, and its purpose was to prevent the enemy, even if he gained the gateway, from shooting straight into the courtyard. Visitors to the Khalifa's house in Omdurman (built after the death of Gordon and the Mahdi in 1885) will find ample evidence of the extent to which this device of Arab military building had travelled by the end of the nineteenth century.

Neither painting nor sculpture is to be found in Arab art. This fact is largely but not entirely explained by the religious ban on all representation of the human figure mentioned earlier – not entirely because, first, the ban was disregarded in the non-Arab but equally Muslim art of Persia and the Mogul Empire and, second, the Arabs did not develop either landscape or architectural painting, to which there was no religious objection. The exclusion of the human form, however, must have acted as a general discouragement, for purely landscape or architectural painting is a comparatively late development in the history of art, having been preceded by the use of nature and buildings as a background for human figures. Nor must it be forgotten that in both classical sculpture and Renaissance painting the first subjects were the objects of worship themselves – a trend which Islam specifically set out to repulse.

Abstract design and decoration in the minor arts, however, including lettering, reached high levels of excellence among the Arabs and in many ways influenced artistic developments in Europe.

6

There were three areas of sustained Arab-European contact, leading to the steady penetration of Europe by Arab civilization in the various manners we have noticed: Spain, Sicily, and Syria.

Spain was by far the most important of the three channels, for not only was it occupied by the Arabs continuously for eight centuries, but it was here that Arab civilization reached its most mature and influential expression; and geography, of course, decreed that, until the Crusades, Spain should be the principal route by which both original Arab ideas and Arab translations from the Greek, wherever they originated, could reach Europe. The Byzantine gateway was closed to the Arabs, and even the glories of Baghdad in the time of Harun al-Rashid had to travel by the western route, via Sicily and Spain. In Toledo and Cordova the Arabs founded two of the oldest universities of Europe, and to them came scholars from all over the Continent to study Greek philosophy and science in Arabic, as well as the work of the Arab thinkers themselves. Notable among these were Gerard of Cremona from Italy, Robert the Englishman, and Michael the Scot, of whom the last-mentioned subsequently visited and died in Sicily. The reconquest of Toledo by Alfonso VII in 1085, far from putting an end to the process of spreading Arabic learning in Europe, enhanced it. Alfonso was a liberal who proclaimed himself 'King of the Two Faiths', so that under his rule Muslim Arab teachers and scholars continued to flourish and more Christian students than ever before came to Spain from across the Pyrenees to acquire the knowledge that came from the East.

The same thing happened in Sicily a century later when the island was captured by the Normans after a long period of Arab occupation. Roger II (1130–54), to whom al-Idrisi dedicated his famous geographical work, patronized Arab learning, maintained Arab customs at his court, used the Hijra date on his coronation robe (itself of Arab make), and continued to strike coins in Arabic. Even a century after this, under the Emperor Frederick II, the culture of the island was still largely Arab, and its influence was still reaching the Italian mainland through the University of Naples (where St Thomas Aquinas studied for some time) and other centres of learning.

In both Spain and Sicily the Arabs effected important changes in land tenure and established advanced systems of agriculture by irrigation. Among the plants they introduced into the one country or the other were the orange and mulberry trees, sugar cane, date-palms, and the cotton shrub. Agricultural terms of Arabic origin abound in both countries, and there are fountains in Palermo that still bear Arabic names, only slightly corrupted.

Perhaps next to Aristotle and the Arabic numerals the most important gift which the Arabs brought to Europe (it reached it via Spain) was paper, the making of which they had learned from the Chinese. Even before the printing press came to exploit the full potentialities of the new material, its use by the Arabs and introduction into Europe offered enormous facilities for the copying of manuscripts and the dissemination of knowledge.

In the third contact-region, Syria, it was the Crusades that brought the Europeans and the Arabs together during a total period of some two hundred years – between the end of the eleventh and that of the thirteenth century. The Arab impact on Europe through Spain and Sicily was more vigorous and creative than that which they made through the Crusades, the main reason being that Arab civilization in the east had entered upon its decline by the time the Crusaders arrived, whereas in Sicily and Spain the Europeans had encountered that same civilization at its apogee. Yet there is no doubt that the Crusades had an educational and liberalizing effect on Europe, and particularly on those of its sons who took part in them and sometimes lived for many years in close contact with the Arabs of Syria. They found, in the words of H. A. L. Fisher, 'a society … in many respects more refined and dignified than their own', and 'under the seductive influences of an eastern climate, the rigidity of the Latin settlers insensibly relaxed. Syrian women, Syrian dishes, and Syrian ways of life began to appeal to these rude adventurers from the west and to temper their fanaticism.' Many of them adopted local dress and customs. Some formed friendships with Arab chieftains; others married Christian Arab women. They learned some of the medical and chemical knowledge of the Arabs, and acquired skill in many of their arts and crafts – including, as we have seen, the art of military building. They went back to Europe with a more liberal and humane outlook, with sharpened minds and with many specimens of Arab textiles, glass-ware, woodwork, and metal-work which were to suggest new ideas of development and improvement to European craftsmen. Lastly, they went back with vivid memories of the honourableness and magnanimity of Saladin, their most redoubtable opponent and the final destroyer of their Latin kingdom – a figure which has ineffaceably stamped itself on the mind of the world as the possessor of those qualities that later came to be most closely associated with the European tradition of chivalry.

7

The pinnacle of Arab civilization was reached, alike in the east and west, some five centuries before its final collapse with the capture of Cairo by the Turks in 1517. The golden age of both Baghdad and Cordova stretched roughly from the ninth to the eleventh century, and we cannot end this section of our survey better than by casting a look at the life of the two cities before we take leave of medieval Arab life and turn to the Arab revival in the nineteenth century.

For two hundred years the two capitals of the Arab world were the centres of world civilization. The standards of culture in them, of municipal amenities and of ordinary civic life were far in advance of anything Christian Europe could show. The reign of Harun al-Rashid in Baghdad coincided with that of Charlemagne over Western Christendom, and the two monarchs are reported to have exchanged embassies and presents, Charlemagne thinking of Harun as a useful counterpoise to the power of Byzantium in the east, and Harun anxious to have the friendship of Charlemagne against the Umayyad Caliphate of Spain. But whereas Harun, and more particularly his son al-Mamun, were scholars themselves as well as patrons of learning and the arts, Charlemagne and the nobles of his court were, in the words of Professor Hitti, 'still dabbling in the art of writing their names'.

The courts both in Baghdad and Cordova were magnificent, standing as the apex and supreme emblem of a prosperous, cultured and, among the upper classes, a very luxurious way of life, which in the eastern capital at least tended to become self-indulgent and intemperate. The Koranic ban on intoxicating drink (which already under the Umayyads in Damascus had begun to be disregarded) now became all but a dead letter. Dancing and singing revels, liberally stimulated by wine, were held by the Caliph himself in Baghdad. The chief court poet of Harun al-Rashid, and one of his boon companions, was the famous Abu Nawas, who anticipated in practice as well as in song Omar Khayyám's devotions to the grape. The palace thronged with wits, poets, scholars, as well as singers and dancers of both sexes. Merriment and the festive arts and social refinement were splendidly cultivated. But the picture has its ugly side: slaves, eunuchs, growing harems. Nevertheless, when we are told by the Arab chroniclers that the seraglio of the Caliph al-Mutawakkil consisted of four thousand concubines we must, despite the assurances of the reporters to the contrary, conclude that this establishment, unlike that of Gibbon's noted Roman emperor, was designed rather for ostentation than for use.

It was not, however, till the end of the tenth century that the segregation of women in Baghdad became complete. In the earlier Abbasid days many Arab women took an active part, side by side with men, in the cultural and political life of the city, some of them becoming famous as scholars or poetesses.

Baghdad was built after a circular pattern. At the centre stood the Caliph's palace and the chief mosque; and from there four roads joined the city to the four corners of the empire. The goods that came along these roads, as well as in the numerous ships that crowded the river moorings, furnished the bazaars with every luxury which the citizens of their acropolis might desire. The upper stratum of society consisted of merchants, civil servants, scholars, and the representatives of the various liberal professions that were beginning to appear. There was the House of Wisdom with the libraries attached to it and the observatories, where the work of translation and research proceeded; and there were many bars, or rather wine parlours, kept by Jews and Christians – the bootleggers of the time', as Professor Hitti calls them – who ostensibly catered for their own co-religionists, but were mainly patronized by the uninhibited Muslims. Mosques and public baths abounded in the city, though the figure of twenty-seven thousand for the latter must, like the index-number of the Caliph's uxorious potency quoted earlier, be taken with the pinch of salt necessary to swallowing the boast-ful exaggerations of the Arab chroniclers.

By contrast, the three hundred public baths claimed for Cordova sounds well within the bounds of the credible. The water for these establishments and for the other needs of the city's five hundred thousand inhabitants was supplied by an aqueduct built by the first Umayyad prince of Spain, Abdarrahman I, towards the end of the eighth century. It was not, however, till the reign of the third Abdarrahman, in the tenth century, that Cordova reached the height of its glory and came to be known to some of its admirers in Western Europe as 'the jewel of the world'. Its two chief monuments were the Great Mosque (which the first Abdarrahman had started to build more than one hundred and fifty years before) and the Caliph's palace – Abdarrahman III was the first Umayyad ruler of Spain to assume the title of Caliph in open rivalry to the Caliph of Baghdad – named al-Zahra, meaning 'the flower', and containing four hundred rooms, with columns and basins brought from as far away as Constantinople. The court, to which envoys from the Byzantine emperor and the rulers of Europe were accredited, was here too the patronage-centre of learning and the arts. A university was founded and many free schools. Seventy libraries, including a state one rich in books and manuscripts from all over the world, are said to have existed in the city, together with many bookshops. Mosques and palaces rose in profusion among its one hundred and thirteen thousand homes; and miles of its streets were paved and illuminated, whereas mud and darkness were not banished from the streets of London and Paris till eight or nine hundred years later! The standards of culture in the neighbouring and contemporary Christian kingdoms of Leon, Navarre, or Barcelona were so acknowledgedly inferior to Cordova's that whenever the rulers of these countries needed a master architect or surgeon they sought him in the Arab capital; while the Arabs had such a poor view of the Europeans that a learned Toledan judge delivered himself of the opinion that 'their temperaments have become cold and their humours rude, while their bodies have grown large, their complexion light and their hair long. They lack withal sharpness of wit and penetration of intellect, while stupidity and folly prevail among them.'

8

So much for the place of the Arabs in history. In Spain their monuments endure, but they themselves have vanished

altogether. The French and the Spaniards rule their descendants in Morocco. Baghdad was destroyed by Hulagu in the
thirteenth century, and Damascus all but destroyed by his
descendant Timur Lenk in the fifteenth. Yet there, and particularly in Baghdad (where the complete absence of stone
rendered buildings peculiarly vulnerable to the ravages of
conquerors and time) it was the monuments and the civilization they housed that perished. The people remained to live
under Ottoman rule. In Egypt, which built in stone and was
spared the Mongol invasions, both the people and their
buildings survived. So did they in Jerusalem and Tunis. As
for Mecca and Medina, twin sources of the whole mighty and
brilliant drama, they remained in the distant and obscure
holiness to which they had been reduced, as a shrine of pilgrimage – they and the nomad population that continued to
live and travel between and around them.

Three centuries were to pass after the Ottoman capture of
Cairo before a new life began to dawn for the Arabs.

CHAPTER THREE

THE ARAB RENASCENCE

I

IF any one date is to be chosen as marking the end of this long Arab sleep, it will be the day on which Napoleon set foot on Egyptian soil in 1798.

Until that day the Arabs were still living in the Middle Ages. Socially and intellectually their life had become ossified. They had gradually lost the ability to think their way into fresh fields of endeavour and discovery. Disputations over the rules of grammar had long since replaced the creative literary urge. A narrow obscurantism ruled in religion. Learning by heart had come to be mistaken for learning, and empty words to be accepted instead of ideas. Ibn Sina, al-Farabi, al-Ghazali, and the other great thinkers of the past were no longer read. Polygamy, concubinage, and segregation had degraded the position of women among the vast Muslim majorities, created a lopsided social life for the men, and rendered unhealthy the atmosphere in which children grew up. The Ottoman genius, purely military and political, did not impart to the Arabs any of those spiritual qualities which, though carried on the point of the sword, had often fertilized a conquered people; nor were the Ottomans themselves fertilized by the Arab heritage, as the Romans had been fertilized by Greece, or the Goths by Rome. Moreover, Ottoman rule became, after the seventeenth century, economically oppressive and destructive. Under it the Arab world was reduced to

73

extreme poverty, and poverty contributed to the prevailing ignorance and spiritual aridity.

Meanwhile the Europeans, whom the learned judge of twelfth-century Toledo found 'lacking sharpness of wit and penetration of intellect' had had their Renaissance and Reformation; had discovered the great ocean routes to India and the New World and embarked on their imperial careers all round the globe; they had accomplished the scientific revolution of the seventeenth century, had had the enlightenment of the eighteenth and were, as Napoleon arrived in Egypt, going through the Industrial and French Revolutions.

Napoleon's expedition was more than a military invasion; it was also a cultural incursion from the West into the heart of the Arab world, comprising as it did many scholars and scientists, among whom was Champollion who deciphered ancient Egyptian hieroglyphic writing, and engineers who studied the project of joining the Mediterranean and Red Seas by piercing the Suez Isthmus. With it there also came the first printing press to reach Egypt.

The results of Napoleon's expedition were seen in the amazing career of Mohammed Ali, himself not an Arab but a man of genius destined to play a decisive role in ushering in the new Arab age, both as the founder of modern Egypt and the near-founder of a modern Arab Empire including Syria, Arabia, and the Sudan.

Mohammed Ali was an Albanian officer in the army sent by the Ottoman Sultan to resist the French occupation of Egypt, which for many centuries had been ruled locally by the Mamluk military caste under the remote suzerainty of the Sultan. The Ottoman forces had failed to offer any effective opposition to the French until Napoleon reached Acre, but all the time Mohammed Ali was establishing his personal ascendancy over the Albanian troops with whom he had come, and so successful had he been that when, in 1801, the French finally evacuated Egypt, he emerged as its virtual ruler, owing only a nominal allegiance to the Sultan. For the next forty years he and his son, Ibrahim Pasha, dominated the Middle Eastern scene, conquering new territories, clashing with the European Powers (particularly Palmerston's Britain), threatening the position of the Sultan himself, and administering various stimulants to the Arab mind.

In the first place, Mohammed Ali had been impressed by the skill and efficiency of the French; and in creating the structure of a modern state in Egypt he employed many Frenchmen and sent missions of Egyptian students to France to learn European techniques. Though many of his schemes ended in failure, he did establish a cultural contact with Europe, and thus laid down one of the main lines along which the Arab revival was to develop. The fertilizing influence of Europe on the Arab world, first experienced through Napoleon's expedition and as a result of Mohammed Ali's policy, was to grow later, both in Egypt and the Levant, through mission schools and printing presses – French, American, and British – on a vast scale.

Secondly, by putting an end to Mamluk rule, gaining for Egypt effective independence from Turkey and giving her the shape of a nation-state, he set the stage for the later growth of Egyptian nationalism – though, indeed, when that nationalism came eventually, and before the descent of the British on the scene – it was a protest by the native Arabic-speaking Egyptian population against the progeny of Mohammed Ali and the ascendancy, over the army and the government, of the Turkish aristocracy they represented.

Thirdly, it was under Mohammed Ali, and as a result of his ambitious and visionary policy, that the germ was first introduced from which the idea later developed of a general liberation of the Arabs from Ottoman rule and the setting up of an empire or all-embracing state in the eastern Arab world.

Ironically enough, it was at the Sultan's own request that Mohammed Ali launched the policy which, but for the intervention of Britain and Russia (France was favourable to him) would probably have led him in triumph to Constantinople itself and established him as the new sovereign of the Arabs. In Arabia, an alliance between the Wahhabis (a puritanical

sect preaching a return to the austerities of early Islam) and
the house of Saud (ancestors of the present king of Saudi
Arabia) had acquired early in the nineteenth century
enough power to threaten the Turkish position in Iraq and
Syria. The Sultan pressed Mohammed Ali, as his loyal
vassal, to suppress this movement. In 1811 Mohammed Ali
dispatched an army charged with fulfilling the Sultan's bid-
ding; and after a campaign of seven years, his son, Ibrahim,
was brilliantly successful against the Wahhabi ruler. Some
time later, the Sultan appealed to Mohammed Ali to suppress
a revolt of his Greek subjects in the Morea. Again Mohammed
Ali responded by dispatching Ibrahim; but this time, when
Ibrahim had won another splendid victory, Mohammed Ali
demanded from the Sultan the overlordship of Syria as a
reward for his services, and, on the Sultan's refusing his demand, sent Ibrahim to seize Syria by force. The Syrian Arabs
– both Muslim and Christians – welcomed Ibrahim with enthusiasm, being discontented with Ottoman rule and believing that Mohammed Ali and his son would bring them
liberty.

It was only Britain's vigorous intervention that forced
Ibrahim back from the gates of Constantinople in 1833. For
seven years, however, Ibrahim was allowed to retain the
governorship of Syria on behalf of his father, before a second
intervention of the Powers compelled him to withdraw from
the country, unregretted by the local population who had
been alienated by many of his policies and measures – particularly the heavy taxation he imposed.

In the meantime a more lasting Egyptian position had
been established elsewhere. In 1820 Mohammed Ali, in
search of ivory, gold, and new recruits for his expanding
army, had sent another of his sons to conquer the Sudan – a
country whose northern half was Arab, having been several
centuries earlier invaded by Arab tribes coming up from
Egypt who intermarried with the local black population and
left behind them a racially mixed progeny, but speaking
Arabic as their mother tongue and practising Islam – that is

to say, an Arabized people despite their partly negroid complexion and features. The country was conquered by Mohammed Ali's forces, who added to the northern Arab region a large part of equatorial Africa inhabited by an extremely primitive population of negroid tribes who had nothing Arab about them, racially or culturally. This was the manner in which the Sudan, as it is known to-day, was constituted as a political entity. Over the whole of it Mohammed Ali established a common Egyptian administration which, unlike his rule in Syria and Arabia, was not resisted by the Sultan or the European Powers and, though corrupt and oppressive despite all the efforts made by Mohammed Ali's successors to reform it, survived till 1885, when it was overthrown by the famous revolt of Mohammed Ahmed al-Mahdi, but only to be restored, in partnership with Britain (who by then was in control of Egypt itself) in 1898, and to lead to the present close association between Egypt and the Sudan.

Not only was Mohammed Ali himself not an Arab and did not speak Arabic, but in trying to create an Arab Empire he had no thought for Arab nationalism or freedom; his aim was merely to wrest power from the Sultan and aggrandize himself. It was different, however, with Ibrahim – his chief instrument in this vast undertaking. Ibrahim had come to Egypt as a boy and grown up in Arab surroundings, learning to speak Arabic with some fluency. Moreover, his outlook as a ruler was different from his father's, partly no doubt because he came in direct contact with the native Arab population he was sent to rule over in Syria. He tried, according to Antonius, from motives of sentiment as well as policy, to identify himself with the Arab tradition, to think of the Arab Empire he and his father aimed at as being based on an Arab national movement. In this Ibrahim was seeing visions of the future rather than actualities, for, in spite of the demonstrations of joy with which he was received in the country, there was as yet no general Arab consciousness to inspire a political movement and, as we have seen, the Syrians themselves came to resent his rule by the end of his sojourn among them. But, though premature, Ibrahim's ideas – and even his father's policies of personal aggrandizement – sowed seeds that were to germinate later. For seven years the Syrian Arabs had lived independent of Ottoman rule, and this experience was to suggest possibilities undreamed of before. The whole of Mohammed Ali's career had demonstrated how feeble the structure of the Ottoman Empire had become, not merely *vis-à-vis* the great military powers of Europe, but even when faced by revolt from within.

Nor was Mohammed Ali's revolt the only internal blow that shook the Ottoman structure. The Wahhabi assault in Arabia, which the Sultan had only been able to suppress with the help of Mohammed Ali, was another, and it was a blow delivered by purely Arab leaders from within the very heart of Arabism. Both these challenges, however, had come too soon to lead to a general Arab movement. It was only later in the century that Arab national consciousness began to awaken throughout the Arab world, called to life not by the exploits of a military leader, but by the message of a rediscovered culture.

Meanwhile the evolution of Egypt herself as a modern state continued, leading to the birth of Egyptian nationalism which preceded that of general Arab nationalism, ran parallel with it for many decades after the emergence of the latter and finally coalesced with it in the Arab League. It is therefore to events in Egypt that we must now turn.

2

Egyptian nationalism began as a reaction to the French occupation in 1798, turning later, in the next century, against the Turkish followers of Mohammed Ali and his successors, and finally becoming fully mobilized against the British occupation and the Capitulations (financial and legal privileges) enjoyed by the European Powers.

Partly through expenditure on modernization and eco-

nomic development under European influences (the Egyptian
Government bore half the cost of digging the Suez Canal)
and partly through ostentatious extravagance, the rulers of
Egypt after Mohammed Ali became heavily indebted to the
capitalists of London and Paris, thus opening the way to
European intervention in Egypt's internal affairs. During the
reign of the Khedive Ismail (1863–79) a dual control (Anglo-
French) was established over the country's finances, as well
as the *Caisse de la Dette* into which the interest on Egypt's
foreign loans was to be regularly paid. A new development
took place under the Capitulations. These privileges or immunities dated back to the Crusades and were subsequently
conferred by the Ottoman Sultans on European subjects.
According to them, Europeans could only be taxed with the
consent of their governments, and could only be tried on a
criminal charge by their consular courts. Ismail's reign saw
the creation of the 'mixed' courts, with European and
Egyptian judges, for the trial of civil actions involving Europeans. Lastly, a new factor was introduced into the Egyptian
situation with the completion of the Suez Canal in 1869 – a
factor which ultimately may have been the decisive motive
that impelled Britain to occupy Egypt, since the Canal
seemed to Britain to make of Egypt a route to India too
dangerous if not controlled by British arms.

In 1882 a nationalist movement led by an Egyptian officer
of native peasant stock, named Arabi, broke out in revolt
against the Khedive Tewfik, son of Ismail, who had finally
been deposed by the Sultan, at the instance of the Powers,
and exiled to Italy. Arabi's revolt was principally an attack
by nascent politically conscious Egyptian elements against
the Turkish oligarchy that monopolized all the senior posts
in the administration, both on the civil and military sides. In
a secondary and general sense it was a protest against all
foreign intervention in Egyptian affairs. There is some suspicion, however, that the British and French representatives
in Egypt at the time deliberately misinterpreted the movement and, as some writers have suggested, even acted as

latter could achieve full independence.

It was in Egypt that the most sustained, vocal, and powerful movement of Arab nationalism against Western rule was
to develop in this intermediate period. And it was a characteristic of this movement that it drew a fair measure of its
inspiration from European ideas. For, together with armies,
the West was also exporting teachers and books to the Middle
East. Under Mohammed Ali and his successors many schools
with a modern outlook had been opened in Egypt. The nineteenth-century European concepts of nationalism, freedom,
and democracy were therefore circulating among a small
intelligentsia class, which was further inspired by the
Europeanizing policy of the Khedive Ismail, himself educated in Paris.

3

A parallel movement of intellectual revival had been started
in Syria, and particularly in Lebanon, during the rule of
Ibrahim Pasha, who had allowed American and French
mission schools to be opened in the country. Within a few
years more than thirty schools came into being and printing
presses were established in Beirut. By 1866 the movement had
made such progress that the Americans were founding the
Syrian Protestant College, later to become famous throughout the Middle East as the American University of Beirut. A
few years later, the Jesuits founded, in the same city, their
University of St Joseph, which had started in a humbler form
a few years earlier at another place in Lebanon. English,
Scottish, German, and even Russian schools were to follow;
but the predominant influences remained American and
French. The schools were open to Muslim as well as Christian
Arabs, but naturally the main demand came at first from the
Christians.

From the beginning there was a marked difference between the American and the French educational approach to

the Arabs. The purpose of the French schools was principally to foster the Lebanese Christian community, teach the French language, disseminate French culture, and attach the Maronite and Catholic Arabs to France. Also, their university was intended to be, and remained, principally a local centre of education for the Lebanese, who were a predominantly Christian community. Judged by academic standards, the French achievement has been superior to the American. Not only have they imparted to the Lebanese and Syrians who flocked to their schools a far better command of the French language (which indeed often puts them on a level of complete equality with Frenchmen at the highest level) than the American schools and university ever succeeded in giving their pupils; but they have generally attained a higher standard of pure scholarship than their American counterparts and, in so far as the Arab intellectual revival drew its inspiration from the West, they did more for it by putting the Arabs into communion with the spirit of the West at a greater depth than that to which any of the other foreign schools were able to penetrate.

But the Arab revival, though largely launched by Western agencies, did not derive its inspiration solely or mainly from the West. The Arabs had, in their own language and past culture, a great and stimulating heritage on which to draw for the revivification of their faculties, the restoration of their self-respect *vis-à-vis* both the Turks and the Europeans, and, above all, the recapture of their sense of identity as Arabs. It was in this field that the Americans rendered their greatest service to the Arab peoples. They helped the Arabs to rediscover their past by laying the greatest emphasis on the revival of classical Arabic and its adaptation to modern needs, and on the printing and dissemination of Arabic books. Moreover, the American University of Beirut came to be the principal educational centre for the whole Arab Middle East (with the exception of Egypt, which in the main found its own schools and universities sufficient for its needs). In the course of time, the university came to receive as many students from Palestine, Jordan, Iraq, and Syria as from the Lebanon itself, and had more Muslims in its family than Christians.

But we are now still in the early days of its life, and of the Arab intellectual renascence. At that time the Lebanese Christians played the leading role, in and around the university, in reviving Arabic learning and awakening Arab national consciousness on the basis of a common language and a common culture. This is not surprising since, if Arab nationalism was to have a religious, as opposed to a lingual, basis and follow some such path as Pan-Islamism, which was being preached by Jamal-ud-Din al-Afghani in Egypt, the Christian Arabs would have no part in it. Their only chance was to launch Arab nationalism as a cultural movement, and though this was difficult in view of the close and subtle connection between the Arab tradition and the Muslim religion, it offered a chance well worth trying for the Christian minorities. This is not to say that the interest of the Lebanese Christians in the revival of Arabic learning was in any way insincere. Far from it. Arabic was their language as much as it was the language of the Muslim Arabs; and their joy and pride in reviving its literature and the power of its expression through the labour of such scholars and teachers as Yaziji and Bustani (both of whom, incidentally, were Maronites and therefore belonging to the majority Christian sect that was being specially cultivated by France) was undoubtedly genuine, as was also the hope that in their common Arabism they and the Muslims would find the basis of a movement aiming at emancipation from Ottoman rule, which had become distasteful to both and was, in the days of Abd-ul-Hamid II, an obvious bar to progress.

About 1880 the first political expression of this cultural nationalism was seen in the formation in Beirut of a society which included Christians, Muslims, and Druses; and which displayed a series of placards, in Beirut and other cities, demanding the use of Arabic as an official language, the abolition of press censorship, and the granting of self-government to Syria and Lebanon.

Three years later the members of the society became alarmed at the activities of the Turkish secret police. They dissolved their organization and the leaders among them made their way to Egypt, where British rule had just been established, opening for the cultural and even the nationalist activities of the Arabs new and freer fields.

It was not only, however, these active Arab nationalists that took the road to Egypt. From the middle of the nineteenth century emigrants in increasing numbers had been leaving Syria and Lebanon for the New World. By far the greater number of them were Christians, since in their case a powerful combination of considerations – some of which were unknown to the Muslim Arabs, or even acted as a deterrent upon them – urged the exodus. To the Muslims Ottoman rule, even at its worst, had the saving grace of being the rule of an Islamic imperial power; whereas to the Christian Arabs the fact that the Turks were Muslims made their rule even more odious than mere corruption, oppression, and racial alienness could have done. Then, again, the great outside world to which the emigrants went was a Christian world, more attractive to the Christian than to the Muslim Arabs.

The British occupation of Egypt (and later the Sudan) opened a new territory – much nearer home – for the Syrian and Lebanese Arabs to emigrate to in search of the security, freedom, and economic opportunities which they could not find under Ottoman rule. Here, again, the bulk of the emigrants were Christians, since the ruling power whose protection (and often service) they came to seek was Christian. Also, the first few generations of Syrian and Lebanese Arabs to take advantage of the education offered them by the Western missionaries were, naturally, in the main Christians; and it was this Western-educated class that provided most of the emigrants to Egypt and the Sudan where, for many years, they performed under the British administration a very useful function as doctors, administrative officers, clerks, and accountants, not to mention their general service, in the very early days, as intermediaries between the British rulers and their non-English-speaking subjects.

On the political plane, the Christian Arab immigrants did not – at the beginning at least – enter the stream of Egyptian nationalism. They had come to Egypt precisely because the British were there, and they tended to identify themselves with Britain and support her occupation of the country. Moreover, even when later some of them espoused the cause of Egyptian nationalism, they found the Egyptians loath to accept them as fellow-citizens on terms of equality. A Muslim Syrian or Lebanese established in Egypt could become fully assimilated in one generation, whereas his Christian compatriot might find himself still regarded as an alien even if his great-grandfather had been born in Egypt.

On the cultural side, however, the Syrian (and particularly Lebanese) Christian immigrants fused into the nascent Egyptian movement, and some of them, indeed, played a prominent part in promoting it. The proprietors and editors of the first Egyptian newspapers and magazines (some of which occupy a leading position in the Press not only of Egypt but of the whole Arab world to-day) were Christian Arabs from Lebanon.

Two paramount facts, in particular, made possible a general Arab intellectual and literary revival: classical Arabic had remained structurally the same, preserved in unalterable form by the sanctity of the Koran, since the days of the Prophet; and the spoken dialects of the different Arab peoples – from Morocco to Iraq, and from northern Syria to the Sudan or Nejd – had not become separate languages like the Romance descendants of Latin. They were, despite much local alteration and the influx here and there of foreign elements, still recognizably Arabic, so that with a little initial difficulty the Egyptian could understand the Lebanese, the Syrian the Iraqi, and so forth. Moreover, these spoken dialects were never used for writing; they had not developed forms capable of being written, so that the intellectual unity of the Arab world had been preserved through the common

possession of the written language, which was now being
revived.

Clearly, however, the revival had to pay attention to the
requirements of a new age. A new style, less elaborate and
more flexible, had to be evolved – a style influenced by modern
European modes of expression, eschewing archaic vocabulary, adopting foreign words where necessary in a world
dominated by Western political concepts, by Western science,
and Western inventions; or fusing new meanings into old
Arabic words so that they could represent new ideas.

Alike in Cairo and Beirut this process was developing
rapidly in the last two decades of the nineteenth century and
at the beginning of the twentieth. New scholars, writers, and
poets were appearing. More and more books were being
printed and circulated – some presenting the old masterpieces of Arabic literature, others being translations of European works, and others still being original contributions by
the leaders of the revival. The poets Ahmed Shawqi (an
Egyptian) and Khalil Mutran (a Lebanese), apart from a
massive output in the traditional ode form, attempted something entirely new. The former, inspired by Shakespeare,
wrote a number of poetic dramas, including one on the subject of Antony and Cleopatra; the second actually translated
Othello and *The Merchant of Venice* into Arabic verse. Jurji
Zaydan (another of the Lebanese immigrants in Egypt),
under the influence of Walter Scott, wrote a number of
novels (a new literary form in Arabic) on themes taken from
Arab history. Many years later, the blind Egyptian scholar,
Taha Hussein, went to the Sorbonne after completing his
studies at the Azher and, under French influence, initiated a
new school of Arabic writing and began to apply Western
canons of criticism to Arabic literature.

From across the Atlantic came a third stream of Arab
thought, revitalized by Western influences. A number of the
Lebanese emigrants to America became prominent writers –
some of them, like the traveller Amin Rihani and the mystic
writer and painter, Khalil Jibran, writing in both Arabic

and English – and their works influenced the course of literary development in both Cairo and Beirut.

Nor was the cultural movement in Egypt confined to literature. It included among its leading figures a great and courageous religious thinker in the person of Sheikh Mohammed Abdu, who tried to give to Muslim theological interpretation a liberal and rational direction in opposition to the dogmatic conservatism of the Azher Ulema; and an equally courageous social reformer, Qasim Amin, who called for the emancipation of women.

4

From 1882 to 1919 British policy in Egypt was, except for a short period between 1907 and 1911, one of Olympian paternalism. Cromer and Kitchener established a just and efficient system of government, rehabilitated the country's finances, extended irrigation, and protected the fellah against oppression; but they belonged to a passing imperial age, and had little understanding of, or sympathy with, the forces of the new, literate middle-class nationalism that were beginning to gather on a wider basis after the collapse of Arabi's revolt.

Discontent against the British occupation continued to develop and spread, embracing, as it did so, elements of Turkish origin as well as Arab Egyptians. The leader of the extreme left wing or Hizb al-Watani (Nationalist Party) was a French-educated and French-encouraged young lawyer, Mustapha Kemal; while a leading figure (commended, ironically enough, by Cromer in his farewell speech in 1907) in the comparatively moderate Hizb al-Umma (Party of the Nation) was Saad Zaghlul, to become famous in 1919 as the leader of the Wafd Party and chief representative of militant Egyptian nationalism.

Until 1904 France, who had never forgiven herself for letting Britain intervene alone in Egyptian affairs in 1882, had not been averse to causing the British embarrassment by supporting the forces of Egyptian nationalism. But the *Entente Cordiale* put an end to that phase in Anglo-French relations, and the cause of Arab nationalism thereby suffered a serious set-back in Egypt. It was, however, to receive a great and unexpected encouragement in Syria four years later from the Ottoman capital itself.

In 1908 the Young Turk movement forced the Sultan Abd-ul-Hamid to restore the constitution which he had suspended in 1876, decreed the equality of all races in the Ottoman Empire, and offered the Arabs a share in the imperial cabinet and parliament. The offer was accepted, and one of the Arab deputies who sat in the joint parliament at Constantinople was to become famous later as King Abdullah of Jordan. For a short while there was an exhilarating Turco-Arab honeymoon, the Arab nationalists believing that their aspirations were thus going to find a brilliant fulfilment. Soon, however, they were to be bitterly disappointed, as the Young Turk movement began to develop along racialist lines. Although the Arabs far outnumbered the Turks in the empire, electoral districts were so framed as to give the Turks a dominant majority in the parliament. The Turco-Arab Brotherhood Society founded in Constantinople in 1908 was dissolved, and the Arab nationalists began secretly to reorganize themselves as a separate entity, though their final breach with the Turks was delayed for some time even after the outbreak of World War I in 1914, because of their fears of European designs on the Middle East.

During the years 1909–14 the underground Arab movement formed a number of secret societies, the most important of which were al-Fatat (Young Arab) and al-Ahd (Covenant), in which Arab officers in the Turkish army appeared for the first time as champions of Arab nationalism. Shortly before the outbreak of the 1914 war, al-Fatat held a congress in Paris. Muslim and Christian delegates were present in almost equal numbers; but as far as geographical representation was concerned, Syria was still far in the lead, though two members came from Iraq, and three from America to represent the emigrant Arab community there.

Although this nationalist ferment was growing in various parts of the eastern Arab world, communications between the different centres were still a major difficulty in the way of bringing together the forces of the movement. The journey by camel caravan from Damascus to Baghdad (and that was still the only means of land travel between the two cities) took three weeks. There was an alternative maritime route from Beirut to Basra, through the Suez Canal, Red Sea, and Persian Gulf, but sailings were infrequent and seldom direct; and the time taken, in the most favourable circumstances, no shorter than that required for the land journey.

. Until 1908 communications between Syria and the Arabian Peninsula itself were also slow and precarious. The land journey from Damascus to Medina might take as long as forty days, and even when a ship was found going from Beirut to Jeddah, the journey could not be accomplished in less than ten or twelve days. In 1901, however, the Sultan Abd-ul-Hamid, by one of those ironies with which history mocks the cunning of man, had launched the Hejaz railway project, which was to link Damascus and Medina by a regular train service covering the distance between them in well under a week. Abd-ul-Hamid had two objects in planning this link. On the face of it, his action was a devout service to Islam, making the pilgrimage (it was intended to prolong the railway to Mecca) easier for millions of Muslims, and therefore calculated to earn for the Caliph the gratitude of all believers. A deeper and more mundane motive was the Sultan's need to establish a closer military control over his subjects in the Arabian Peninsula. As it turned out, however, the railway, when it came, proved of great service to the Arab nationalist movement that was to culminate in the Arab Revolt of 1916. But before we reach that event we must cast a look at the rest of the Arab world.

In 1911 Italy annexed Tripolitania after a brief war in which she defeated the Turks; and in the following year

Morocco, which had never been occupied by Turkey but had remained a separate and independent Sultanate since the Arab expulsion from Spain, became a French protectorate. Thus, as Tunisia and Algeria had already passed under French rule (the former also as a protectorate retaining formally its autonomous government under the Bey, and the latter by direct annexation to Metropolitan France as a number of *départements*), and as Egypt was, for her part, under British rule, the whole of Arab North Africa (using that term in its unrestricted geographical sense) was now a zone of continuous European colonies or semi-colonies. Its last official link with the Ottoman Empire was severed in 1914 when, on Turkey entering the war against Britain and her allies, Ottoman suzerainty over Egypt was terminated and replaced by a British protectorate. But whereas in Egypt the British were to be found only in the temporary capacity of administrators, soldiers, and a town-dwelling business community, in the Italian and French sections of north Africa colonization was proceeding in the sense of seizure of, and settlement on, the land.

The imposition of European rule over Egypt and the other Arab countries of north Africa before 1914 meant that when the war came the sentiments of the politically conscious sections of the population in this part of the Arab world were different from those of the nationalists in Syria, Iraq, and the Arabian Peninsula. For these last were still under Ottoman rule and aspiring to freedom from it, with British assistance, as a result of Turkey's defeat; whereas Arab nationalists west of Suez had new masters who, moreover, were Christians, so that they tended to sympathize with Turkey. In the Western Desert the Senussi leader of Libya led a rising against the British in Egypt; and the majority of the Egyptian Muslims were at heart enthusiastic about the Turkish attack on the Suez Canal and disappointed at its failure. It was not till after the war, when the expulsion of the Turks from the eastern Arab world was followed, not by Arab independence, but by the imposition of British or French rule in Syria and

Iraq, together with the added outrage of British-sponsored Zionism in Palestine, that Arab nationalism on both sides of Suez became identical in its opposition to Western domination.

In the Arabian Peninsula itself, the Ottoman power – as we have seen from Abd-ul-Hamid's eagerness to reach the Hejaz by railway – had never been very effective, and for the most part the various local princes and sheikhs enjoyed a large measure of autonomy, if not virtual independence. Those of them along the eastern and southern shores of Arabia (Kuwait, Qatar, Oman, etc.) had in the latter half of the nineteenth century been induced to conclude treaties with Britain, whereby they accepted British protection in some form or other. In Nejd, the Wahhabi movement and its secular ally, the House of Saud, had completely recovered from the defeat inflicted upon them by Ibrahim Pasha nearly a hundred years before; and in the early years of this century Abd-ul-Aziz Ibn Saud (later the famous king of Saudi Arabia) had established himself as the undisputed ruler of the whole region, befriended and subsidized by Britain.

But it was Hussein, the Sherif of Mecca (and father of the late King Abdullah of Jordan and King Faisal I of Iraq) who, on the eve of World War I, took an initiative that gave him the leadership of the Arab national movement, and gave the movement itself the opportunity of shaking off Turkish suzerainty.

Hussein, a descendant of the Prophet's family, had been in Constantinople for sixteen years virtually as a political prisoner when the Committee of Union and Progress came to power in 1908. The new rulers of Turkey sent him back to his home in the Arabian Peninsula, there to be the new Sherif of Mecca, or Custodian of the Holy Places of Islam. Hussein, an astute and ambitious man, was not content to hold the office as the empty dignity which his predecessor had allowed it to become. He set about the task of gaining control of the tribes of the Hejaz so as to give himself a position of political power in the Peninsula. The Ottoman authorities in Constantinople learned of what he was doing, and tension began to develop between them and him. It was in these circumstances that Hussein sent his son Abdullah to Cairo in February 1914 to sound Lord Kitchener as to whether he could expect British support in the event of an open breach between him and the Turks. Several months were yet to elapse before World War I broke out and the Young Turks led their country into it on Germany's side; and meanwhile, Britain was still Turkey's traditional friend and protector. Kitchener and his Oriental Secretary, Sir Ronald Storrs, with whom Abdullah was much more outspoken than with the proconsul himself, returned to Hussein a discouraging reply.

Naturally, the British attitude was completely reversed after November 1914. A revolt of the Arabs could now be turned to good account in the British offensive against Turkey in the Middle East. Moreover, a revolt led by the holiest figure in Islam (in virtue both of his descent and official position) would be a useful retort to the Caliph's appeal to all Muslims to join in a *jihad*, or holy war, against Britain.

On the Arab side, however, as contact developed between Hussein and the nationalists of Syria and Iraq, there was some reluctance, in which Hussein's son Faisal shared, to break with Turkey before making sure (i) that Arab national aspirations could not be realized within the frame-work of the Ottoman Empire, and (ii) that the Arabs would really obtain their independence from the Western Powers, and not merely fall under their domination. Protracted negotiations – the famous Hussein-McMahon correspondence – followed between the Sherif, speaking on behalf of the Arab nationalists on the one hand, and Sir Henry McMahon, who had succeeded Kitchener in Egypt, on the other.

All through these negotiations the Arabs (whether Hussein and his sons or the societies that represented the Syrian and Iraqi nationalist movements) were thinking in terms of one Arab kingdom east of Suez, uniting the Arabian Peninsula with Syria, Lebanon, Palestine, and Iraq. This project, inspired by dreams of past glory and intended to re-create as much of the Umayyad or Abbasid Empire as was possible, may not have been practically realizable in 1918, even if Britain had not by then become committed to policies that made the fragmentation of the eastern Arab world inevitable. The region was too large and lacking in good communications to be capable of being held together by inexperienced politicians against the unstable and separatist forces of Arab life, especially when no common and efficient administrative machine existed for its governance as a whole. Moreover, there were certain important differences between the Arabian Peninsula and the Arab countries to the north of it. Arabia had not changed much since the time of Mohammed; it was largely nomadic and pastoral. Whereas Syria and Iraq had several millennia of urban civilization behind them. Even Mecca and Medina were very backward as compared with Beirut, Damascus, Jerusalem, Haifa, Baghdad, and Basra. They were still medieval and theocratically minded, untouched by the Western influences that had been at work for nearly a century in Syria. Nor did the Syrian nationalists necessarily think that Hussein would be the most suitable head for the projected Arab state. But Hussein, being more or less beyond the reach of the Ottoman power, was in a position to launch a revolt, while the nationalists of Syria and Iraq, under centralized Turkish rule and even martial law during the war, could do little for their cause except die on the scaffold, when they were found out – as many of them did, including a few Christians. Another reason why Hussein could lead a revolt while the Syrian nationalists could not was that in Syria the movement had not reached popular dimensions yet, but was still confined to the intelligentsia class, while in the Hejaz Hussein could mobilize a large number of tribesmen.

At first, when Hussein defined the frontiers within which Britain should recognize Arab independence after the war, Sir Henry McMahon tried to evade the issue on the grounds that it was profitless to argue over such matters until the war was won. But Hussein was adamant, and in the end

McMahon informed the Sherif that his conditions were accepted by the British Government subject to reservations concerning Britain's desire to have a position of influence in the province of Baghdad, and concerning the traditional interests of France in the Levant. Though, some twenty years later, Sir Henry McMahon was to say that at the time of the correspondence Palestine was intended by him to be excluded from the area of Arab independence, there was no specific mention of Palestine whatever in the letters exchanged, nor of any region that could, without downright casuistry, be interpreted to cover Palestine. Certain it is that the Arabs themselves had no suspicion at all that the independence promised them was not to extend to Palestine, which was an integral part of the Arab world, indistinguishable from Syria, its population being 90 per cent Arab. This is obvious from the fact that as soon as King Hussein (with increasing vanity, the Sherif had assumed first the title of King of the Arabs, and then Caliph) heard of the Balfour Declaration in 1917, he asked the British Government in some alarm for an explanation of the meaning of this document, and was assured in reply that Britain's undertakings to the Jews would not be allowed to interfere with either the economic or the political freedom of the Arabs. But this is to anticipate the future. The agreement between Britain and the Arabs was concluded in January 1916, and the Arab Revolt (which in England at least will always be associated with the name of T. E. Lawrence) launched later in the year.

Lord Wavell, among others, has borne testimony to the great importance of this revolt in protecting the flank of the British forces in Palestine, diverting large numbers of Turkish troops to the Hejaz, and counteracting German propaganda in Muslim countries. If the revolt failed to bring about civilian uprisings in Palestine, Syria, and Iraq as the allied forces advanced to liberate them, there were several reasons for that: the ruthlessness of the Turkish military dictatorship; the sapping of the physical strength of the population by a devastating famine that had carried off several hundred thousand people in Syria, Palestine, and Lebanon during the years of the war; the fact, already touched upon, that the national movement was still confined to a small intelligentsia minority and had not yet spread to the masses; and, last but not least, the disinclination of the British authorities (particularly the Government of India) to give much publicity among the local people to the Revolt, from fear that it might over-stimulate the desire for immediate independence which Britain, both for reasons of her own and in the interests of the French and the Zionists, was unwilling to concede in 1918.

CHAPTER FOUR

CONFLICT WITH THE WEST

—

I

I T is a characteristic of the Arab mind to be swayed more by
words than by ideas, and more by ideas than by facts. Trans-
cendental principles, especially when put into resonant
speech, seem to the Arabs to have a power capable of conquering the greatest practical realities. Nowhere was this
weakness more glaringly demonstrated than in the Arabs'
attitude towards the Palestine question: so imbued were they
with the justice of their cause in that conflict that they were
unable to assess the power of the forces arrayed against
them and would never admit to themselves the possibility of
defeat.

The grandiose project for establishing a united and independent Arab state in Asia after World War I suffered from
this radical weakness. The Arab nationalist movement that
aspired to this goal had little physical strength with which to
oppose European ambitions and policies in the Middle East.
As we have seen, some of the Arab leaders were mistrustful of
European designs and insisted on exacting *effective guarantees*
of independence as the price of their revolt. Their lack of
realism, however, can be seen in their touching belief that
the guarantees they exacted must inevitably be effective,
despite the powerlessness of the Arabs to enforce them against
the victorious might of Britain and France. This belief, apart
from being an expression of the transcendentalism of Arab
thought, rested on an abounding faith in the word of Great

Britain. Through honest commercial dealing in the Arab world over a long period of time, the British had established the conviction that an Englishman's word was his bond. Both Hussein and his son Faisal held this belief and maintained it despite repeated revelations to the contrary. It was a long time before they could bring themselves to believe that the explanations and assurances which the British Government gave them, as one disturbing fact after another leaked out, were valueless if not positively deceitful.

Many excuses can be adduced for Britain's failure to honour, in their entirety, the pledges she had made to the Arabs during World War I. Britain was fighting for her life, and a country in that position is apt to make promises to anyone who will help her without prying too closely into the compatibility of all these promises with one another. Also, Britain, as a world power, with diverse and complex connexions, had many claims on her which she could not disregard but must try as far as possible to bring to a common, harmonious fulfilment. Then, again, statesmen in war-time are harassed by the number of different problems they have to deal with and may be pardoned if they fail to give to each the full consideration it deserves, particularly when they have several agencies operating from different angles on a common region or a common question. This certainly was the case in the Middle East between 1914 and 1918, when the Foreign Office, the Arab Bureau in Cairo, and the Government of India were often ignorant of the activities or opposed to the intentions of one another. Lastly, the British Government did not realize to what extent Hussein was acting as the spokesman of a general Arab movement covering Syria, Palestine, and Iraq; they were inclined to think that his insistence on Arab independence throughout these countries was largely an expression of personal and dynastic ambition, and that if at the end of the war they presented him with an independent kingdom in the Arabian Peninsula, he would be well enough pleased with that to accept the British interpretation of the reservations made with regard to the *vilayet*

of Baghdad and the French position in Syria, as well as the
policy of the Balfour Declaration.

The fact remains, however, that within a few months of
concluding her agreement with the Arabs, Britain proceeded
to negotiate with France a treaty which made Arab unity
and independence at the end of the war impossible; and
worse still, she made in the following year a promise to the
Zionist Jews which could not, on any interpretation, be
honestly fulfilled except by a shocking sacrifice of Arab rights
and interests.

In embarking upon the negotiations with the French,
Britain was probably doing no more than was necessary to
reconcile the Arab aspirations she had promised to satisfy
with the claims which she knew the French laid to a position
of predominance in the Levant. These French claims could
be traced back, emotionally, to the Crusades, in which
France had played the leading part, and which had led to the
Europeans in general becoming known in the Arab countries
as the *Franj*. The presence in Mount Lebanon of a large
community of Christian Arabs belonging to the Catholic
Church had always interested France, partly from spiritual
and partly from political motives, since it gave her potential
adherents in the Ottoman dominions and might, in certain
circumstances, afford her an opportunity of territorial ac-
quisition. Since the reign of Francis I, in the sixteenth century, France had tended to assume the position of protectress
of the Catholic Christians in Syria and Lebanon. It was in
that monarch's reign that the Ottoman Sultan was induced
to grant to French citizens the first of the privileges which
came to be known as the Capitulations; and gradually France
tried, through her friendship at that time with Turkey, to
have these privileges extended to all Catholics in the Ottoman Empire. The first French schools were opened in
Lebanon in the second half of the seventeenth century, and
though the connexion was temporarily suspended as a result
of the French Revolution and Bonaparte's invasion of Egypt,
the Catholic missions began to come back during the rule of

Ibrahim Pasha, and French cultural influence grew in the Lebanon throughout the nineteenth century. The massacre of the Christians in 1860 nearly led to a French occupation of the country; and though the French troops had to withdraw, and the Mountain was placed under a collective European guarantee, the claim of France to be in a special sense the protectress of the Catholic majority continued to develop. By 1912 the French had so far succeeded as to gain from Britain a recognition of their 'special position' in Syria and Lebanon. What this diplomatic language meant was that, in the event of the demise of the Sick Man of Europe and the partitioning of his territory, the Levant would be France's share. The agreement between Britain and Hussein contained a reservation more or less to this effect, which Hussein did not accept but agreed to leave pending till the end of the war so as not to embarrass Britain in her relations with France. It was not, therefore, surprising or reprehensible that Britain, immediately after concluding the agreement with the Arabs, should open negotiations with France with a view to finding a formula that would reconcile, as far as possible, all the interests involved and rights recognized.

What was surprising and reprehensible, however, was the result of these negotiations. In the Sykes-Picot Agreement, as it came to be called, Britain and France agreed to partition the Arab countries north of the Peninsula (that is to say, geographical Syria, which included Palestine and Jordan as well as Lebanon; and Iraq) into British and French spheres of influence. The Lebanon and Syria (including the Mosul region) were to be the share of France; Iraq (but without Mosul) and what is now the kingdom of Jordan, the share of Britain; while Palestine, in that first agreement (Tsarist Russia was still in the war and claimed certain rights of protection over the Greek Orthodox part of the Holy Places of Jerusalem) was to be placed under an international regime. In the Levant, the coastal regions of Syria and Lebanon were to be administered directly by France; while an independent Arab state, under French protection, was to be set up in the

99

less developed and politically conscious regions of the interior. Similarly, in the British portion, the more mature region, including Baghdad and Basra (the Iraq of to-day) was to be placed under British colonial rule, while in the less advanced country to the east (roughly Transjordan) Britain was to 'protect' an independent Arab state.

While negotiating this agreement with France, Britain did not tell her ally of the pledges she had given the Arabs; nor did she let the Arabs have any inkling of the negotiations with the French. It was only when the Bolsheviks, on their accession to power and withdrawal from the war, published the text of the Agreement in order to embarrass the Colonial Powers, that the Arab nationalists knew of the real shape of things to come.

This alarming discovery for the Arabs, however, roughly coincided with another shock of an even more portentous nature, namely the issuing of the Balfour Declaration by the British Government on 2 November 1917.

2

It is one of the tragic facts of modern history – a fact that has caused much trouble and suffering already, and may still cause a great deal more – that Jewish nationalism and Arab nationalism started about the same time, and that the goal of the former could not be attained without bringing it into a mortal conflict with the latter in one of the most vital regions of the Arab world. In a way this is not surprising, since both Arab nationalism and Jewish nationalism stemmed from the nationalist ideology of nineteenth-century Europe.

By no means the whole of Jewry had remained in Palestine until Titus expelled them from it and destroyed the Temple in A.D. 71. The incorporation of Palestine in the Roman Empire had opened all the Mediterranean world to Jewish enterprise, and a large number of Jews had taken advantage of the opportunities thus afforded them and left

Palestine from choice long before the forcible dispersion of 71. Even after that event, however, and more particularly throughout the Arab and Ottoman periods, there probably had never been any time during which a small Jewish community did not exist in Palestine – varying between 5 and 10 per cent of the total population. But the vast majority of the inhabitants since the Arab conquest in the seventh century had been Arabs (both Muslim and Christian); some in the ethnic sense and some in the broader cultural sense defined in the first chapter of this book. Many of them, indeed, were the descendants of the autochthonous people of the land – the Canaanites of the Bible – who had survived the Jewish conquest under Joshua, retaining possession of the coastland, and lived on under the Romans and Byzantines to become finally the Arab population of medieval and modern times. Even the Jews among this population became Arabized, adopting Arabic as their mother tongue.

Until the birth of Zionism, however, the Jews who came to live in Palestine (it would be inaccurate to say 'came back', since many of these Jews were not the descendants of the old Hebrew population of the country, but the progeny of European gentiles converted to Judaism) belonged to one of two classes: pious, orthodox Jews who from religious motives wished to live and die in the Holy Land, and refugees from persecution in other countries who, as individuals, found tolerance under Arab or Turkish rule. A new phenomenon appeared in the eighteen-eighties when, following an outbreak of anti-semitism in Russia, many Russian Jews came to Palestine and established agricultural settlements, though still only as individuals, preferring no political claim to the country, willing to live under Ottoman rule and to employ Arab peasants on their land. It is significant, however, that before 1914 the size and prosperity of these settlements had begun to arouse the alarm and hostility of the Arab population.

By then the Zionist movement – in other words the Jewish national movement which aimed at statehood in Palestine –

had made considerable progress in England and America. Highly placed Jews were able to plead its cause in Press and Parliament, in church circles and among the members of the two governments. The establishment of a Jewish National Home (it was really intended from the beginning to be a 'state', but the word 'home' was adopted as a form of intermediate camouflage necessary to lull Arab suspicions) was represented to the liberals as a great humanitarian measure that would at once solve the Jewish problem and help to modernize the Near East; to the conservative and empire-minded politicians as a valuable contribution to British imperial strategy; to the pious Christians, and particularly the nonconformist section of them, as a fulfilment of the word of God. These general pleadings were reinforced by a direct personal appeal to Lord Balfour and Mr Lloyd George from Dr Chaim Weizmann, a Jewish scientist of Russian origin, whose chemical researches in England were helping the Allied war effort. But perhaps the two most potent considerations of all were the hope of winning away from Germany the Jews of Central Europe, and of enlisting the maximum amount of support for the war from American Jewry.

Not only Balfour and Lloyd George were won over to the Zionist cause, but also Winston Churchill, Woodrow Wilson, Smuts, and other leading Allied figures. None of these statesmen seems to have given any serious consideration to the existence and rights of the Arabs of Palestine. They were either completely ignorant of the facts and thought of the Arabs as some Bedouin tribes that could be moved about, or out, without much difficulty, to make room for the Jews (and this is the most charitable explanation that can be offered); or they were cynical enough to regard the Arabs as an inferior people whose rights did not have to be respected in the same way as the rights of Europeans and Americans. Whichever was the case, the British Government finally issued the following Declaration:

H.M. Government view with favour the establishment in Palestine of a national home for the Jewish people, and will use their best endeavours to facilitate this object, it being clearly understood that nothing shall be done to prejudice the civil and religious rights of other non-Jewish communities in Palestine, or the rights and political status enjoyed by Jews in any other country.

In a way the most outrageous part of this document was the very clause put in ostensibly to safeguard the position of the Arabs. To call them, who formed 90 per cent of the population of the country, the 'non-Jewish communities' was, in J. M. N. Jeffries' unforgettable phrase, tantamount to 'calling the grass of the countryside the non-dandelion portion of the pastures!' It indicated either such unawareness of the numbers and status of the Arabs in the country as cannot be pardoned in the framers of such a document, or a deliberate attempt to play them down by disingenuous phrasing. Besides, 'civil and religious rights' was itself an equivocal phrase. To the Arabs it could be represented as meaning political independence; while to the Jews and their supporters in Britain and America it obviously meant something less, something that would not prevent the eventual establishment of a Jewish state. In fact, General Smuts made it quite clear during the drafting of the Mandate for Palestine that no autonomous government would be allowed in the country until the Jews had become a majority through British-sponsored immigration.

Thirty years later, Ernest Bevin, when Foreign Secretary, admitted that the Balfour Declaration contained two mutually irreconcilable undertakings: furthering the invasion of Palestine by immigrants, and providing for the protection of the native population against the consequences of this invasion!

The Arabs, both in Palestine and outside it, sensed immediately the real danger to them of this British move. With the sureness of the instinct of self-preservation they apprehended that, to quote the words of George Antonius, 'a national home can be established for one people in the country of another only by dislodging or exterminating the people in possession'. The British Government did their best to delay the 'breaking' of the news of the Balfour Declaration among the Palestine Arabs for as long as possible. But when the news eventually reached the intended victims their fears and resentment (not to be allayed even temporarily by the assurances of the British Government and some of the Zionist leaders, as had been those of King Hussein and his son Faisal) were expressed in the strongest terms to the King-Crane Commission in 1919.

The dispatching of this Commission to Syria and Palestine while the Peace Conference was sitting in Paris was the only attempt made by any of the Allies to ascertain the wishes of the Arabs concerning their destiny under the League of Nations Mandatory system, which was being evolved as a substitute for Colonialism. President Wilson's Fourteen Points had included the principle that the Allied Powers should not acquire any new colonies, or annex any of the countries of the liberated peoples. To reconcile this principle with the terms of the Sykes-Picot Agreement, Class 'A' Mandates were to be created by the League of Nations in respect of 'certain provinces of the Ottoman Empire' which were deemed to be sufficiently advanced for their independence to be recognized subject to their receiving temporary assistance from one of the Great Powers. Further, the Covenant of the League stipulated that the wishes of the peoples concerned should be the principal consideration in the choice of the Mandatory Power. Wilson invited Lloyd George and Clemenceau to join him in sending an Allied commission to Syria and Palestine to ascertain the wishes of their people. The British and French Premiers declined the invitation, but Wilson was not to be put off, and sent an all-American commission, consisting of two distinguished and impartial persons – Dr Henry King and Mr Charles Crane, both members of the American Peace Delegation and of the Peace Conference's Mandates Commission.

The Commissioners spent six weeks in Syria and Palestine, during which they received a very large number of deputations and petitions. They found that there was an overwhelming majority for a united Syria (i.e. including the Lebanon and Palestine). They recommended that this strong desire for unity should be respected, subject to the autonomy of Lebanon (within Syrian unity) as a predominantly Christian country, which already under Ottoman rule had enjoyed a large measure of self-government. They also found that the great majority of the people wanted America to be the Mandatory Power (because they believed her to be disinterested and free from imperialist designs); and failing her, Britain. Only the Catholics of Mount Lebanon – a small proportion of the total – expressed a preference for France. But it was when they came to deal with Zionist aspirations that the Commissioners recorded their most significant and prophetic opinions. Saying that they 'began their study of Zionism with minds predisposed in its favour', they proceeded, under the impact of 'the actual facts in Palestine, coupled with the force of the general principles proclaimed by the Allies and accepted by the Syrians' to recommend 'serious modification of the extreme Zionist programme for Palestine of unlimited immigration of Jews, looking forward to making Palestine distinctly a Jewish state.'

In this last sentence the Commissioners put their finger on the raw reality of the Zionist project, adding by way of confirmation, 'the fact came out repeatedly in the Commission's conferences with Jewish representatives that the Zionists looked forward to a practically complete dispossession of the present non-Jewish inhabitants by various forms of purchase'. In conclusion, the Commission uttered a solemn warning: 'The Peace Conference should not shut its eyes to the fact that the anti-Zionist feeling in Palestine and Syria is intense and not lightly to be flouted. No British officer consulted by the Commissioners believed that the Zionist programme could be carried out except by force of arms. ... That of itself is evidence of a strong sense of the injustice of the Zionist programme, on the part of the non-Jewish population of Palestine and Syria. Decisions requiring armies to carry out are sometimes necessary, but they are surely not gratuitously to be taken in the interests of injustice.'

No notice was taken of this report by the Peace Conference. Instead, the Supreme Allied Conference, meeting at San Remo in the spring of 1920, took a series of decisions which completely disregarded both the wishes of the Arabs and the recommendations of the King-Crane Commission. Geographical Syria was to be broken up into Palestine, Lebanon, and a reduced Syria (roughly the Syrian state of to-day) consisting of the cities of Damascus, Homs, Hama, Aleppo, and their hinterland as far as Iraq. France was to have a Mandate for Lebanon and Syria; but while occupying and directly administering the Lebanon, she was to allow the existence, 'under her protection' of an Arab state in Syria centred on Damascus. Britain was to have a Mandate for Palestine, with the obligation to establish in it the Jewish national home promised in the Balfour Declaration. She was also to have a Mandate for Iraq, as an undivided territory to be directly administered by Britain, and to include the Mosul region, ceded by Clemenceau to Lloyd George under pressure.

These decisions produced a violent psychological reaction among the Arabs, who felt that they had been betrayed, that their wishes had been cynically set aside in the interests of the rival imperialistic claims of Britain and France, that even the promises given to them in writing by Britain had been violated. That reaction, confirmed and accentuated by later events in the period between the two wars, was unfortunately to condition Arab feelings towards the West until the present day.

The first event to confirm and accentuate this reaction came very shortly after the San Remo decisions. King Hussein's son, Faisal, who had led the Arab Revolt in the field, as an auxiliary ally of the British forces that entered Syria, was in Damascus by 1920, heading the promised independent Arab state. The French, who had officially promised to recognize this state, were fundamentally hostile to it. In their eyes the whole Arab movement was suspect as a British-sponsored creation inimical to French interests in the

Levant. Friction arose soon between the French in Lebanon and Faisal in Damascus, as a result of which the French presented Faisal with an ultimatum so crushing to Arab national aspirations and so humiliating to Arab feelings that one can only suppose they hoped he would reject it and so give them an excuse for occupying Syria in addition to Lebanon. That was Faisal's own view. Hence, his acceptance of the ultimatum (despite the advice of many of his followers) in the hope of saving Damascus from French military occupation. But even his surrender did not avail. After a valiant but vain attempt by the Arab nationalists to repulse the advancing French columns, Damascus was occupied and Faisal compelled to leave the country.

Thus the stage was set for a long and bitter conflict between the Arabs on the one hand and the French, British, and Zionist Jews on the other, in Syria and Lebanon, Iraq and Palestine respectively. France's part in the struggle came to an end in 1945, with the full realization of Syrian and Lebanese independence. Britain, as far as Palestine is concerned, withdrew from the conflict in 1948 by laying down her Mandate, while her differences with Iraq may be considered as virtually over. In Jordan (detached from Palestine in 1922 and placed under the Emir – later King – Abdullah) there has never been an Anglo-Arab clash. But the conflict between the Arabs and the Zionists has not ended in any real or final sense, despite the Zionists' success in 1948 in establishing their state of Israel.

We shall look briefly at the course of all these conflicts, but at this moment we must turn back to Egypt; for the end of World War I saw the beginning of the Egyptian movement for independence on a national scale and in a militant and sustained manner. From that moment the current of Egyptian nationalism began to run parallel with the current of Arab nationalism. Psychologically, they were like two rivers running into and out of one another.

3

The war had stimulated Egyptian nationalism in many ways. The abolition of Ottoman suzerainty and the proclamation of the British protectorate was the first sting. Then came the swarming of British troops in large numbers over Cairo and Alexandria as well as the Canal zone, the conscription of Egyptian fellahin to form a labour corps and the requisitioning of their animals for the British forces. This personal impact helped to spread anti-British feeling among the masses; while the intellectual middle-class nationalists received encouragement from President Wilson's Fourteen Points and the general proclamation of democratic ideals by the Allies.

No sooner was the war over than a delegation (in Arabic *Wafd*; hence the name of the nationalist party that grew out of this occasion) called on the British High Commissioner to ask for the country's independence, and for leave to proceed to Paris to put their case before the Peace Conference. The leader of the delegation was no other than Saad Zaghlul, in whom the departing eye of Lord Cromer had, in 1907, discerned the promise of future achievement. Instead of acceding to their request the British Government deported the delegates to Malta. Widespread popular risings, in which the alienated peasantry supported the urban nationalists, greeted this measure. Communications were attacked and destroyed, British officers and civilians killed, Cairo for some time isolated. The British authorities had failed to assess the importance of the movement, and both its character and extent took them completely by surprise. They had been still thinking of the nationalists as a group of urban politicians without any support in the country; adhering to the old legend that the people at large were contented under British rule because all they wanted was justice and security. Against this complacent and out-dated belief something suddenly struck that could be called a national revolution. It was the first of a series of rebellions that were to break out in the Arab world against Britain or France in the inter-war years – a manifestation of nationalism as a popular emotional force; a portent of a new era in modern Arab development.

With that outbreak commenced a lengthy ding-dong battle between Egyptian national aspirations and the requirements of British imperial security as seen by the Foreign Office and the Chiefs of Staff – a battle in which negotiations for a peaceful settlement alternated regularly with the use of violence and counter-violence, in which both sides repeatedly passed from intransigence to accommodation, and again from accommodation to intransigence but which, in its over-all effect, has resulted in the fulfilment of Egypt's aspiration to independence.

First came the release of the deported leaders and Zaghlul's journey to Paris where, however, his demand for complete independence could gain no hearing from a peace conference dominated by Lloyd George and Clemenceau, especially as President Wilson had already recognized the British protectorate. More fruitful was the dispatch to Egypt by the British Government of a mission headed by Lord Milner, then Colonial Secretary, to report on the situation and make recommendations for the future. It was Milner and his colleagues who indicated the road along which not only Anglo-Egyptian but also Anglo-Iraqi and even, up to a point, Franco-Syrian and Franco-Lebanese relations were to develop in the inter-war years. Their solution, propounded in 1920, was a treaty of friendship and alliance between Britain and Egypt, whereby the former would recognize the independence of the latter subject to receiving in return certain rights (including that of maintaining British troops on Egyptian soil) necessary to the protection of her interests. The Egyptian nationalists were too deeply committed to the goal of independence and the total evacuation of British troops from Egypt and the Sudan to be able to accept Milner's offer. But the way had been shown, and every effort that has been made since to settle the Anglo-Egyptian dispute has consisted in taking a step along that road.

In 1922 the British Government recognized the independence of Egypt by a unilateral declaration (the Egyptians still refusing to accept, by an agreement binding on them, anything less than complete independence) which reserved for future settlement the questions of the Sudan, the security of Britain's imperial communications, defence, and the protection of foreign residents and native minorities. The office of Khedive, which on the proclamation of the Protectorate in 1914 had become a Sultanship, now underwent a further verbal transformation in the interests of democratic evolution. Egypt became a constitutional monarchy, and its head of state a King who, however, was granted by the constitution considerably wider powers than those associated with kingship in democratic Europe. These powers meant, in fact, that the King could dismiss a prime minister with a majority behind him in the chamber of deputies, and rule through minority governments either without parliament or with a parliament produced by rigged elections. The position thus created between the monarchy and the majority party (the Wafd) was to establish a recurring pattern of government that lasted for nearly thirty years. Free elections would return a large Wafdist majority. Sooner or later the King (both Farouk and his father, Fuad, were autocrats who, with the old Turkish mentality of their dynasty, despised the Egyptian people, believing that the whip was still the best instrument for ruling them) would dismiss the Wafdist prime minister, dissolve the chamber of deputies, and appoint a 'strong man' to rule the country by either open or camouflaged dictatorship. In time the dictatorship, especially when exercised openly by a Palace man and resulting in flagrant abuses perpetrated in the King's interest, would become intensely unpopular. On the advice of the British – sometimes under strong pressure from them – the King would finally consent to another free election bringing in another enormous Wafdist majority, and so on. What ultimately broke up this pattern and, *inter alia*, led to the military *coup* of 1952, was, ironically enough, the final peace concluded between the

King and the Wafd in 1950. The ageing Wafd leader, Nahas Pasha, tired of long sojourns in the political wilderness, determined to avoid further clashes with the King. This gave Farouk a free rein until the abuses of his regime became a crying public scandal that gave the military junta their opportunity.

The nationalist extremists, resenting the restrictions placed on Egypt's independence by the Declaration of 1922, resorted to violence of a new kind in fighting the British – a campaign of individual assassination. This culminated in a major crisis in 1924 when Sir Lee Stack, Sirdar of the Egyptian Army (the post was still held by an Englishman under the 'defence' reservation) and Governor-General of the Sudan, was murdered in Cairo. The British retort was an ultimatum to the Egyptian Government (headed at that time by the Wafdist leader Zaghlul) requiring the evacuation of the entire Egyptian army from the Sudan (where the bulk of it had been stationed since the reconquest of that country and the establishment of the Condominium Government) and the payment of an indemnity of £500,000. In addition, the British note threatened that the area of cultivation in the Sudan requiring Nile water irrigation would be no longer limited to the figure agreed upon with Egypt. Egypt paid the indemnity and recalled her army from the Sudan. She also trembled with a new fear, which ever since has been a dominant factor in her attitude to the Sudan question: the fear that the British might use their position in the Sudan to establish a stranglehold over her through their control of the Nile.

This episode was important for another reason. It marked the beginnings of nationalism in the Sudan, and initiated the Egypto-Sudanese alliance against the British which was eventually to determine the results of the elections to the first Sudanese parliament in November 1953. The Sudanese intelligentsia had been, since 1898, growing up under the influence of Egyptian teachers, Egyptian Sharia judges, Egyptian officers, and junior officials in the administration. Since 1919 Egyptian nationalists had been active in the Sudan, and,

when the 1924 crisis came, a pro-Egyptian Sudanese movement staged a number of anti-British incidents, including a
mutiny of military units in Khartoum. Thus a new Arab
people entered upon the modern political scene.

The Egyptian surrender to the British ultimatum and the
almost total elimination of all Egyptian influences from the
Sudan for a decade after 1924 caused a certain reorientation
among the Sudanese nationalists towards the goal of independence rather than union with Egypt. Their slogan became
'the Sudan for the Sudanese'. This attitude partly represented a genuine revulsion of feelings. Partly, also, it was
calculated to win British approval for the development of
Sudanese national aspirations under British tutelage, since
their development in alliance with Egypt was, for the time
being, out of the question.

Attempt after attempt was made by British and Egyptian
statesmen after 1924 to settle the Anglo-Egyptian dispute by
reaching agreement on the four reserved questions. The two
immovable rocks on which all these attempts foundered were
the questions of the Sudan and the Suez Canal. Egypt
claimed sovereignty over the Sudan and the right to defend
the Suez Canal herself; in other words, the termination of the
British occupation of both countries, regarded as a political
unity under the Egyptian Crown. Britain would not concede
either point. The two sides faced one another like two
elements whose coming together was impossible. But in 1936
a formidable catalyst appeared in the shape of Mussolini's
growing ambitions in the Mediterranean. If the Egyptians
found the presence of British troops on their soil disagreeable,
the idea of its incorporation in a new Italian Empire – for
which they could not entertain even the respect they felt
for the British – was utterly abhorrent. A united front was
formed, headed by the Wafd but including all the country's
leading figures, to negotiate with Britain. Success was
achieved in the Treaty of Friendship and Alliance of 1936.
Without prejudice to the question of sovereignty over the
Sudan – shelved for the time being – Britain and Egypt agreed

that the principal object of their administration of that country was the welfare of its people. Priority was to be given to qualified Sudanese in all appointments to government service; and where no qualified Sudanese were available Egyptian candidates were to be given equal consideration with British. Britain undertook to withdraw her troops from Cairo and Alexandria within ten years; and Egypt agreed to place at the disposal of her ally a zone in the Suez Canal region, where Britain would have the right to maintain, in times of peace, a force of not more than 10,000 ground troops and 400 R.A.F. personnel. If war came, Britain would defend Egypt, and Egypt would give Britain all necessary help and facilities. Finally Britain agreed to the return to the Sudan of a number of Egyptian troops. The treaty was to be for twenty years, though either party might ask for a revision of it in ten.

A very important consequence of the treaty for Egypt was the abolition, with Britain's help, of the Capitulations – the financial and judicial immunities which European residents in the country had enjoyed, to the increasing and scandalous detriment of the national interest with regard to revenue and public security.

4

The second Arab rebellion against Western rule in the inter-war period was that of Iraq.

When the British promised to recognize Arab independence, one of the reservations they made was for 'special administrative arrangements in Basra and Baghdad', by which they meant direct British control of lower Iraq. The Sherif Hussein had insisted that Iraq must be included in the area of Arab independence, but agreed that the lower part of the country might be temporarily occupied by the British 'for a period to be settled by negotiation'. Thus the matter stood till the end of the war, with the Government of India, on the other side, thoroughly disapproving of the encouragement

given by Britain to Arab independence, and crudely favour-
ing outright annexation of Iraq.

In Iraq itself (whose Arabs had provided the majority of
the officers forming the secret society *al-Ahd*) nationalism
was quiescent during the war. Its representatives were mainly
scattered abroad, many of them joining Faisal in the Arab
Revolt and taking part with him in forming the Arab state
in Damascus after its liberation; while communications
between the country and the rest of the Arab world were
completely severed.

The position, however, changed immediately as soon as
the war was over. Communications were restored and transformed by the introduction of motor transport. The nationalist leaders began to return, and newspapers appeared. Public
opinion among the politically conscious elements was greatly
stimulated by the Anglo-French Declaration of 7 November
1918, reaffirming to the Arabs the promise of independence
and 'national governments and administrations that shall
derive their authority from the free exercise of the initiative
and choice of the indigenous populations.' Under these influences Iraqi nationalism was quickly reborn. Across the
desert, in Damascus, Faisal had formed his kingdom, and
from there a stream of nationalist Arab inspiration reached
Baghdad and Basra.

The British found themselves being pulled in two opposite
directions. On the one hand, they were committed to the
liberal policy of the Anglo-French Declaration. On the other,
the Indian Government and the representatives of Britain in
Iraq itself believed in the necessity of direct British rule. The
latter influences won the day to such an extent that the administration they produced was acidly described by no less
an imperialist than Lord Curzon as 'not an Arab government inspired and helped by British advisers, but a British
government infused with Arab elements'. The British made
here the same mistake as they had made in Egypt. They
failed to understand the nature of nationalism or to assess its
power. They ignored it as being a frothy agitation made by

an insignificant minority. They believed that the mass of the people wanted only an efficient government that would give them security and justice, and that they would support a British administration against the nationalists of their own kin.

The truth of the matter was that the Iraqi Muslim Arabs resented the descent upon them of foreigners and Christians in the capacity of authoritarian rulers. Their resentment was fanned by propaganda from Bolshevik sources, as well as from Turkey with whom the Allied peace negotiations dragged interminably, and from Damascus, where Faisal's elder brother, Abdullah, was proclaimed by the members of the *al-Ahd* society King of Iraq.

There were many non-political causes of discontent, such as the legacy of economic conditions under the old Turkish regime, and the strictness of the British authorities in collecting taxes; but the force that gave an underlying unity and direction to the general discontent and eventually fired it into armed rebellion was nationalism – in other words, the desire of the educated class for independence. The rebellion broke out in the summer of 1920, soon after the announcement of the San Remo decisions giving Britain a Mandate over Iraq, and lasted for nearly three months. Its fighting power came chiefly from the tribes, who had been influenced both by political and religious propaganda, and from the Iraqi officers who had returned to the country after the expulsion of Faisal from Damascus.

It cost Britain £40,000,000 (as heavy reinforcements had to be brought from India) and 400 fatal casualties in British and Indian troops to suppress the insurrection; while the rebels themselves suffered more than 8000 casualties. The damage caused to the country through the destruction of buildings, railways, etc., was estimated at £400,000.

Although Britain had, before the outbreak of the rebellion, declared her intention of setting up an Iraqi state with independence as its goal, there is no doubt that the rebellion caused a profound alteration in the British attitude towards the country. It was realized that the promised state had not only to come very quickly but also to have much more reality and to move towards the goal of complete independence with much more visible speed than had been intended. Just as the Egyptian revolution of 1919 had resulted in the Milner Mission and the Declaration of Independence of 1922, so the Iraqi rebellion led to the decisions taken at the conference held in Cairo in 1921 by Mr Churchill, who had succeeded Milner as Colonial Secretary. Iraq was to become a constitutional monarchy with a council of Iraqi ministers and elected assemblies. Though the British High Commissioner was to wield great powers for some time and the Iraqi ministers were to have British advisers, the government was to be an apparatus of genuine Iraqi institutions. Moreover, despite her having obtained from the San Remo conference a mandate over Iraq, Britain now proposed that the relationship between her and the new state should be expressed in the terms of a treaty of friendship and alliance rather than in those of a mandate imposed from above and deriving no validity from the will of the Iraqi people.

King Faisal, whose Syrian state had been destroyed by the French, was put forward as a candidate for the throne of Iraq and accepted by a large majority of the people. He was to reign for twelve years, steering his kingdom through difficult times, holding a delicate balance between the British on the one hand and the Iraqi nationalist extremists on the other, and gradually, by his dignity, sincerity and tact, winning genuine respect and popularity despite the general prejudice that existed against the House of Hashem and the personal handicap, in nationalist eyes, of having been helped to the throne by the British.

The treaty which was concluded between Britain and Iraq in 1922 fell far short of Iraqi nationalist aspirations. Britain retained direction of Iraq's foreign relations, together with a large measure of control over the country's finances. Ultimate power rested not with the ministers but with the British 'advisers'; not with the King but with the High Commissioner. The nationalists, with whom Faisal tended to associate himself, resisted these conditions and only surrendered at the last moment when presented with an ultimatum by the High Commissioner. However, the principle had been established that Iraq was, potentially at least, an independent, sovereign state; and though the terms of this first treaty were substantially those of the Mandate itself, the treaty provided for its own future revision and thus opened the door to a succession of modifications culminating in the treaty of 1930 which terminated the Mandate and all British control over the Iraqi Government. Instead of being a ward of the League of Nations, Iraq (whose candidature was sponsored by Britain) became in 1932 a member of that organization, and so was the first Arab state to appear upon the stage of modern international politics on terms of equality with the nations of the West – even those of them, including Britain herself, who still held colonial possessions and were becoming increasingly known to the Arabs as the 'Imperialists'.

The only restrictions on Iraq's independence after 1930 were the obligations she assumed as Britain's ally. These included her acceptance of two British military bases on Iraqi soil and her undertaking to give Britain all assistance and facilities in the event of war. Yet the Iraqi nationalists were to protest later (as did the Egyptian nationalists concerning the Anglo-Egyptian treaty) that they had had to accept these conditions, since the alternatives before them were not independence with or without a treaty, but independence with a treaty or no independence at all. Thus, though a body of moderate opinion in Iraq was satisfied with the treaty to a point that made Nuri Pasha es-Said assure the British Foreign Secretary of his country's 'sincere and abiding gratitude to the British people', there was, in general, little enthusiasm for the alliance or love for Britain. The facts that Britain had given Iraq the services and institutions that made her a modern state and that she had finally recognized her independence, helped her to be rid of the Ottoman Capitulations, and brought about her admission to the League of Nations were outweighed in the nationalist mind by memories of the Sykes-Picot Agreement, by the imposition of the Mandate in the first instance instead of the immediate recognition of independence in 1918, by the resentments which twelve years of British rule had left behind, and finally by the obligatory alliance and the maintenance of British military bases. Enhancing all these direct causes of hostility to Britain was the steady imposition of Zionism, under a British administration, on the Arabs of Palestine – a situation to which, from the beginning, the Iraqis reacted with violent sensitiveness.

Iraq under the Mandate, and at the demand of her own politically conscious class led by the old liberals of the pre-1914 Arab movement, had been given a democratic form of government. Indeed, there was no possible alternative to this, although the bulk of the population was still illiterate and the gulf between the forms and the spirit of democracy, as practised in the West, was bound to be, for many years, considerable. As long as King Faisal lived there was a hope that his prestige and wisdom would tend the frail democracy of his new state along the paths of healthy growth. But this hope was tragically shattered by the King's unexpected death shortly after Iraq gained her independence. In the absence of an educated electorate, with none of the sanctions established by a long parliamentary tradition, amidst growing social abuses that called for reform and the intrigues and counter-intrigues of cliques of political personalities competing for office, a power vacuum began to develop into which the army was inevitably drawn. Both Persia and Turkey, Iraq's neighbours, provided examples of successful military dictatorship which were not without a certain influence on Iraqi politics. But no great military dictator emerged in Iraq. Instead, the army intervened in support of one political clique against another. The period between 1936 and 1941 has been described as one of 'government by *coups d'état*'. Seven times in these five years the government was changed under military dictation, and the country lived in a state of permanent instability. Iraq was thus the first Arab state in which the weakness of democracy and its inability to effect the needed social and economic reforms brought the army into politics. We shall see how the same phenomenon occurred later in both Syria and Egypt. But now it is time to look at another conflict between Arab nationalism and the West.

5

Basically, the history of Syria and Lebanon in the period between the two wars was the same as that of Iraq and Egypt as regards the development of national consciousness in the two countries and the evolutions through which they went in their relationship with the ruling European Power – in their case France. Dissatisfaction with an autocratic alien rule that did not take their national sentiments sufficiently into consideration broke out finally in armed rebellion, which gave a severe shock to the ruling Power and inflicted heavy losses on her. Although the rebellion was finally suppressed or fizzled out, it achieved the fundamental object of bringing about a reorientation in the policy of the foreign rulers. Increasing recognition of national aspirations expressed itself in substituting for the Mandate a treaty of friendship and alliance conceding the full independence of the two countries, subject to their placing at the disposal of France certain military facilities.

To begin with, however, the situation in the Levant was, in one important respect, unlike that of either Iraq or Egypt. Although the Arab idea had largely originated among the Christians of the Lebanon (some of whom, indeed, forfeited their lives in its cause under Turkish martial law in the 1914–18 period) the majority of the Lebanese Christians welcomed the advent of France as a Mandatory Power at the end of the war, as against the establishment of an independent Arab state in which the Muslims would be in a majority. These were principally the Maronites and other Uniates, who were not only in communion with Rome but had been

119

impregnated with French culture and pro-French sentiments by the many Jesuit and Frères schools in the country; though even among the Greek Orthodox and Protestant sects there was a certain mistrustfulness of Arab nationalism as a predominantly Muslim movement, and a preference therefore for the protection of a Christian Power. Neither the Copts in Egypt nor the Assyrian or Kurdish minorities in Iraq presented an analogy to the Lebanese Christians. Many of the Copts might in their hearts – at that time – be glad of the British occupation, but publicly they espoused the nationalist cause with great enthusiasm and played a leading part in the Wafd under Saad Zaghlul. The Assyrians in Iraq were a very small minority – a community, but certainly not a people capable of statehood. As for the Kurds (who of course are Muslims and only a minority in the racial sense), though they were far more numerous than the Assyrians and cherished at one time aspirations to autonomy, they had never in fact formed an autonomous enclave in the modern Ottoman Empire, like the Lebanese Christians.

France therefore came to the Levant in the confident belief that in the Lebanon she would find a willing dependency and a loyal ally. She also came with feelings of definite hostility towards the Arab movement. The British in Iraq might be high-handed, might fail in the manner and speed of fulfilling their undertakings to the Arab nationalists; but fundamentally they were the friends and not the enemies of Arab nationalism. Not so the French in Syria. We have seen how they destroyed Faisal's Arab state in Damascus and expelled him from the land. Their opposition to Arab national aspirations did not cease with that action. France continued to regard the Arab movement with animosity, partly because it was in its inception a British-sponsored movement, and partly because of the fear that any success achieved by the Arab nationalists in Asia would have anti-French repercussions among the Arabs of North Africa.

To weaken Arab nationalism in the Levant, France pursued a twofold policy. On the one hand, she enlarged the

Lebanon, with its Christian majority, by adding to it predominantly Muslim districts along the coast (including Sidon and Tripoli) and inland, so that she made of it a substantial barrier to stand between the Arab nationalism of Syria and the sea. On the other hand, she tried to kill Arabism as such by dividing Syria itself into four separate administrations following parochial lines of segregation. Thus Jebel Druse became one administration; the region of the Alawis (an offshoot of the Shia) around Latakia, another; Alexandretta, on the grounds that its population contained a large proportion of Turks, a third; while the fourth and principal administration was set up in Damascus representing what remained of Syria, with its majority of Sunni Muslims. No more blatant demonstration of the policy of 'divide and rule' had ever been presented to the world. Everything that could be done to intensify the fears of minority groups, whether religious or racial, was done. That these fears existed and were, up to a point, justified, does not exonerate the French, who should have tried to allay them – in the interests of the country as a whole – instead of playing upon them.

Discontent at the high-handed methods of the French – even when well-intentioned – came to a head in Jebel Druse in 1925. A rebellion broke out which soon came to be national in character if not in extent, for it was joined by many nationalists from other parts of Syria. The rebels inflicted heavy defeats on the first French forces sent out against them. They even reached Damascus, and though they failed to occupy the city their bands remained active in its outskirts for many months. In order to drive them out the French actually bombed and bombarded, without warning, some quarters thickly populated by the normal inhabitants.

The Druse leader, in order to win the Lebanese Christians to a friendly attitude towards the rebellion, if not active participation in it, proclaimed the slogan: 'Religion belongs to God; the Motherland to all!' But by and large the Christians both in Lebanon and Syria were not at heart with the rebellion. They still had not forgotten the massacre of 1860;

they mistrusted the Druses; they were loath to relinquish the security which the occupation of a Christian Power had given them since 1918. Many more years were to pass before Christians, Druses, and Muslims combined in a national movement seeking complete independence of the French and the establishment of indigenous governments without foreign protection for the Christian section of the population.

The French Government had to send heavy and costly reinforcements to deal with the rebellion. They also changed their High Commissioner in Syria and Lebanon and abandoned their former policy of autocratic rule for one of manifest concessions to Arab nationalist feelings. Republics were proclaimed, first in the Lebanon and then in Syria, the latter country becoming subsequently unified after her initial parcellation, but losing Alexandretta which France, with British support, ceded to Turkey as a *douceur* some time before the war in order to gain her good-will. Above all, the French began to move in the direction of a treaty relationship to replace the Mandate, as the British had done in Iraq and were trying to do in Egypt. The treaties were finally negotiated in 1936 with the Popular Front Government of Léon Blum. Syrian and Lebanese independence was recognized and France was to sponsor the admission of the two countries to the League of Nations. There was to be a military alliance, whereby France undertook to defend Syria and Lebanon, and they to give her all assistance and facilities in time of war. But there was a difference between the two treaties in one important respect. The treaty with Syria gave France two permanent air bases but did not provide for the presence of French troops, except in two specified regions and for a period of five years; while the treaty with Lebanon permitted the indefinite presence of any number of French air and land forces anywhere in the country. This difference reflected both the greater complaisance of the predominantly Christian Lebanon towards France and the greater importance France attached to the Lebanon as a permanent stronghold of French power in the Middle East.

The two treaties were ratified by the Syrian and Lebanese parliaments, but in France the Blum government had fallen and the French senate failed to ratify them. However, the entire position created by them was to be altered by the war three years later.

Despite the readiness of the Lebanon to accord France greater privileges under the treaty than Syria was willing to accord her – or than any predominantly Muslim Arab country would at that time have been prepared to concede to a European Power – a marked change had come over the attitude of the Lebanese Christians, both in regard to France and to Arab nationalism, since 1918. A section of the Maronites still adhered to their original extremely pro-French attitude. They were mistrustful of the Muslims and of Arab nationalism to the extent of wanting the Lebanon to remain permanently, in effect, a French protectorate. By culture and spiritual affiliation these Maronites were more French than Arab. Some of their more extravagant polemists denied the Arab heritage altogether, maintaining that the Lebanon was, in terms of ancient ancestry, Phoenician and not Arab. But another section of the Maronites, headed by some of their most enlightened and influential leaders, was becoming increasingly disillusioned about the French connexion and convinced that the Lebanon could not isolate itself from the Muslim Arab world. As a result of this reorientation a new kind of Lebanese Arab nationalism was coming into being – a movement which integrated Muslims and Christians on the basis of reciprocal concessions: the Lebanese Christians would join the Muslims in seeking independence; the Muslims would accept the special identity of the Lebanon, with its largely Christian and Westernized complexion, as a separate Arab country, not to be incorporated in Syria or any larger Arab unit in which the Muslims would be a vast majority.

Another movement developing at the same time, but destined to fail, was that of the Syrian Popular Party. The leading personalities of this party were young Lebanese

Christian men and women whose object was to unify Lebanon and Syria on a basis of nationalism transcending sectarianism, but emphasizing *Syrian* nationalism as something distinct from Arab nationalism.

In both movements, however, the Muslim and Christian Arabs of the Lebanon were being brought together in an alliance against the French, the impact of which was to be felt in the years of World War II.

6

We have so far dealt with three Arab rebellions against Western imperialism – the Egyptian rebellion of 1919, the Iraqi rebellion of 1920, and the Syrian rebellion of 1925; and we have noted that 1936 saw intermediate solutions of both the Anglo-Egyptian dispute and the dispute between Syria and the Levant States. It was that same year, however – 1936 – that witnessed the fourth (if for the moment we exclude Morocco), the bitterest, and the most determinedly prolonged armed struggle of the Arabs for their national rights in the inter-war years – namely, the Palestine rebellion.

If, however, the rebellion in Palestine did not come till such a late hour, disturbances and minor outbreaks had been a common feature of the history of the country since 1920; and from the beginning the Palestine question had become the common concern of all the Arab countries – the burning issue of Arab nationalism as a movement transcending the artificial boundaries established by the Sykes-Picot Agreement and the 1919 Peace Conference. The reason for this was that Zionism involved, as the Arabs were not slow to realize, a more deadly and lasting injury to the Arab world than the imposition of temporary European rule on this country or that. If the British army did not evacuate Egypt, if independence was not immediately proclaimed in Syria or Iraq, it could not matter very much in the long run. These countries were not being invaded by foreign settlers; they remained the property of their peoples; their indigenous populations were in no danger of becoming a minority in their own home-land, still less of losing it altogether. Sooner or later, the British would leave Egypt and Iraq, the French Syria, and that would be the end of the matter. But it was not so in Palestine. Here, the native Arab population was being held down by the British (for that really was what the fulfilment of Britain's Mandate in Palestine amounted to) so that Jewish nationalists from all over the world might be able to come into the country in sufficiently large numbers to establish ultimately an alien state, in which the Arabs would occupy a subordinate position or from which they would be expelled altogether. Naturally, it was the Arabs of Palestine who felt the impact of the injury most directly and acutely, but all the peoples of the surrounding Arab countries were alarmed and outraged by what was happening in Palestine, sharing with the Palestine Arabs their immediate tragedy, and seeing in the forcible intrusion of Jewish nationalism into the Middle East a danger to them all.

The Arab reaction to Zionism was not an anti-Jewish manifestation. As we saw in the earlier chapters of this book, the Jews had played a welcome and distinguished part in the scholarly and scientific labours that produced Arab civiliza-tion under the Caliphs of Baghdad and Spain. All through the history of the Arab and Ottoman Empires, Jewish min-orities had been tolerated in the Arab countries. Often when the Jews were being persecuted in Europe they had found refuge under Muslim rule. When the Zionists began to arrive in Palestine there were several thousand native Jews in the country who had been living in it for centuries. They were accepted as part of the population and did not suffer persecution. Such prejudice as may have been felt towards them did not exceed the anti-semitism that is still encoun-tered to-day in Britain and the United States. If they suffered from any civil disabilities, these were no greater than those suffered by the Christian Arabs as second-class citizens in Muslim society. What the Arabs opposed in Zionism, therefore, was not the race or religion of the Jews. It was the nationalism that claimed Palestine for the projected Jewish state; and the struggle that ensued was essentially a political struggle between the old-established population of a country and a host of foreigners arriving as invaders with the object of dispossessing that population.

That this was the intention of the Zionists was very clear from the beginning. It was clear, as noted already, in 1920 to the King-Crane Commission, who were shocked by the discovery. It was clear to the personnel of the British Military Administration that ruled the country in the period between the expulsion of the Turks and the establishment of civil government under the Mandate. It was made embarrassingly clear in 1922 by the Zionist witnesses who appeared before the Haycraft Commission – the first of the many commissions that were futilely sent by the British Government to inquire into the causes of the tension and trouble in Palestine and recommend a solution for what was in the nature of things an unresolvable conflict created by the British Government themselves.

For twenty years the British Government were to maintain the manifestly untenable view that no such conflict need exist in Palestine, that the obligations they had assumed towards the Zionists were not incompatible with their pledges to protect the rights of the Arabs, that a national home for the Jewish people could be established in Palestine without injury to the native population. They adhered to this deception or self-deception despite the frankness with which the Zionists were making it clear, time after time, that the kind of 'national home' they wanted was utterly irreconcilable with the legitimate and natural aspirations of the people of the country, and which compelled the British Government to issue two statements of policy, the first in 1922 and the second in 1930, calculated to curb Zionist ambitions, or at least to allay Arab fears.

In the first statement, for which Mr Churchill was responsible, the British Government rebutted Zionist assertions that

'Palestine is to become as Jewish as England is English', denied the intention to eliminate or subordinate the Arab population of Palestine, and affirmed that their policy was not to convert the whole of Palestine into a Jewish national home, but to create a Jewish national home *in Palestine*. But at the same time they enunciated the principle that the foreign Jews that came into Palestine under the terms of the Mandate and the Balfour Declaration were in the country 'as of right and not on sufferance', and that their continued immigration was to be allowed in accordance with *the country's absorptive capacity*, thus establishing an economic criterion which could well undermine the entire political and moral position of the Arabs as owners of the country.

Mounting tension and Arab opposition to the Zionist invasion caused another outbreak of violence in 1929. In 1930 came the second British statement of policy (issued this time by the Labour Government of which Ramsay Macdonald was Prime Minister and Sidney Webb Colonial Secretary) denying Zionist claims that the obligation to establish the Jewish national home, assumed by Britain under the Mandate, took precedence over her obligations towards the 'non-Jewish communities' of Palestine, and once more affirming, in blind disregard of realities, that the two undertakings were not irreconcilable and could be brought to parallel fulfilment.

Never perhaps was the power of the Zionists in Britain, and the powerlessness of the remote and impalpable Arabs, so spectacularly demonstrated as in the prompt and unedifying sequel to this proclamation of majestic impartiality. Stormy Zionist remonstrances elicited from Ramsay Macdonald a document – nicknamed by the Arabs 'the Black Letter' – in which the substance of the White Paper just issued was virtually swallowed back by the British Prime Minister.

It was not, however, until the Nazis came to power in Germany and launched their policy of barbarous anti-semitism, that the Palestine problem was suddenly blown up into unmanageable proportions. The exodus of Jews from

Europe caused thousands of them to converge upon Palestine, so that in the three years between 1933 and 1936 the number of immigrants rose by leaps and bounds, reaching finally the figure of sixty thousand per annum – and that in a country whose total population was below a million and a half.

The Arabs were appalled at this incursion which threatened to swamp them. In Britain and America Zionist propaganda, always highly organized, ubiquitous, and in sole possession of the field, deliberately confused political with humanitarian issues by playing on the sympathy of the civilized world for the victims of Hitlerite persecution in order to further the expansion of the Jewish national home in Palestine. Further, the Zionists argued that the Palestine Arabs themselves would benefit by Jewish immigration, since the superior enterprise and technique of progressive European Jews would help to improve economic conditions in the country and raise its people's standard of living. Uninformed Western opinion was influenced by these specious arguments, but the Arabs saw their status and very existence in Palestine being blasted. With every prompting of the instinct of self-preservation they understood – and how rightly in the light of subsequent events! – that the matter was not one of economic development and standards of living, but of the ultimate ownership of their native land, of whether Palestine was going to remain an Arab country or become a foreign state peopled mainly by central European Jews.

At last came the explosion of 1936. The Arabs proclaimed a general strike, which was carried out successfully for a period of over two months. At the same time armed bands, joined by Syrian and Iraqi Arabs, launched a campaign of violence which did not finally die down, though 20,000 British troops were employed to deal with it, until shortly before the outbreak of war in 1939.

Soon after the beginning of the rebellion the British Government dispatched a Royal Commission to make one more inquiry into the causes of the Palestine conflict and recommend a solution. This commission did two decisive things.

First, it confronted the British Government with the bitter truth that the conflict between Jewish nationalism and Arab nationalism was incapable of reconciliation, and that therefore the entire policy which Britain had followed since the issue of the Balfour Declaration was hopelessly unrealizable. Secondly, the commission drew the conclusion that since the claims of Jews and Arabs were irreconcilable within one state the only solution was to divide Palestine into two states, one Arab, one Jewish. Thus was first propounded the idea of the partition of Palestine – an idea which, on the face of it, and to people in the West constantly subjected to Zionist propaganda, seemed just and reasonable, but which was ultimately to culminate in 1948 in the Jews seizing almost the whole of Palestine.

The Arab reaction to the partition scheme was one of profound outrage and alarm. They saw in it, with regard to a large part of Palestine, the realization of their first and worst fears: the vaguely outlined 'home' of the Balfour Declaration was to be an independent, sovereign state – an alien state forcibly established in an Arab country. It was no longer the thin end of the wedge, but the thick end in all its fullness about to be rammed in. In Europe the Nazi persecution of the Jews continued, and the threat of thousands upon thousands of them coming to Palestine had to be faced.

From all the Arab countries came protests against the proposed partition of Palestine; while in the country itself the campaign of violence started in 1936 became more bitter and intense. The Arabs had two principal demands: that Jewish immigration be stopped, and that Palestine as an undivided entity (that is to say with its native population as the majority) should be given its independence.

Arab opposition to the partition proposal degenerated in the end into terrorism practised by one Arab faction against another. But this does not alter the fact that fundamentally the troubles in Palestine between 1936 and 1939 were an armed uprising by the Arabs against Zionism and, later, against the specific recommendations of the Royal Commission. Those actively engaged in the campaign of violence did not exceed some two thousand, but they had the sympathy and support of the bulk of the Arab population. The number of fatal casualties included 69 British, 92 Jews, 486 Arab civilians, and 1138 armed Arab rebels; while about 100 rebels were convicted by the military courts and hanged.

At last, with the storm clouds gathering for World War II, the British Government, anxious not to have a hostile Arab world to face throughout the Middle East on account of Palestine, decided to shelve the partition proposal and make a fresh approach to the Arabs. In this decision they were supported by the findings of the Woodhead Commission which, having been sent to Palestine to make concrete proposals for partition following the general recommendations of its predecessor, had bluntly announced that partition was not feasible. In 1939, therefore, the British Government invited both Arabs and Jews to come to London for a Round Table conference. The invitation to the Arabs was interesting in that it was not confined to the Arabs of Palestine but extended to representatives of the surrounding Arab countries, including Egypt and Iraq, who had shown an increasing concern in the fate of Palestine. In inviting these states Britain admitted that underlying unity of the Arab world which had been set at naught by the peace settlement of 1919, and foreshadowed the support she was to give to the idea of the Arab League a few years later.

No agreement by negotiation proved possible at the Round Table conference, so that Britain had to fall back on a unilateral declaration of policy similar to those of 1922 and 1930. This was the famous White Paper of 1939. In it the British Government announced their intention of setting up, within ten years, an independent Palestine state, in which Arabs and Jews should share in government in a manner guaranteeing the interests of each community. During the ten years pending independence a total of 150,000 more Jewish immigrants would be allowed to enter Palestine, so that the proportion of Jews to Arabs in the country would roughly reach one to three. Also, the purchase of land by Jews in certain parts of the country (another Arab demand) was prohibited.

Although both Arabs and Jews formally opposed the White Paper when it was issued, the Arabs in their hearts were not hostile to it; and indeed gradually came to accept it openly and take their stand on it as an acquired right. While disliking the prospect of having to receive another large quota of immigrants annually for the next ten years, they were gratified by the abandonment of partition, by the British repudiation of the intention to set up a Jewish state in Palestine, and above all by the promise of independence, though it was not to become complete for another ten years. Their most serious worry was that Zionist pressure would once again compel the British Government to abandon a proclaimed policy. And again, how right they were!

But there was one respect in which the Arabs were grievously wrong. The issue of the White Paper marked a very crucial change in the triangular relationship between British, Arabs, and Jews. The Zionists were quick to understand the implications of the White Paper and effect a major change in their strategy to meet the future; the Arabs had no comprehension of what that future was going to be, and continued to behave as in the past. What the Zionists realized was that Britain was not going to establish a Jewish national state in Palestine by employing British arms against the Arab population, and that if they wanted to have their state they must prepare to fight for it themselves, first against the British and then against the Arabs. The Arabs, on the other hand, did not contemplate having to fight for Palestine against the Jews. Until that moment the Jews, though growing in numbers and strength, had not been in a position to wrest the country from its people without the support of British troops. The fear of the Arabs had always been that *Britain* would impose a Jewish state upon them, that *Britain* would cut off a part of Palestine for this purpose, that *Britain* would hold them down until the Jews became a majority through ever-increasing immigration. In other words, they had always thought of their problem in the terms of a political three-cornered tussle between them, the British, and the Jews; and their strategy had been to bring sufficient pressure to bear on Britain to prevent her from doing any of these things. The mistake they made after the issue of the White Paper was that they continued to adhere to this strategy: they would win their independence from Britain by means of negotiations, conferences, and sustained political pressure, helped when necessary by nuisance-value violence. That the Jews would become strong enough to compel a British withdrawal and then seize Palestine themselves never occurred to the Arabs. This, perhaps more than any other, was the mistake that cost them Palestine; though it is arguable that even had they foreseen their real danger, their inherent weaknesses and divisions would have doomed them to the same defeat in the end.

7

The inter-war period saw the creation of two other Arab states, similar to one another in political and social complexion, and different from those we have considered already in sophistication and cultural standards. These were the kingdom of Saudi Arabia and the principality of Transjordan, later to become the Hashemite kingdom of Jordan.

The creation of Saudi Arabia was the single-handed achievement of King Abd-ul-Aziz Ibn Saud, a redoubtable scion of that Arab dynasty which we have encountered before as rulers of Nejd and allies of the puritanical Wahhabi sect. When we first met Ibn Saud himself in this narrative, he had established his supremacy over Nejd and become a semi-vassal of Great Britain. Both the British Government and the Arab nationalists in Iraq tried to enlist his support for the Arab Revolt against the Turks in 1914, but there were two reasons why the support he gave was no more than moral. First, his traditional enemy, Ibn Rashid, the Emir of

Jebel Shammar, immediately to the north of Nejd, was pro-Turkish and strong enough to neutralize Ibn Saud. Secondly, relations between Ibn Saud and the Sherif Hussein of Mecca, who led the Revolt, were unfriendly. Ibn Saud, with his Wahhabi principles, regarded Mecca and Medina as little better than centres of idolatrous worship contrary to the teachings of Islam; while Hussein, with his Turkish culture, regarded Ibn Saud as a primitive tribal chief and behaved towards him with open contempt. Matters became worse when Hussein proclaimed himself King of the Arabs in 1916, and eight years later assumed the title of Caliph.

The first clash between Ibn Saud and the Hashemites occurred in 1919, when Hussein's son, the Emir Abdullah, attacked Nejdi territory and was severely defeated by Ibn Saud, who was only deterred from invading the Hejaz by Britain, still the ally and protectress of Hussein. The end of the war, bringing about the collapse of Turkey, deprived the Emir of Shammar of the power which had supported him, so that Ibn Saud was able to overthrow him and annex his territory to Nejd. By 1925 Hussein had quarrelled with Britain over the Palestine question, and so lost her protection. At the same time he became involved in a dispute with Egypt over certain questions relating to the Pilgrimage, while his assumption of the Caliphate had aroused jealousies and resentments in many parts of the Arab and Muslim worlds. This sinking of his international stock gave Ibn Saud an opportunity to attack him, while the *casus belli* was provided by certain rash intrigues which Hussein had entered into against the Nejdi Prince with some of his neighbours. Ibn Saud invaded the Hejaz, compelling Hussein to abdicate and leave the country. This new conquest added the Holy Cities of Islam to Ibn Saud's realm, and gave birth to the kingdom of Saudi Arabia.

Shortly after this victory Britain concluded a treaty with the new monarch, recognizing his full sovereignty. In return Ibn Saud undertook to maintain friendly relations with the various British-protected Arab sheikhdoms round the coasts of Arabia, and agreed that Britain should fix his frontiers with Iraq and Transjordan, where he had already recognized the rule of two of Hussein's sons – Faisal and Abdullah.

Ibn Saud was a big figure, but in the old tribal tradition. In spite of granting oil concessions to American companies and importing motor-cars to replace the camel along the main routes of communication, he and his kingdom remained largely medieval. A substantial proportion of the people were nomads, and the King himself was an Arab of the desert and a theocratic Muslim ruler, untouched by Western civilization or modern influences except in the most superficial manner. His failure to master the pronunciation of 'Czechoslovakia' during the Munich crisis was a joke among the British diplomats who had to deal with him – and had, indeed a great respect for his personality and native sagacity. He would begin with 'Czech ...' and end with a smile and a despairing wave of the hand. In his family and domestic habits he might have been one of the less restrained Caliphs of the eighth or ninth centuries – so large was his harem, so numerous his offspring. He established peace and security throughout his kingdom and was, in the old Arab way, accessible to any of his subjects, who could appear before him with his complaint and address him simply as 'Abd-ul-Aziz'; but his law was a law of blood and iron under which the Sharia was applied in criminal jurisdiction and robbery was punished by the amputation of the robber's hand. The state apparatus, in spite of its success in maintaining order, was rudimentary and ramshackle, controlled in the last resort by the absolute power of the King. There was no educated, politically conscious middle class in Saudi Arabia, no possibility of establishing parliamentary institutions, even if Ibn Saud had been willing to grant them. The King's relations first with Britain and then (through the oil connexion) with the United States were extremely friendly and, essential point to remember, the King and his country were really independent. No foreign forces of occupation were to be seen anywhere on Saudi Arabian land; no foreign High Commissioners or advisers were there to exert any political pressure on the ruler or his ministers. Partly because of this, and partly because of the pastoral and undeveloped character of the country, there was no anti-Western nationalism in Saudi Arabia.

Transjordan was that part of geographical Syria that fell to the share of Britain under the Sykes-Picot Agreement, and lay to the east of the river Jordan. It was a poor, mainly desert country, inhabited by some four hundred thousand Arabs, most of whom were nomads. Soon after the destruction of Faisal's kingdom in Damascus by the French in 1920, Britain informed the small urban community in Transjordan that her intention was to grant the country immediate self-government through a number of municipal councils. A short while later, Faisal's elder brother, the Emir Abdullah, who had been playing a prominent part in the Arab movement since 1913, appeared in Transjordan with the declared intention of leading an armed rebellion against the French in Syria. From this purpose he was turned away by Britain who, with the consent of the Transjordanian councils, offered to recognize him as Emir of the country, subject to his accepting British protection and help in establishing a modernized administration. Abdullah accepted the offer, and immediately after the British Government obtained the agreement of the League of Nations to the exclusion of Transjordan from those clauses of the Mandate that provided for Jewish immigration into and land purchase in Palestine. In this manner Britain tried to make feeble amends to the Arabs for encouraging Jewish immigration into western Palestine on the one hand, and for letting the French expel Faisal from Damascus on the other.

Abdullah was an autocratic ruler like Ibn Saud, but he had the superior polish and Muslim cosmopolitanism of an upbringing in Constantinople, as well as a wider knowledge of the Arab world in general. Moreover, though he would not allow any real democracy in his principality, in the sense of sharing power with elected councils, his British advisers created, in a modest form, the machinery of a modern state and an excellent small modern army – the famous Arab Legion. As in Saudi Arabia, there was no 'nationalism' or conflict with the West in Transjordan in this first phase of its existence. Abdullah himself became unpopular with the nationalists both in Palestine and in Syria and Iraq. He was regarded as a British stooge, and suspected of lacking fervour in the fight against Zionism – even of being willing to compromise with the Jews by allowing them to have autonomous rule in a part of Palestine, if the remainder of the country would be added to Transjordan to make a kingdom for him. Indeed, at one time he propounded a solution for the Palestine problem along some such lines; and after the Palestine debacle he defended this solution to the present writer on the grounds that it would have set definite limits to the expansion of the Jews, instead of leaving the whole of Palestine at their mercy. It is, however, doubtful whether anything short of united and adequate Arab military force (which at the crucial moment was not forthcoming) could have contained Jewish nationalism in a small part of Palestine, or in a form less obnoxious to the Arabs than that of an independent, sovereign state.

The establishment of Ibn Saud as the major power in the Arabian Peninsula, and the fact that his kingdom marched with Transjordan and Iraq to the north, was to create one of the chief tensions and causes of division in the Arab world. For though Ibn Saud had recognized both Abdullah and Faisal, he could never forget that they were the sons of his old enemy, Hussein; and the fear that they might some day seek to recapture the Hejaz from him was always one of the prime considerations that dictated his policy. As we shall see later, this situation, reinforced by other factors, caused an anti-Hashemite 'Axis' to be formed within the Arab League.

Apart from Saudi Arabia, the Peninsula now included only the Yemen, the Aden Protectorate, and the various sheikhdoms that lay strung along its southern and eastern coasts. The Yemen was another medieval theocracy ruled by its obscurantist Imam in almost complete seclusion from the modern world; Aden was a British colony; the sheikhdoms puny and, until the discovery of oil in Kuwait, Bahrein, Qatar, etc., poor countries in treaty relations with Britain, who 'protected' them but did not interfere much in their primitive tribal administration. With the single but unimportant exception of Aden, none of these countries had as yet entered the stream of the twentieth century, nor played any part in the Arab revival, though by race they were almost purely Arab (Indian and Jewish communities existed among them) and had never forgotten their Arab identity.

8

So far we have looked exclusively at the eastern Arab world, beginning with Egypt. But west of Egypt lies the western Arab world, stretching all the way to the Atlantic, and including Libya, Tunisia, Algeria, and Morocco, the last of which is known in Arabic as *al-Maghreb al-Aqsa*, or 'The Farthest West'.

For a long time the French, after the establishment of their rule in North Africa, professed to regard the peoples of Tunisia, Algeria, and Morocco as Muslims rather than as Arabs, to emphasize their Berber origin and so prevent the growth of any sense of Arab nationalism in the three territories or of kinship between them and the countries of the eastern Arab world. This French attitude was particularly accentuated after World War I, which witnessed the Arab Revolt against Turkey and the general emergence of Arab nationalism throughout the Middle East, partly with the approval and help of Britain, often in hostile reaction to her 'imperialism' as well as to the imperialism of France in Syria.

It is true, of course, that the racial basis of North Africa is predominantly Berber. But then the racial basis of all the Arab countries outside the Arabian Peninsula is predominantly non-Arab. The countries of North Africa became

Arabized, like those of the eastern Arab world, as a result of the Muslim Arab conquests. Their Berber population received a certain proportion of Arab blood and, more important still, was converted to Islam and adopted Arabic as the language of culture, government, and urban life in general, even though in tribal areas away from the coast the people continued to speak Berber. The proportion of Berber-speakers varied from 2 per cent in Tunisia to about 40 per cent in Morocco.

Algeria and Tunisia, like all the Arab countries to the east of them, were embraced by the long, if not always tightly gripping, arms of the Ottoman Empire. But Morocco never came effectively within this clasp. It remained for a thousand years a medieval Arab state, ruled over by a Sultan and loosely called in English 'the Moorish Empire'. It contained a large proportion of descendants of the Arab or Arabized Muslims who from time to time were expelled from Spain on its reconquest by the Christians. Even to this day the sons of some of these expatriates are alleged to possess the keys of the houses their ancestors were forced to leave on the other side of the straits of Gibraltar. The continued independence and complete segregation of Morocco under its medieval institutions kept it in some ways more picturesquely Arab than any of its sisters in North Africa or the Middle East, and prevented it from acquiring even such elementary modern cosmopolitanism as the Ottoman Empire possessed through its various connexions with Europe. Until the arrival of the French, the people of Morocco were almost as untouched by Western influences (though there was always some trade between them and Europe) as those of Yemen or Nejd at the other extreme of the Arab world.

Algeria was the first of the North African countries to be occupied by the French, and colonized in the literal sense of receiving a steady stream of French settlers. Although the French found it easy enough to depose and expel the semi-Turkish Dey from Algiers, it was many years before the resistance of the native population, led by the Emir Abd-el-Kader, was overcome and the country finally passed under French rule. This resistance of the Algerian people to the French invasion was the first reaction of the western Arab world to European imperialism. It cannot be called an expression of Arab nationalism, for the Arab idea had not been born yet in the modern world; but it was the rising of an Arab people in defence of its freedom and its land against invaders of another race and religion; and it is an interesting coincidence that this first fight of the Western Arabs for their freedom took place while Ibrahim Pasha was making his bid to create an Arab Empire in Syria.

The beginnings of the Tunisian question were similar to those of the Egyptian question, in that indebtedness to Europe led to bankruptcy in 1869 and the establishment of financial control over the country by Britain, France, and Italy. European settlement in Tunisia had been in progress for some time, and at first the majority of the settlers were Italians. This and other signs of Italy's designs on Algeria's neighbour excited the jealousies of the French who, after reaching a secret agreement with the British, took military action in 1881. A force crossed the frontier from Algeria and compelled the Bey of Tunis (roughly the equivalent of the Khedive of Egypt) to accept a French protectorate. But here again the control of the country was only secured against the resistance by the native population – another portent of future nationalism.

Financial need also played its part in the occupation of Morocco by France. Soon after their establishment in Algeria, the French began to interest themselves in the Empire of the Farthest West, where backwardness, insecurity, and an inefficient central administration were creating conditions of anarchy and bankruptcy that opened the way to foreign intervention. The 'Empire' was not a homogeneous, compact state, but a loosely held association of Arab cities, Berber tribes, and powerful feudal nobles. Diplomacy, military enterprise, and loans to the Sultan had given France, despite British influence and competition, a strong position in the country before the end of the nineteenth century. By the *Entente Cordiale* of 1904 – a precursor, in a sense, of the Sykes-Picot Agreement – the French obtained a free hand in Morocco, in return for their leaving Egypt to the British. France also agreed that Tangier should be an International Zone, and Spain was given a portion of the northern coast-land, part of which is known as the Riff. In 1912 the Sultan accepted a French protectorate similar to the one established over Tunisia. In theory his sovereignty still extended to the Spanish zone, where he was represented by a deputy – the *Khalifa*, and to Tangier where he was represented by the *Mandub* (delegate).

The Sultan's acceptance of the protectorate was greeted by a violent rising in Fez, and the tribes of the Central Atlas continued to trouble the French for a considerable time, so that the 'pacification' of the whole country was not completed until 1934. In Morocco, the French followed a policy not of general assimilation, as they did in Algeria, trying to Frenchify the whole country as much as possible; but rather of diarchy. Leaving the old Arab cities and the Sultan's traditional government, the *Makhzen* alone (but, of course, under French supervision) they created new cities apart, in the European style, and a modern administration to function in them.

No sooner, however, had French Morocco been completely 'pacified' than trouble on an altogether new scale broke out in the Spanish zone. Here, in 1923, the Emir Abdel Krim launched such a heavy and sustained attack upon the colonizers that it became known as the 'Riff war'. After defeating the Spaniards, Abdel Krim turned against the French in 1925 – the year the Syrian revolt was raging in Jebel Druse and around Damascus. Although racially a Berber, Abdel Krim became one of the big figures of Arab nationalism. Altogether he fought the forces of Spain and France for three years, inflicting on them heavy losses, before he was finally defeated by the combined efforts of the two Powers in 1926 and deported to the island of – names can have a curious irony sometimes – Reunion. After World War II, the French agreed to his coming back from there on condition that he would live permanently in Paris; but when his ship reached Port Said he was persuaded by nationalists to seek refuge in Egypt, where he was received by Egyptian and other Arab leaders as one of them, and where he took part in founding the Maghreb Office in Cairo – an establishment designed to further the cause of nationalism in the western Arab world and to co-ordinate the western and eastern national movements as much as possible.

Italy, frustrated in Tunisia, began to turn her attention to Libya. She did a deal with France similar to the one by which Britain had obtained a free hand in Egypt in return for recognizing French aspirations in Morocco; and having thus secured French connivance, she embarked upon the conquest of Libya in 1911.

was symptomatic of the growth of the sentiment of Arab nationalism, and of its spreading as between east and west, that both Egyptian and Tunisian nationalists fought with the Libyans against the Italian attack. The Turkish authorities gave up the struggle in 1912. Arab resistance, however, continued, especially in Cyrenaica, until 1928, when Mussolini's agent, Marshal Graziani, finally subdued the whole of Libya. This was achieved 'acre by acre', as he put it, and took nearly ten years, in the course of which nearly half the population of Cyrenaica perished by mass executions and other means.

Meanwhile, all through the inter-war period, nationalism as a middle-class urban movement was spreading in Tunisia, Algeria, and Morocco. Its growth was most vigorous and best organized in Tunisia. The first Tunisian nationalist party had appeared in 1904, with a newspaper of its own. Thaalbi, the leader of this party, was exiled to Paris in 1911. At the end of World War I, encouraged by President Wilson's declarations, and stimulated by the independence movements in the eastern Arab world, he submitted a memorandum to the Peace Conference, demanding independence.

In Tunisia itself, a delegation of notables (similar to the Egyptian *Wafd*) presented itself at the French Residency, asking for a constitution to be granted to their country. As the Arabic word for 'constitution' is *Destour*, this occasion gave to the Tunisian nationalist movement the name it was to carry to this day, whether in its first form, as the Destour Party, or, in its later form, after its reorganization in 1934, as the Neo-Destour Party. Most of its members were graduates of French universities; and though their ultimate aim was independence, they were prepared to co-operate with the French in a policy of gradual evolution towards that goal if the French showed any sincerity of intention. French policy, however, vacillated between a tentative liberalism and, under the influence of the settlers supported by imperialistic circles in Paris, frequent lapses into stern repression, involving the imprisonment or flight of the nationalist leaders.

In Morocco, the phase of rebellion by tribesmen was being succeeded – only four years after the defeat of Abdel Krim – by the growth of a politically conscious town intelligentsia. In 1930 (following an open attempt by the French to withdraw large sections of the Berber-speaking population from the influence of the Sultan's jurisdiction) the first political party came into being. Called the *Action Marocaine*, it had three leaders who hailed, respectively, from the Sorbonne, the Geneva University, and the traditional Arab Mosque-University of Qayrawan. Their demand was not independence but the acceptance of a moderate programme of reforms, including the end of direct administration by the French, equality between Frenchmen and Moroccans, more Moroccan officials in the administration and elected municipalities. Later they added other demands, including the cessation of official colonization. In 1936 and 1937 there were disorders and police action resulting in a considerable number of Moroccans being killed. The *Action Marocaine* was ordered to dissolve, and Allal al-Fasi, one of its three leaders, exiled from Morocco.

It was becoming clear from these beginnings of nationalist opposition to the French regime that two grievances were more deeply felt by the Moroccans than any other: the privileged position and increasing number of French settlers who were occupying more and more land in the country, and the complete control of French officials over policy, together with the confining of Moroccan officials to the lowest posts in the administration. As Nevill Barbour, writing in the *Political Quarterly* in 1951 puts it: 'Morocco might have been a Sleeping Beauty restored to the waking world by a French Prince Charming. But the Prince was not of her race or religion and it appeared that his relatives were to be advanced and her property to be developed for their advantage.'

The position in Algeria was in some important respects different from that in Morocco or Tunisia. For one thing, Algeria, unlike its sisters to the west and the east, had never formed a separate, self-contained Arab state, or been the seat of one; it had always been part of empires based on Morocco or Tunisia, or under Turkish rule, so that no sense of Arab or Muslim statehood existed in it to the same extent as it did in its neighbours. For another, the French constitutional relationship with Algeria, as well as their policy and system of administration in the country, were all different from what they were in Morocco or Tunisia. In these two states the French position was based on a treaty accepted by the existing native rulers and, nominally at least, establishing merely a French protectorate. Algeria, on the other hand, was conquered outright and annexed to Metropolitan France as a *département*, with representatives in the French Chamber and Senate. Moreover, the country came under French occupation half a century before Tunisia, and eighty years before Morocco, so that by the time the inter-war period of nationalism was setting in, French influence and assimilation had gone much deeper in Algeria than in either Tunisia or Morocco. Thus we find that the first assertion of Algerian nationalist sentiment in the middle thirties came from a completely assimilated leader, Ferhat Abbas, the aim of whose movement was, at first, thorough assimilation to France, subject to the retention by Algerians of their personal status as Muslims. Curiously enough, the French settlers – with a glaring lack of that French logic which is internationally proverbial but which is often absent from the colonial policies of France – denounced Ferhat Abbas's movement as 'nationalist', with the result that a few years later he abandoned the idea of assimilation for one of an Algerian state within the French Union.

Other Algerian Muslims, however, opposed the idea of assimilation from the beginning and gave their support to a more popular movement, led by a kind of working-class prophet, Messali Hajj, and aiming at a Muslim Algerian state.

Yet a third movement developed during this period. Cultural rather than political, it was an attempt by the Ulema of Algeria to raise both the Arabic language and the Muslim religion from the low levels to which they had sunk as a result, *inter alia*, of a century of French rule which discouraged the use of the former, and used the latter for its own ends. This movement, which directed its efforts towards the founding of schools and the provision of good teachers and books in Arabic (of which there was a great dearth in Algeria), bore some resemblance to that of the Muslim Brotherhood in Egypt, in that both aimed at an internal reform and uplift of Muslim society; but whereas the Muslim Brotherhood was a lay popular movement with political ambitions, the Algerian movement has not only remained non-political in any immediate sense, but continued to operate at the professorial rather than the demagogic level.

CHAPTER FIVE

GAINS AND LOSSES

===

I

ALTOGETHER, the quarter-century that passed between the outbreak of World War I and World War II saw profound changes and a great deal of progress in the Arab world. The most significant single phenomenon was the universal rediscovery by the Arabs of their identity as a world society, within the limits of which each local group – Syrians, Egyptians, Iraqis, Tunisians, etc. – was striving for the fulfilment of its national aspirations, and in many cases had achieved a large measure of success. In the second place of importance was the entry of this Arab society, in many fundamental respects, into the modern age; the mixing, here and there, of the Arab world with the world of Europe and America. This process, as we have seen, started before 1914. It had started with the employment of Frenchmen by Mohammed Ali in his Egyptian administration; in the coming of Western missions to the Lebanon to open schools and printing presses; in the going of many young Arabs to Europe or America for higher studies. But all these had been rather individual and local contacts. By and large, the Arab world had remained, in relation to the outside world, like a Muslim woman in *purdah*. It was only in the period between the two wars that the secluded lady began to cast off the veil and come out into the open spaces of cosmopolitan society.

The process extended to every department – social, cultural, political, economic. In the social and cultural fields the wireless, the cinema, and air travel formed a mighty triumvirate of barrier-breaking forces. There was a great expansion of education and of the Arabic Press which, despite its faults of xenophobia and national self-flattery, helped to link the Arab countries with the centres of world civilization. In particular, the education of women made great strides among the middle classes, stretching as far afield as the Sudan; and Muslim Arab girls began to enter the universities, side by side with boys. Some of them studied for the liberal professions; and in the more sophisticated cities of Egypt, Palestine, Lebanon, and Iraq the life of the educated middle-class Muslim family began to follow the Western pattern. Polygamy ceased almost entirely among this class. Many of the women dropped the veil (if not completely and publicly, at least on all informal occasions) and began to go out with their husbands and lead an ordinary cosmopolitan social life. The home and the family, in the Western sense, were thus substituted for the harem.

The national struggles of the various Arab countries put them in the centre of the international picture, and a two-way traffic was opened of European commissions visiting the Arab countries, and Arab delegations going to Europe to attend international conferences until, on reaching independence like Iraq, they were admitted to the League of Nations and sat on the world's principal political platform.

In the economic field, the most important development was the discovery of oil in Iraq, Saudi Arabia, Kuwait, and other parts of the Arabian Peninsula, as well as in Egypt, and the laying of the foundations of a tremendous industry (developed by European and American companies holding concessions from the Arab states) for the extraction of the oil and its transportation in pipe-lines across the desert to Mediterranean ports for refining and shipment to world markets. The full development of this industry to the point at which it was to bring untold wealth to some of the Arab countries was not achieved till after the War, but the beginnings were there well before 1939, introducing into some of the Arab countries Western influences in a new shape, and giving the Arab world a new economic significance for the world at large.

This considerable economic and cultural progress was, however, confined to the upper and middle strata of society – landowners, merchants, and the professional and civil servant class. The masses of the people, whether as peasants or city workers, whether the craftsmen employed in the traditional occupations of the Middle East, or the new artisans of the modern light industries that were beginning to develop, still lived in conditions of great poverty, ignorance, and squalor. Much of the land (particularly in Egypt and Syria) was owned, in the form of huge estates, by old families who constituted a kind of feudal aristocracy (among this class the splintering of land by inheritance according to Sharia law was prevented by a legal fiction enabling landowners to entail their property as though it were a religious endowment for charitable purposes). The peasants' earnings and the workers' wages were still very low, the education and health services available to them meagre, their political influence insignificant. Trade unionism was raising a tentative head in Egypt, Palestine, Lebanon, Syria, and Iraq; and there were new political parties, influenced by Communist, Socialist, or Fascist thought from Europe, that put forward programmes of social and economic reform. But the older political parties – e.g. the Wafd in Egypt, the Nationalist Bloc in Syria – still held the field, and these parties had come into being as the champions of national freedom against 'colonialism' and the forces of foreign occupation. Their object was independence, not social reform; their slogans those of an emotional nationalism which, at moments of crisis, united landowners, merchants, professional men, peasants, and workers against the 'Colonizers'. Indeed, because of the issue of independence and the strong appeal of emotional nationalism, the ruling and propertied classes were often able to turn the discontent of the peasants and workers against the French or the British, and so gain a respite for themselves.

In spite of the Anglo-Iraqi treaty of 1930 and the Anglo-Egyptian treaty of 1936, the general trend of Arab feeling when war broke out in 1939 was anti-Western, and particularly anti-British. This tone had been set by the 1919 Peace settlement, which continued to be viewed by the Arabs as a betrayal. Further, anti-Western feeling had been exacerbated by the various conflicts that broke out between the Arab countries and the Western powers, and that continued to drag diplomatically, even when their first violent phase was over, for the greater part of the twenty years between 1919 and 1939. Towards the end of this period Axis propaganda became very active in the Arab countries, making the most of its opportunities by dwelling upon and magnifying every grievance the Arabs had felt in their dealings with Britain and France since 1919.

One of these grievances needed no exaggeration: the Palestine question. For twenty years, as it seemed to the Arabs, Britain had been helping a foreign people to possess itself of an Arab country, occupying the heart of the eastern Arab world and containing some of the most holy shrines of Islam. The bitter effects of this sustained and continuing policy could hardly be wiped out by the belated White Paper of 1939. For although this White Paper did attempt to set limits to the expansion of the Jewish national home, the limits were not to be attained for another ten years; and the Arabs were not even sure that Britain would stand by those limits when the time came. Moreover the people which Britain was thus helping to establish itself in the heart of the Arab world was the people against which the Nazis had declared relentless war, so that a certain community of feeling between the Arabs and the Germans was inevitable at the outbreak of the war. Few Arabs paused to reflect that but for Hitler's persecution of the Jews the Zionist pressure on Palestine might never have become a serious threat to the Arabs. What the masses in all the Arab countries felt was that they and the Germans had a common enemy in the Jews and, it almost seemed, a common enemy in Britain and

France who, as a result of their victory in World War I, had occupied their countries, sent troops to shoot them when they demanded freedom, and wounded their *amour propre* with their airs of social and national superiority.

It was not, therefore, surprising that the prospect of a German victory should have had a certain appeal for many Arabs in 1939 – particularly when it was still only a distant prospect, involving dream-satisfactions without the impact of reality. The proclamation of freedom and democracy as the causes for which the Allies fought sounded a hollow mockery in Arab ears. The Allies were the great 'Imperialist' powers of the world; while the Germans had never been known to the Arabs as rulers. They could therefore pose as potential liberators.

When the fateful moment for a decision came, however, only one of the Arab countries, or rather one particular clique in it that seized power against the lawful government, took arms against the Allies or did anything to hinder their war effort. That country was Iraq.

2

Various reasons contributed to the Iraqi internal rebellion and the short-lived war against Britain in 1941.

Of all the Arab countries Iraq had consistently been the one to react the most bitterly to British policy in Palestine; so that although in so far as her own national aspirations were concerned she had obtained a large measure of satisfaction as early as 1930, she was by 1939 the most hostile to Britain on account of Zionism. This hostility was actively fanned by the arrival in Baghdad, shortly after the outbreak of war, of Hajj Amin al-Husseini, the Mufti of Jerusalem. Having been compelled to leave Palestine some time before the war (as a result of the part he had played in directing the 1936-9 Arab rebellion) he had sought asylum in the Lebanon – an asylum at first accorded by the French, but terminated after the commencement of hostilities. Driven from Lebanon, the Mufti repaired to Iraq, where his influence weighed heavily against the Allied cause and the British alliance.

Secondly, constitutional government in Iraq had been virtually destroyed (as we have seen) by the repeated interference of the army in political affairs and the establishment of one *coup d'état* government after another. Not only had the country prematurely lost its first king, the wise and influential Faisal I, but also his son, the second king, had been killed in a motor accident a short time after his accession, so that for a number of years Iraq had been going through the difficulties of a royal minority, with the infant king's uncle, the Emir Abd-ul-ilah, acting as Regent.

Lastly, Axis propaganda, conducted by the German minister, Dr Grobba, had been very active in Iraq immediately before the war, and had won over to the Nazi cause a number of Iraqi officers and politicians. The devastating German victories of 1940–1 did the rest by convincing this Iraqi group that Germany was bound to win the war.

Four colonels, known as the Golden Square, in league with the politician Rashid Ali al-Gaylani, carried out yet one more *coup d'état*, the object of which was to range Iraq on Germany's side in the war. The Regent was first placed under duress by the army; then he, together with Nuri Pasha es-Said (the biggest figure in Iraqi politics and a lifelong believer in friendly relations with Britain) and a few other leaders who had remained faithful to the Anglo-Iraqi treaty, fled from Baghdad to save their lives, the Regent being eventually taken aboard a British warship at Basra, and remaining outside the country until the revolt and the army's 'thirty days' war' against Britain was defeated by the British forces.

Many of the civilian politicians left in Baghdad were at heart loyal partisans of the Regent, but power was now entirely in the hands of the army commanded by the Golden Square who, expecting immediate and adequate help to reach them from the Germans by air via Syria, attacked the British air bases and garrisons in the country. The British forces, though small in number and occupying only a few isolated and exposed positions, stood their ground and, rapidly reinforced by the landing of more troops at Basra, counter-attacked to much greater effect. The help expected from the Germans did not arrive. The Iraqi army and air force were outclassed by the British. The civil population of Basra, at first hostile to the landing of reinforcements, became gradually reconciled to the return of peace and order. The whole business lasted a month. When the signs of defeat became clear, the officers and politicians who had engineered the rebellion, headed by the Mufti, hastened to leave the country, seeking refuge in Persia or Saudi Arabia. The Regent and Nuri Pasha returned, and Iraq, now under her lawful government, proceeded with loyal determination to fulfil the terms of the alliance with Britain, and to punish those who had caused the rupture. Every assistance was given to the Middle East Command in the prosecution of the war, and one of the columns that attacked the Vichy French in Syria was enabled to proceed from Iraq. Later, Iraq signed the United Nations declaration, and declared war on the Axis powers in January 1943.

However, Iraqi nationalism in the sense of hostility to Britain and a desire to terminate the last traces of the British occupation was not dead. It had merely received a deep and galling wound from the ignominious failure of the 'war' it had sought to wage in – as it seemed to it – the cause of national liberation. An extremist minority wing of the nationalists remained, bent as ever on breaking every tie with Britain. But at the end of the war, to quote Stephen Longrigg: 'The objectives of all politicians were the removal of all limitation to their independence and free choice, the end of all treatment of the country as a junior partner, and the abolition of provisions which, offensively to their *amour propre*, left Habbaniya and Shuayba as British cantonments in the heart of Iraq.' Negotiations were therefore opened with Britain in 1947 for a revision of the treaty of 1930 in a way that would maintain the alliance but on a basis of much more real parity than before. The British Government were favourable, and so much progress was made that in December of that year a delegation, including Nuri Pasha es-Said, visited London in order to conclude the revised treaty, the draft of which was, indeed, signed ¦at Portsmouth on 15 January 1948 by the Iraqi delegates and Ernest Bevin, then Foreign Secretary. This treaty provided for immediate mutual help in time of war, but the two British bases in Iraq were to be handed over to the Iraqi state, Britain to leave in them only limited British personnel at British expense but under Iraqi command. British combatant forces could only reoccupy the bases in case of war. The British Military Mission, a relic of the 1930 treaty, was to be replaced by a mixed Council which would co-ordinate strategic plans.

On the assumption that the majority of Iraqi leaders wished to have some kind of alliance or protective connexion with Britain, the Treaty of Portsmouth was as reasonable an offer as they could hope to have. The Iraqi Government, however, made two fatal mistakes regarding the presentation of the treaty to their public. First, they allowed the text of the treaty to be published before the return of the Prime Minister and his colleagues from England to Baghdad, so that the chief government leaders were not present to explain and defend the treaty when it was published, and to see that things did not get out of hand. Second, the English version was published in England before an Arabic translation of it was published in Baghdad. This achieved the double and unfortunate effect of wounding Iraqi *amour propre* and opening the door to suspicion, damaging speculation, and the deliberate attacks of the government's opponents, who sought not only the rejection of the treaty but also the overthrow of the government for other reasons.

A very serious situation ensured in Baghdad, and the country was once more on the brink of revolution. The Regent, having at first expressed approval of the treaty and exchanged telegrams of good-will with the British sovereign on the occasion of its conclusion, was compelled by the menacing turn of events to denounce it as showing, on closer examination, that it was not in the country's interest. The Treaty of Portsmouth was dead, and there the matter stood. Both in international law and in fact the British position in Iraq continued to be that of the 1930 treaty, which was far less favourable to Iraqi nationalism than the Treaty of Portsmouth. Yet the Iraqi nationalists found it easier to acquiesce for the time being in an established position which they were unable to reverse and which they could denounce in words at any moment, than to put their signature to a new treaty which gave Iraqi sanction to the continuance of the British alliance and the continued presence on Iraqi soil of joint bases including British personnel. Following the conclusion of the Turco-Iraqi pact early in 1955, however, and the adherence to it of Britain, the 1930 Treaty was terminated by agreement between the British and the Iraqi governments and new arrangements even made for mutual help in time of war.

3

When the war came in 1939 the treaties negotiated between France and the Levant countries in 1936 had still not been ratified by the French Senate. Moreover, shortly before the outbreak of war the constitution of Syria was suspended by the French and the country placed under a Council of Directors controlled by the High Commissioner. Its unity was broken up once more, separate administrations being re-created in Jebel Druse and the Latakia region (the Alexandretta region had already been ceded to the Turks – a step which caused much resentment in Syria against both France and Turkey). In Lebanon, the constitution was suspended soon after the outbreak of war, and the country placed under a direct administration like that of Syria.

From the moment of France's collapse in Europe in 1940, the French position in Syria and Lebanon became doomed. Though under the Vichy regime the French authorities were able to maintain their physical grip on the two countries, their moral position – with France herself a beaten nation that had lost its independence – became vulnerably hollow. Both Syrians and Lebanese felt sure that they were about to see the end of French rule, whichever side won the war. In the Lebanon the *entente* between the Muslims and a large section of the Maronites together with the other sects created now an overwhelming majority in favour of independence; and in both Beirut and Damascus the nationalists waited for their opportunity.

The opportunity – or rather the first instalment of it – came in 1941 when British forces, including a Free French contingent, attacked the Vichy forces in Syria and Lebanon. At the moment that the campaign was launched General Catroux issued a proclamation, on behalf of General de Gaulle, ending the mandatory regime and declaring Syria and Lebanon to be independent sovereign states, with whom France would conclude treaties to guarantee their freedom. This French declaration was officially and publicly endorsed by the British Government, who became thus the guarantors of Syrian and Lebanese independence. The peoples of the two countries, having been already once bitten – during World War I – by the Anglo-French declaration, were now twice shy of accepting such assurances at their face value. Above all, they were very suspicious of all talk of a 'treaty' to be concluded between them and France, believing, not unjustifiably, that the French would, by the terms of the threatened treaty, once the war was over, try to place limitations on the independence and sovereignty which they were now proclaiming, and which both Lebanon and Syria intended to secure unconditionally.

From the beginning, the Lebanese and Syrians, with their eyes fixed unshakably on the realities of the situation, regarded the British as the effective source of power and tended to address themselves to them in seeking both redress of temporary grievances and the satisfaction of their ultimate aspirations. The British found themselves in an extremely delicate position as between their Free French allies and the Syrian and Lebanese nationalists whose independence they had guaranteed. On the one hand, they did not want the people of these liberated countries to become so disappointed with the results of their 'liberation' as to adopt an unfriendly attitude that might prejudice the war effort; on the other, they knew that the French felt profoundly mistrustful of Britain's entry into the Levant – always France's 'special sphere' – and acutely sensitive about the inferiority of their position *vis-à-vis* Britain in the three-cornered relationship that had thus been established. At first the attitude of the British was to let the Free French take over all the powers which the Vichy French had exercised, and to tell the Syrians and Lebanese that they must wait till the end of the war for the realization of their guaranteed independence, reiterating that they had come into the Levant merely to prosecute the war and not to supersede the French in any way.

Syrian and Lebanese discontent at this state of things, and particularly at the British attitude, mounted steadily with the irritation of war-time restrictions and shortages adding to the anger of nationalist frustration. An agitation began for the holding of elections and the restoration of constitutional life. The French at first resisted this, but finally were persuaded by the British to allow elections to be held in 1943.

The first blow to the French was the overwhelming victory, in the Lebanese elections, of the party that favoured the participation of the Lebanon in the Arab movement against the party that stood for a special connexion with France. But worse was still to come. As soon as the new parliaments met and the new governments were formed the nationalists in both countries began to demand the abrogation of all laws restricting their independence and giving France the special powers she had enjoyed under the Mandate. The French, while professing their desire to recognize the full independence of the two countries at the end of the war and by means of 'treaties' to be concluded between them and France, opposed any unilateral action by the Syrians or Lebanese in that direction, and denied their right to do so. For their part, the Syrians and Lebanese did not trust France to give them full independence once the war was over and she recovered her position as one of the great powers. They wanted to realize their independence immediately, taking advantage of France's weakness and of the presence in the Levant of British forces, for whose intervention they could appeal if necessary on the strength of Britain's guarantee of their independence.

After a short period of diplomatic tussling, the Lebanese Parliament took the initiative and challenged the French by passing legislation which ended all restrictions on the country's independence. The French authorities on the spot retaliated by arresting the President of the Republic and the majority of the ministers, suspending the constitution, dissolving the Chamber, and declaring the laws passed by it null and void.

An acute crisis followed, during which Muslim-Christian national solidarity reached a greater depth of reality than ever before. A general strike was maintained throughout the country for over a week. Two ministers who had escaped arrest established themselves in a village in the mountains and continued to issue orders in the name of the government. The leader of the extreme pro-French party, summoned to form a government, was unable to do so and had to content himself with setting up a council of civil servants.

Sympathy and support were promptly extended by all the surrounding Arab countries, and particularly Egypt, where the Egyptian Premier and veteran president of the Wafd, Nahas Pasha, had assumed the leadership of the movement for forming a league of the Arab states. Such a league, it was obvious, could not be formed unless Syria and Lebanon were included in it, and the two countries could not be included if they were not independent and so able to carry out any decisions in which they took part. In addition, the predominantly Muslim Arab countries, like Egypt and Iraq, were extremely gratified at the decision of the Lebanon, with its Christian majority, to cut completely adrift from France and identify itself with national independence in the Arab world.

As for Britain, she was not only concerned to retain, or recover, Arab good-will, but also to see that the conduct of the war was in no way prejudiced by a break-down of order in the Levant. She therefore brought pressure to bear on the French to alter their course of action.

Faced with all this opposition, the French submitted to the inevitable. The arrested President and ministers were released, the constitution and national government restored, the unilateral steps taken by the Lebanese (and shortly afterwards by the Syrians) to establish their independence accepted.

There was, however, one more round to be fought before the two countries became not only completely independent but also free from French occupation in any form. In 1945, as the war was ending in Europe, the French, with De Gaulle installed as head of the Provisional Government in Paris, insisted that they must maintain bases in Syria and Lebanon. Ships began to arrive in Beirut with new troops. The French claimed that they were mere replacements, but the Syrians and Lebanese saw in them reinforcements intended to back a high-handed policy. Tension grew, riots and fighting occurred in the principal Syrian cities, and the French bombed and shelled Damascus once again as they had done twenty years before.

As the war with Japan was still on, and security in the Middle East was a vital concern to Britain, she stepped in at this point to stop the fighting and restore order. The following year Syria and Lebanon, now members of the United Nations, appealed to the Security Council, demanding the withdrawal from their soil of all French and British troops. The Security Council adopted an American resolution expressing the hope that this would be done; and in fact it was done within the next year. Thus Syria and Lebanon emerged from the war as independent states, with no foreign military bases or troops on their territory, and owing no treaty obligations to France as Egypt and Iraq still owed to Britain. They owed their new status partly to the collapse of France during the war and partly to the guarantees and active assistance they received from Britain and for which the French, for a long time, found it difficult to forgive their ally, suspecting her for having deliberately engineered their expulsion from the Middle East.

4

Britain had had her own troubles in Egypt (as well as in Iraq) during the war.

When hostilities broke out King Farouk had once more dismissed the Wafd and was ruling the country through minority governments. He himself was known to have Italian sympathies inherited from his father (who had been brought up in Italy) and imbibed from the court his father had left him; while some of his ministers and trusted private advisers became convinced, as a result of Germany's resounding victories in 1940, that the Axis Powers were going to win the war, and therefore counselled only a reserved and partial fulfilment of the treaty, as, for instance, the breaking off of diplomatic relations with Germany but not with Italy. Though Britain secured the dismissal of the ministry that had followed this particular course, and received loyal co-operation from its successor, the situation generally continued to deteriorate in the absence of a popularly supported and strong government. Matters got completely out of hand in the dark days of 1942, when the British forces were retreating for the second time in the Western Desert. Students demonstrated in the streets of Cairo, shouting 'We are Rommel's soldiers'. Behind all this confusion of weakness and hostility stood Nahas Pasha, the leader of the Wafd, ready and able to implement the treaty faithfully and with full effect. But Farouk still refused to have him. Britain decided to use compulsion against the King. While tanks surrounded Abdin

Palace he was presented with an ultimatum: either he would accept Nahas as Prime Minister, or he would be deposed and deported. The King yielded, so that during the Alamein crisis of 1942, when Rommel stood at the gates of Alexandria, Egypt had a strong government maintaining order and giving every assistance to the British forces. Indeed, when the time of testing came, the vast majority of the Egyptian people showed by deeds (or rather the absence of them) that it preferred Britain to the Axis. No sabotage or anti-British action or agitation of any kind was attempted during the crucial weeks of that summer. Nahas Pasha and the Government refused to leave Cairo, and by their calm and steadfastness prevented panic and made a substantial contribution to the success of the British armies, first in holding the Axis attack, and then in winning the great victory of Alamein.

However, the coercion of the King by a display of military force had administered one more humiliation to Egyptian *amour propre*; it added to the grievances of Egyptian nationalism, and was later felt vicariously, even by people who had no great liking for the King himself.

The end of the war found Egypt one vast military base for the Allies, with British troops, in tens of thousands, occupying not only the Canal zone but also swarming over Cairo and Alexandria and retarding the return of the country to normal life. By the terms of the 1936 treaty, Britain was entitled to keep in Egypt, in peace-time, a maximum of 10,000 troops, confined to the Canal zone. The delay in evacuating the chief cities and reducing the number of troops in the country altogether was a grave mistake on the part of Britain. Nationalist feeling found the presence of such a large and ubiquitous British army in the country a constant irritant, to which it reacted by desiring the total withdrawal of British troops even from the Canal zone. The success of Syria and Lebanon in obtaining an independence not subject to the continuance of French occupation in any form no doubt encouraged this desire. Egypt was now the leader of the Arab League – a fact which enhanced her prestige both among the

Arab countries and in the world at large, and made her more impatient than she had ever been of the restriction on her independence represented by the presence of British troops, in any capacity, on her territory. For not only had Syria and Lebanon succeeded in ridding themselves of foreign occupation, but also two other states of the Arab League – Saudi Arabia and Yemen – who were far behind Egypt in wealth, cultural attainments, and international status, had never, since their liberation from Turkey, been occupied by European troops. It was, moreover, felt and argued that the elimination of the Axis threat and the establishment of general peace in 1945 had removed the only justification for the maintenance of a British base in Egypt. The treaty of 1936 provided for its own revision at the request of either partner at the end of ten years. This revision was now requested by Egypt.

The Egyptian Question, as always, consisted of two principal issues: the Suez base and the Sudan. The ten years that had passed between the conclusion of the treaty and the end of the war saw a great forward surge of political consciousness in the Sudan, where modern education had been in progress for some forty years and had produced a vigorous intelligentsia consisting of merchants, civil servants, and professional men. This intelligentsia and the two principal religious sects (that of Sayed Abd-ur-Rahman al-Mahdi, and that of Sayed Ali al-Mirghani) which provided it with its mass support in the country and among the tribes, was sharply divided on the question of the Sudan's political future. One section thought of independence in terms of freedom from Britain and union with Egypt; the other sought complete independence, *vis-à-vis* Egypt as well as Britain. The British favoured this section, partly because its leaders were for the most part senior government officials with whom they were personally on good terms, partly because the independence it desired was to be gradual and achieved through co-operation with Britain, and lastly because it was opposed to Egyptian claims (the Egyptians having become very unpopular with the

British members of the Sudan Government since the outbreak of 1924) and offered the hope of an independent Sudan
associated with Britain – perhaps through membership of the
Commonwealth.

The Egyptians, for their part, were for a long time convinced that the independence movement in the Sudan was a
British fabrication and did not represent any genuine Sudanese aspirations. In this they were wrong, for though it suited
the British to support the independence movement, the
movement was neither their creation nor their tool, but had
its own reality based in Sudanese historical experience and
sectarian differences.

Immediately after the war negotiations between Britain
and Egypt resulted in the Bevin-Sidky (Farouk having dismissed the Wafd once more and summoned Sidky Pasha to
head a minority government) Protocol of 1946. Britain
offered complete withdrawal from Egypt, subject to satis-
factory arrangements being made for mutual assistance in a
new international crisis threatening the Middle East. As for
the Sudan, Britain agreed to a formula which, for the time
being and so far as she was concerned, recognized the unity
of Egypt and the Sudan 'under the Egyptian Crown', but
stipulated that the Sudanese should have the right to decide
their own future when they were sufficiently mature to do so,
and that meanwhile the existing administration in the Sudan
should continue to train the Sudanese for self-government.

In the Sudan there was a vigorous protest by the Independence Front (supported by the British officials) against the
recognition of the Egyptian Crown; while in Egypt, Sidky
Pasha, yielding to nationalist excitement on his return from
London after initialing the Protocol, gave an interpretation
of it which denied to the Sudanese any effective right of self-
determination. In these circumstances the British Government repudiated the Protocol. Sidky resigned, and, in the
following year his successor, Nuqrashi Pasha, presented
Egypt's case to the Security Council. This move had no
result. Britain took her stand on the 1936 treaty, and the

Security Council refused to pronounce that treaty as null and void on the grounds that it did not harmonize with Egypt's post-war status and circumstances. All that happened was that a resolution calling for the resumption of direct negotiations between the parties failed, by one vote, to secure the required two-thirds majority.

Britain's position now was that unless a new treaty was negotiated to replace that of 1936 there would be no change in her relations with Egypt. But the 1936 treaty, as we have seen, provided for the withdrawal of British troops from Cairo and Alexandria and their concentration in the Canal zone. This movement had indeed already started – though belatedly – and before long there were no British troops left anywhere in Egypt except in the agreed region by the Canal, though their number was far in excess of the ten thousand permitted by the treaty. Finally, the Egyptian Government abrogated the treaty by unilateral action in October 1951, and a period of tension, agitation, and terrorism followed, culminating in the horrific events of 'Black Saturday', 26 January 1952.

In the Sudan, Britain proceeded in 1948 to the establishment of a Legislative Assembly and an Executive Council consisting of British and Sudanese members in equal numbers, though later the Sudanese were given a majority of one. These steps were boycotted by Egypt and the pro-Egyptian party in the Sudan.

The deadlock with Egypt over the Sudan continued until 1952. In the spring of that year the Sudan Government issued a constitution for Sudanese self-government by means of a bi-cameral legislature and an all-Sudanese Council of Ministers. The period of self-government was to last for three years, by the end of which the Sudanese would proceed to decide for themselves their future status in relation to Britain and Egypt. During the three years the British Governor-General would act as Head of State, but the Constitution required of him to act on the advice of his Sudanese ministers in all matters save foreign affairs, questions relating to the mainly non-Muslim and non-Arab southern Sudan and the position of civil servants. Again, Egypt refused to take any part in the promulgation of this constitution, regarding it as a further move intended to complete the severance of the Sudan from her. The elections for the first Sudanese Parliament were to be held in the autumn, and it was doubtful whether the pro-Egyptian parties would take part in them. But then something entirely unexpected happened. The Egyptian military junta headed by General Neguib deposed Farouk and assumed power in Egypt.

The results of this revolution were quickly felt in the Sudan. First, General Neguib had lived in the Sudan for many years and was personally known to (and liked by) the leading figures of the Sudanese Independence Front. Secondly, his movement and the reforms it promised aroused general enthusiasm in the Sudan such as the Egypt of Farouk could never hope to arouse. The mere removal of Farouk, who had always wished to be 'King of Egypt and the Sudan' seemed to open new possibilities for an understanding. These possibilities General Neguib and his colleagues were very quick to exploit. By a master-stroke of diplomacy they relinquished the age-long Egyptian claim to sovereignty over the Sudan and agreed that the Sudanese should have the self-government prepared for them by the British and, at the end of it, proceed to an exercise of the right of self-determination. In return for this great concession, they demanded that before the time came for self-determination all British military and police forces and administrative officers (as well as Egyptian) should be withdrawn from the country, so that the choice of the Sudanese should be really free.

Extremely gratified at the Egyptian renunciation of their claims to sovereignty, the Independence party agreed to this condition, and elections were duly held in November-December 1953. They resulted in a sweeping victory for the parties that favoured union with Egypt. This was due in the first place to the anti-British or anti-imperialist spirit now rampant in the Middle East; the Independence party were compromised by their co-operation with the British and their willingness to seek independence through British help. Other factors that told against them included the general fear that their patron, Sayd Abd-ur-Rahman al-Mahdi, wished to be King of the Sudan, and that under a Mahdist monarchy a dynastic despotism might be established in the Sudan just as the Egyptians had got rid of a peculiarly unpopular one themselves.

With the Sudan question at last out of the way, Britain and Egypt now concentrated on the Suez base issue. After prolonged negotiations agreement was finally reached in the summer of 1954. The seventy-year-old occupation of Egypt by British troops was to end. Britain agreed to withdraw all her combatant units from the Canal zone within twenty months, leaving only 4000 technicians to maintain the installations of the base in peace-time, when it was to be militarily occupied by Egyptian forces. For her part, Egypt agreed that Britain should have the right to reoccupy the base with military forces in the event of an attack on any one of the Arab countries or Turkey.

5

References have been made in the foregoing pages to the Arab League. It is now necessary to retrace our steps in order to tell the story of the formation of the League, describe its character, and give an account of its failure to save Palestine for the Arabs.

The idea of Arab unity, in some shape or other, had been a part of the Arab revival since its early days in the nineteenth century. It was, indeed, implied by such expressions as 'the Arab awakening', or 'the Arab movement'. When they rediscovered their ancient culture, the Arabs dreamed of recreating at least part of the universal political structure within which it had flowered. This vision of a new union of the Arab peoples (even in the great days of Arab civilization in the medieval period unity was not maintained for long throughout the Arab world) did not include Egypt or the countries of the Maghreb, but was confined to the lands of Arab Asia. For this there were several reasons. Egypt had taken the shape of a modern nation-state long before *Arab* nationalism started, and was developing, for the time being, along the lines of a specifically *Egyptian* nationalism. Also, communications between the eastern Arab world and the western Arab world were slow and difficult in those early days of the Revival, and there had been no political intercourse between them for a long time. Above all, when World War I started, Egypt and all the other Arab countries of North Africa were under the rule of Britain and her allies, France and Italy. Not even the visionary and often unrealistic imagination of the most audacious leaders of the Arab movement could envisage yet the expulsion of the European powers from these countries. But it was different with the countries of Arab Asia. They were all still Ottoman provinces. To become independent and form an Arab state was comparatively easy for them; all they had to do was to shake off Ottoman rule. Instead of having to challenge the power of Britain and her allies (as the Egyptians, Libyans, Tunisians, Algerians, and Moroccans would have to do if they desired their independence) they could actually enlist their support in freeing themselves from Turkey as soon as the war broke out in 1914. Moreover, the countries of Arab Asia formed a geographically compact region, which Ottoman rule had kept together under one political and administrative system; and they had, after all, formed the heart of the Arab Empire in the days of the Umayyads and Abbasids. Thus it was that when the Arab nationalists, headed by King Hussein, were negotiating with Britain the terms of the Arab Revolt they demanded what was in effect a unitary Arab state comprising the Arabian Peninsula, geographical Syria (i.e. Syria, Palestine, Jordan, and Lebanon), and Iraq; and Britain agreed to this demand subject to certain reservations.

It has been argued since that even in this region Arab

THE ARABS

unity was unattainable in 1918, regardless of the clash of British and French imperialist interests and the support given to Zionism in Palestine. The proponents of this thesis point to the subsequent conflict between King Hussein and Ibn Saud, which resulted in Hussein being expelled from the Hejaz and a state of permanent tension being created between the Hashemites in Iraq and Jordan on the one hand and the rulers of the Peninsula on the other.

It is even arguable, as suggested earlier in this book, that, quite apart from the conflict between Hussein and Ibn Saud, the Arabs lacked in 1918 the powers of political cohesion and the constitutional equipment necessary to hold together Damascus, Baghdad, Jerusalem, and Medina. However that may be, the division of the region into British and French spheres of influence and mandated territories, together with the establishment of the Jewish national home in Palestine, dealt a cruel blow to the dream of unity which had inspired the Arab movement. Arab Asia was splintered into a number of states, some of them exiguous in territory and population, and of an arbitrary and unreal character. This splintering was in particular unjust and harmful to Arab interests in geographical Syria, which already was a cohesive unit where a stable Arab state might have been set up. Here, there was nothing to justify any division beyond some form of Lebanese autonomy within Syrian unity. The fragmentation of the country into four states (Syria, Lebanon, Palestine, and Jordan) was a policy imposed in the interests of Britain, France, and the Zionists, and utterly unrelated to Arab wishes or the realities of the Arab position.

The period between the two wars witnessed two processes taking place side by side. On the one hand, the struggle for independence in the different Arab countries (including Egypt, which now began to draw closer to Syria and Iraq owing to the similarity of their positions and identity of their aspirations) and the concern which all the Arab countries felt about the fate of Palestine stimulated the growth of pan-Arab feelings; while the Press, the radio, the cinema, and air travel gave these feelings increasingly rapid channels of communication. On the other hand, the barriers which Britain and France had imposed arbitrarily in 1919, and which then had been largely artificial, were, with the passage of time, becoming increasingly real. Dynasties, commercial interests, political groups, armies were consolidating themselves in each state in a manner which, if allowed to continue unchecked, would obviously militate against future amalgamation. Far-sighted Arab leaders were conscious of this danger and sought to check it. Foremost among them were King Faisal I of Iraq and the leading Iraqi and Arab statesman, Nuri Pasha es-Said, who never ceased to think of the Arab movement as a whole and propound plans for co-operation among the various Arab states. Faisal's brother, King Abdullah of Jordan, had his own scheme for a Greater Syria; that is to say, the fusion of Syria, Transjordan, and Palestine (or part of it) under him. Neither the Damascus politicians nor Ibn Saud, however, favoured this plan. To the former, Abdullah's autocratic methods of rule and apparent subservience to the British were distasteful; while the latter disapproved of any step that would aggrandize the House of Hashem.

In the spring of 1941 Mr Eden, then Foreign Secretary in the war-time National Government, made a declaration in which he said:

'The Arab World has made great strides since the settlement reached at the end of the last war, and many Arab thinkers desire for the Arab peoples a greater degree of unity than they now enjoy. ... It seems to me both natural and right that the cultural and economic ties between the Arab countries, yes, and the political ties, too, should be strengthened. His Majesty's Government, for their part, will give their full support to any scheme that commands general approval.'

What were Britain's motives for this move? First, she hoped to cultivate Arab good-will to help her in World War II by repairing some of the damage which Arab leaders, not without justification, had been persistently accusing her of having caused to the Arab movement at the end of World War I. Secondly, she hoped that a confederation of Arab states would contribute to the stability of the Middle East, on a regional basis, after the war. Lastly, the idea had been sometimes mooted that if Palestine became part of a larger Arab unit, Arab fears of Zionism would correspondingly diminish – a result which would help to solve the Palestine problem. Now that the division of the Arab countries into French and British spheres of influence had come to an end with the recognition of Syria and Lebanon as independent states no longer subject to French mandatory control, one of the chief obstacles to an Arab union was removed. Britain still held the Mandate for Palestine and Transjordan, but Iraq, Egypt, Saudi Arabia, and Yemen were all independent states; and in so far as any of them were still under foreign influence, this was exclusively British and could therefore help rather than obstruct the movement for unity.

The first response to Mr Eden's encouragement came from Nuri Pasha es-Said who in 1942 put forward proposals for an Arab Union in two degrees. First, he recommended the formation of a single state (unitary or federal, as might be found more feasible) of Syria, Lebanon, Palestine, and Transjordan. In this state the Christians of Lebanon and the Jews of Palestine would be granted a special, autonomous position. Secondly, Nuri Pasha proposed an Arab League consisting, to begin with, of the new state and Iraq, but open to any other Arab state that wished to join, whether immediately or later. This League would have a council presided over by the head of one of the member states elected in a manner acceptable to all. The council would be responsible for defence, foreign affairs, currency, communications, customs, and the protection of minority rights.

In the course of 1943 the initiative passed from Nuri to Nahas Pasha, from Iraq to Egypt. This was the moment at which Egypt decided definitely to identify herself with the Arab movement, at which the strands of Egyptian nationalism and Arab nationalism became intertwined after having been running separately but parallel to one another for many years. This consummation was the result of a reciprocal desire on the part of Egypt and the countries of Arab Asia. Egypt saw the advantages to her of leading a group of Arab countries in the post-war world, while the other Arab countries, recognizing Egypt's superiority in size, culture, and international status, were glad to accept her leadership.

With this change in leadership came a change in the conception of the proposed League. It was found, as a result of the negotiations that took place in Cairo, that nothing as closely integrated and centralized as Nuri's League was possible in a region that was to include Egypt, Saudi Arabia, and Yemen as well as Iraq and the countries of geographical Syria. There were too many rival dynasties, too many local national policies, too many differences in social structure and standards of political maturity between the seven candidate countries for any close union of them to be practicable. Only a loose confederation, which involved no subordination of sovereign rights, could hold them together. The Arab League, which finally came into being in March 1945, was such a loose confederation. Its seven members 'in order to affirm the close connexions and numerous ties which link the Arab States, and being desirous of maintaining and establishing these connexions on the foundations of respect for the independence and sovereignty of these states, and in order to direct their efforts towards the general good of the Arab States, the improvement of their circumstances, the security of their future, and the realization of their hopes and aspirations, and in response to Arab public opinion in all quarters of the world' entered into a covenant to carry out all these objects. In more concrete terms the objects of the League were 'to strengthen the ties between the participant states, to co-ordinate their political programme in such a way as to effect real collaboration between them, to preserve their independence and sovereignty, and to consider in general the affairs and interests of the Arab countries.' Likewise, the member states were to collaborate in economic and financial affairs, communications, cultural matters, matters relating to nationality, passports, *visas*, etc., and matters relating to social questions and public health.

All these objects were to be the concern of the League Council, a body representing the member states, on which each was to have a single vote regardless of the number of its representatives.

Four features of the League Covenant were of special interest. First, the provision that each independent Arab state should have the right to adhere to the League – a provision which made of the League an expandable organization to be enlarged by the addition of new members in the future (e.g. Palestine, as it was then hoped, and the French-controlled countries of North Africa). Second, the special appendix relating to Palestine and providing that until that country (whose existence and *de jure* national independence as an Arab country was affirmed) had a government of its own to represent it on the League Council, the Council would itself select an Arab from Palestine to participate in its proceedings. Third, the appendix which provides for associating Arab states not members of the League (such as Tunisia and Morocco, for instance, who were debarred from membership by their subjection to France) with the proceedings of the Council by their co-option to some of the Council's committees. Fourth, the article permitting 'those Arab states desirous of closer collaboration with each other and stronger ties than those specified by this Covenant' to conclude special arrangements between themselves to realize this object. This left the door open for the later fulfilment of Nuri Pasha's idea of a single Arab state in geographical Syria, or something similar to it.

The first object of the League, and the first benefit accruing from it, was the appearance of a visible symbol of Arab unity, the fulfilment of a psychological need felt by many Arabs. The League might have many weaknesses in practice; some of its members, though independent, might be so backward as to count for nothing in terms of political and military power. They might be quite out of step, socially and culturally, with one another. Yet their coming together in the League expressed, actually and still more potentially, one of the important facts of political life in the Middle East.

But apart from all questions of emotional satisfaction and symbolical value, there were in the post-war world two concrete and urgent Arab interests which, it was felt, would be effectively served by the joint action of the Arab states through the League. The first was the termination of all French control over Syria and Lebanon; the second, the saving of Palestine from continued immigration and final domination by the Jews, and the establishment in it of an independent state while the native Arab population was still in a majority.

Five of the member states of the League – Egypt, Syria, Lebanon, Iraq, and Saudi Arabia – became members of the United Nations. The admission of Transjordan continued to be vetoed by Russia even after the conclusion of a treaty between that country (under the new name of 'the Hashemite Kingdom of Jordan') and Britain, whereby the Mandate was formally terminated and Jordanian independence recognized under King Abdullah. The Russian argument was that Jordan (since she received a subsidy from Britain to pay for the maintenance of her army, which was also trained and commanded by British officers) was too much under British control to join the United Nations as an independent state. As for Yemen, it both lacked the diplomatic personnel to represent it in an international organization and was too remote from, and suspicious of, the outside world to desire such representation. However, even with only five members in the United Nations, the Arab League emerged from the war as a regional *bloc* whose diplomatic weight was something to be reckoned with. The League of Nations had not, at its formation, contained a single Arab state. The presence of five Arab states as foundation members of the United Nations was a measure of the advance of the Arab countries and the elevation of their international status in the twenty-seven years that had passed between the end of World War I and World War II. Moreover, one of the five states – Egypt – occupied one of the non-permanent seats on the Security Council during its first session, when the dispute between the Levant countries and France was heard. On this issue Arab solidarity, as expressed through the League, was a helpful, though not a decisive, factor in securing a result favourable to Syrian and Lebanese aspirations. It was quite a different matter with regard to Palestine.

6

Many things happened during the war to increase the Zionist threat to Palestine. In the first place, the entry of America into the war and the emergence of the fact that she was going to be the senior member of the Anglo-American partnership after the war made it plain that Britain, even if she herself remained faithful to her pledges, would not be able to carry out the policy of the White Paper of 1939. Strong as the Zionists were in Britain, they were stronger still in the United States, where their *bloc* vote in New York and Illinois could swing a presidential election, and where therefore their 'lobby' could exert the pressure of blackmail on Congressmen and State Governors of the two parties. This pressure was all the more deadly since the techniques of mass propaganda in America, though under private enterprise, had been developed to a totalitarian pitch of intensity, and since, in the absence of an Arab opposition, all the batteries of this propaganda could be mobilized by the Zionists. In addition to all this, there was the fact that whereas Britain, after twenty-five years of bitter and chastening experience, was beginning to know something about the realities of the Palestine question, America – apart from a few experts in the State Department – was completely ignorant of them.

Conscious of their growing power and coming opportunity, the Zionists decided that the time had come to drop the mask of their early days and announce at last their true intentions. Their official organization adopted the Biltmore programme (drawn up in New York in 1942) which demanded the establishment of Palestine as a Jewish state, the creation of a Jewish army, and the opening of the country to unlimited Jewish immigration.

In Palestine itself the Jews were preparing both secretly and openly for the seizure of the country by force at the first opportunity. Openly they pressed for and eventually (in 1944) succeeded in having a Jewish brigade, with its own colours, incorporated in the British forces. Thus, thousands of Zionists obtained military training and experience. At the same time the Jews had their own local defence organization in Palestine (the Hagana) which had an underground terroristic wing. Every opportunity was seized during the war to obtain and hoard arms and ammunition for these forces. British army depots were robbed; British officers and soldiers were bribed, or induced to 'sell' military equipment.

Throughout this period the Arabs of Palestine did nothing to prepare themselves for the coming battle. The rebellion of 1936–9 had left them for the moment exhausted. Their leadership was broken up and dispersed. Their arms had been confiscated; those who had been caught in possession of them, let alone using them, had been executed. The Mufti and some of his colleagues, who had escaped from Baghdad after the failure of the Golden Square rebellion, had eventually sought refuge in Germany and were not doing the Arab cause in the eyes of Britain and America any good by broadcasting pro-German propaganda to the Arab countries. The Palestine Arabs themselves were divided in regard to the Mufti. He had made many enemies towards the end of the rebellion by using terroristic methods against those who opposed him; yet his opponents could say nothing openly against him for fear of creating dissension in the Arab ranks and so weakening the opposition to Zionism.

In this demoralized and leaderless condition, the Palestine Arabs found a new hope in the Arab League – a soporific and therefore injurious hope. Not that there were no prescient individuals among them who were aware of the weaknesses of the League and afraid to see it tested in action. But even these shrewd observers did not envisage a military battle for Palestine; their hope was that the League would be able to exert sufficient diplomatic pressure at the United Nations, and particularly on Britain, to prevent the enforcement of the more outrageous Zionist demands. As for the public at large, it was deceived by the inflated talk of the Arabic press about the 'seven states' and the 'forty million people' who stood ready to save Arab Palestine.

The end of the war brought two shocks to the Arabs. The first was Mr Truman's exhortation to the British Government to allow immediately 100,000 Jewish refugees from Europe to enter Palestine. The second was the coming into office of the Labour Party in Britain. For though several of the Conservative leaders, including Mr Churchill himself, were well known for their pro-Zionist sympathies, the party as a whole had not committed itself so categorically to maximum support for the Zionist cause as had the Labour Party, whose executive, only a few months before the end of the war, had passed a resolution in favour of unlimited Jewish immigration into Palestine, adding the astounding euphemism (which in terms of brute fact could only mean, as has actually happened, the entire destitution of almost the whole native population of Palestine) that 'the Arabs should be encouraged to move out as the Jews moved in'!

Once in office, however, the Labour Party had second thoughts, and Ernest Bevin proved less unjust to the Arabs, if not more able to help them, than any British Minister (with the possible exception of Malcolm Macdonald in 1939) since the Balfour Declaration was issued.

In the face of President Truman's pressure and her own diminished power in the world, Britain decided to associate the United States in one more inquiry into the Palestine situation. An Anglo-American Committee was appointed to hear evidence and make recommendations. In the event, these recommendations shirked the realities which the Committee had been asked to face, and proved utterly unhelpful. The Mandate was to continue 'until the hostility between Jews and Arabs disappears'. President Truman's 100,000 immigrants were to be admitted as rapidly as conditions permitted. Lastly the Committee, flying in the teeth of twenty-five years' experience, repeated the unctuous contradiction-in-terms which had first appeared in the Balfour Declaration and continued throughout the period of the Mandate to be the ostensible basis of Britain's Zionist policy. It recommended further immigration 'while ensuring that the rights and position of other sections of the population were not prejudiced'.

The Arabs found it intolerable that independence should be still withheld from Palestine, with its two-to-one Arab majority, while more and more Jewish immigrants were forced upon the country. A little arithmetic could show them clearly where they were going. Twenty-five years before they had had a nine-to-one majority. Continued immigration would result, not in the disappearance of hostility between Arabs and Jews as the Committee professed to hope, but in the further undermining and eventual overthrow of the Arab majority in the country. Although the Arabs had rejected the British White Paper of 1939 when it was issued, they now appealed to it as a charter guaranteeing their minimum rights against the Committee's recommendations. They demanded the termination of the Mandate, the withdrawal of the British, and the establishment of an independent Palestine state on a democratic basis – that is to say, with the Jews sharing in the government in proportion to their numbers.

The British Government declared that the Committee's report (which had also contained recommendations for the termination of Jewish terrorism) would be considered in its entirety; and they made it a condition of the admission of the 100,000 new immigrants that the Jewish underground organizations in Palestine should be disarmed.

The Zionist leaders in Palestine were indignant at this condition. They adopted from the report the parts that favoured them, as another step towards Jewish statehood, and ignored the rest. Meanwhile illegal immigrants (i.e. those not included in the permitted quota) were arriving from Europe in increasing numbers. Most of them did not fall into the categories of old, sick, and very young, on whose behalf a humanitarian case might be presented to world opinion, but were healthy young men and women chosen with an obvious eye to the reinforcement of the Jewish armed forces in Palestine. Terrorism was on the increase, reaching new peaks of audacity, as with the blowing up of a wing of the King David Hotel in Jerusalem; and it was becoming abundantly clear that when the Zionists said they needed their armed forces for defence purposes, they meant by 'defence' the enforcement of all their nationalist demands, in other words unrestricted immigration, freedom to acquire land anywhere in Palestine, and the ultimate establishment of a Jewish state.

Another Anglo-American attempt (this time one between Foreign Office and State Department experts) to provide a solution on the basis of mainly autonomous but federated Arab and Jewish provinces, proved equally abortive. The Jews declared that they would only accept a 'viable state' – which, according to their own definition, was to consist of the best land in Palestine, amounting to 65 per cent of the total, leaving to the Arabs, 'as a supreme sacrifice', the central and mainly arid plateau.

Following this failure, the Arab states accepted an invitation from the British Government to send delegations for yet one more conference in London in the winter of 1946–7. But no result was achieved. The Arab delegates reiterated the now unshakable Arab demand for an independent, democratic state in Palestine, offering equal rights to all citizens, freedom of education to the Jews, and the use of Hebrew as an official language. But they insisted on the immediate stoppage of all immigration and the enforcement of existing regulations against the sale of land to the Jews in certain parts of Palestine.

Faced with an explosive situation, a surging wave of illegal Jewish immigration and terrorism, and utterly unable to provide a solution that would satisfy Zionist demands without 'causing prejudice' to the rights of the Arab and native population of the country, the British Government decided at this stage to refer the question to the United Nations.

In the spring of 1947 the United Nations set up a committee consisting of the representatives of eleven of the smaller states, presumed not to have a direct interest in the matter, to work out a solution. Reverting to the idea of the Royal Commission of 1937, a majority of seven of this Committee recommended the partition of Palestine into independent Jewish and Arab states. Perhaps it was unavoidable that a United Nations committee should, in principle and given the facts of the situation with which it was faced, decide that partition was the only possible solution at that moment. But the details of the partition project put forward were shockingly unfair to the Arabs. Not only were the Jews – who were only one-third of the population – given the larger and more fertile part of the country with the most useful section of the coastal plain and the only good port, so that the Arabs were almost debarred from effective sea communications, but also 500,000 Arabs (or nearly half the Arab population) were to be left in the Jewish state. A large number of these were the inhabitants of Jaffa, the biggest purely Arab city in Palestine and the Arabs' principal seaport. The two states were to enter into an economic union and remain, for a transition period of two years, under the supervision of the mandatory power, during which 150,000 immigrants would be allowed to come into the Jewish state. 'Partition' was a misnomer applied to this scheme. It was a scheme for the liquidation of Arab Palestine and the establishment of a Jewish state in the greater and only viable part of the country, while a piece of hemmed-in territory that had neither coherent frontiers nor the means of livelihood was left to 700,000 Arabs, and even then only on condition that they accepted economic union with the Jewish state.

Britain announced that she was not willing to undertake the role proposed for her under this scheme. Her policy was not to carry out any solution – either on her own behalf or as the representative of the United Nations – to which both sides did not agree. She decided, moreover, while the United Nations' debate was proceeding, to play the part which had been played once before in Palestine by a Roman proconsul who washed his hands. Having announced that she would lay down the Mandate and withdraw from Palestine by a certain date, she refused to take any part in the debate on partition, wishing apparently to give the impression of a strict neutrality. Yet this silence was scarcely fair to the Arabs, whose 'political and economic freedom' in their country Britain had guaranteed. Having issued the Balfour Declaration thirty years before, and for the whole of that period sponsored the establishment of the Jewish national home in Palestine subject, ostensibly, to the solemn obligations she had undertaken towards the Arabs, she failed at the supreme moment to discharge those obligations by not saying one word of protest against a partition scheme which virtually pronounced the doom of the Arabs. This was not neutrality but a dereliction of duty. Moreover, to make acceptance by both Arabs and Jews a condition of her taking part in any solution could only lead to a chaotic termination of the Mandate, for it was clear then, as it had been clear for years, that no agreed solution was possible, since the Jews were demanding in fact the abolition of Arab Palestine. Britain had been warned, very shortly after the issue of the Balfour Declaration, both by the words and deeds of the Zionists (as well as by the Arabs and by neutral observers like the King-Crane Commission) that this was the aim of Zionism. Yet, for thirty years, she had helped the Zionists in realizing this aim while protesting all the time that she would not allow the rights of the Arabs to be prejudiced; and now, when the inescapable and vicious logic of her policy overtook her, all she would do for the Arabs was to say that she would not use force to compel their acceptance of a Jewish state in Palestine. But it was too late. She had used enough force against the Arabs since 1918 to give the Jews a bridgehead from which, with their superior organization and international connexions, they could do the rest for themselves.

The partition resolution was passed by the United Nations Assembly on 29 November 1947, though some high-handed (and underhand) manoeuvring and lobbying had to be resorted to by the United States Government at the last moment to obtain the necessary two-thirds majority. This fact was acknowledged even by the *Manchester Guardian*, which had always been an open supporter of Zionism; while *The Times* commented that 'the general impression among delegates was ... that the partition scheme would have been carried in no other city than New York' owing to Jewish influence in that city.

Britain persisted in her determination to lay down the Mandate on 15 May 1948 and withdraw all her forces from Palestine. As it was certain that the United Nations were not going to send troops themselves to carry out the partition scheme, it became obvious that there was going to be war between the Jews and the Arabs.

For such a war the Jews were much better prepared than the Arabs of Palestine. For years they had been on a war footing with large, well-drilled and well-equipped armed forces; whereas the Arabs, since the end of their rebellion in 1939, had been disorganized. Moreover, the Arabs were generally backward as compared with the Jews, who came from Europe and America with the latest Western techniques, and even the Arab rebellion had lacked the ruthless military efficiency of Jewish terrorism. Again, the Arabs were in their own country, living their normal lives – a condition in which it is impossible to have the sense of danger and urgency and desperation which impels an invading alien minority, holding a precarious bridgehead. Lastly, with the formation of the Arab League, the Arabs of Palestine were encouraged to believe that the defence of Palestine would henceforth be the concern of the Arab states, some of which, at least, had sizable, regular armies.

However, Arab League policy, at first, was to employ irregulars, consisting of Palestinians and volunteers from the surrounding Arab countries, and forming an 'Army of Liberation'. Fighting started before the British withdrew, and the Arab liberation army proved no match for the Jewish forces.

On the afternoon of 14 May – that is to say, a few hours before the Mandate was due to be officially terminated – the Jews proclaimed their state of Israel, which received instant recognition from President Truman, even while the American delegation at Lake Success was trying to bring about a cessation of hostilities between Arabs and Jews on the condition that nothing should be done to prejudice the future political settlement!

There followed the attempt of the Arab League to intervene in Palestine by using the regular armies of some of its members, namely, Egypt, Jordan, Iraq, and Syria. The Lebanon had only a small *gendarmerie*, while Saudi Arabia and Yemen could make no contribution at all save a few token levies from the former.

From the beginning the Arab states' campaign was crippled by lack of unity among them, the absence of a common general-staff and all-round poor organization. In particular, co-operation between Egypt and Jordan was difficult to achieve because of mutual distrust. Another cause of serious weakness on the Arab side was that Jordan's Arab Legion – which though small in numbers was probably the best trained and best armed of the Arab forces, was subsidized by Britain and commanded by British officers in the employ of King Abdullah. This fact probably undermined the entire reality of the Arab effort in so far as it relied on the co-operation of Jordan. For how, in view of American policy and public opinion and of Britain's post-war dependence on America, could an army which received its funds, its equipment, and its higher command from Britain be allowed to succeed in destroying the state of Israel? There were, indeed, questions in the British press and parliament about the position of the British officers in the Arab Legion; and H.M. Government assured the questioners that all these officers had relinquished their commissions in the British army and were serving Jordan in their private capacity. But there remained the question of the subsidy, which makes it difficult to resist the conclusion that Britain did not envisage anything like the destruction of Israel, but merely a sort of token war which would be called to a halt after a little while and at such a point as to leave the Jewish state established within the frontiers laid down by the United Nations or something approximating to them.

In spite of all these handicaps, however, the Arabs – who enjoyed air superiority in this first phase of the fighting – had the upper hand and were on the point of compelling the Jews in the New City of Jerusalem to surrender, when the machinery of the United Nations was brought into action against them, and a cease-fire for four weeks was ordered. The Arabs were persuaded to accept this order largely under British pressure and the warning that Britain, from whom the Arab states obtained their arms, would suspend supplies if the order was disobeyed.

The Arab states yielded and the cease-fire came into force on 9 June; a condition of it, as is customary in such situations, was that neither side should use the truce period in such a way as to improve its military position or reinforce its armies. Britain maintained, throughout the period, a strict arms embargo against Egypt, Iraq, and Jordan, in spite of the fact that she was under treaty obligation to supply them with arms. And apart from Britain the Arabs had no source from which they could replenish their depots. But the Israelis, on the evidence of the United Nations observers themselves, defied this condition, and the connexions they had in every European country enabled them to smuggle into Palestine arms of every type, including a complete air force, several of the units of which were bought or 'stolen' in England and flown over to Palestine.

The result was that the military position was completely reversed in favour of the Jews during the cease-fire period, so that when the fighting was resumed the Arabs had this new and decisive handicap to contend with in addition to all their other weaknesses.

In a few months the Israelis thoroughly routed the now openly disunited Arab ranks. When Egypt opposed King Abdullah's proposal that what was left of Arab Palestine should be incorporated in his kingdom, the King made a local truce with the Jews on the Jerusalem front, and refused to send the Arab Legion to succour the Egyptians in the south when they were subjected to a fresh series of offensives. The Israelis were now able to obtain by military action far more territory than the United Nations partition scheme had allotted them; and when Count Bernadotte, the United Nations mediator, proposed new frontiers that denied them the full extent of their conquests, a group of Israeli terrorists murdered him, and the Jews proceeded, in spite of several United Nations resolutions, to move their frontiers to the utmost limit of their military power, thus leaving of Palestine to the Arabs only a small triangle of Western Galilee and the Old City of Jerusalem, which the Arab Legion had retained throughout the fighting. King Abdullah chose to plant his flag in half the Holy City in preference to accepting the United Nations scheme for internationalizing the whole of it; though it is doubtful whether the Jews would have agreed to part with the New City except under extreme pressure from America and Britain, which did not seem to be forthcoming, so that partition along the lines of military decision proved to be the fate of Jerusalem as of the rest of Palestine.

But apart from military defeat and the territorial loss of most of Palestine, an appalling human tragedy befell the Arab population of the country during the fighting. Seven or eight hundred thousand of the total Arab population of

Palestine (of one-and-a-quarter millions) fled from the country or were driven out into Jordan, Lebanon, Syria, and Egypt. This wholesale exodus was partly due to the belief of the Arabs, encouraged by the boastings of an unrealistic Arabic press and the irresponsible utterances of some of the Arab leaders, that it could be only a matter of weeks before the Jews were defeated by the armies of the Arab states and the Palestinian Arabs enabled to re-enter and retake possession of their country. But it was also, and in many parts of the country, largely due to a policy of deliberate terrorism and eviction followed by the Jewish commanders in the areas they occupied, and reaching its peak of brutality in the massacre of Deir Yassin.

There were two good reasons why the Jews should follow such a policy. First, the problem of harbouring within the Jewish State a large and disaffected Arab population had always troubled them. They wanted an exclusively Jewish state, and the presence of such a population that could never be assimilated, that would always resent its inferior position under Jewish rule and stretch a hand across so many frontiers to its Arab cousins in the surrounding countries, would not only detract from the Jewishness of Israel, but also constitute a danger to its existence. Secondly, the Israelis wanted to open the doors of Palestine to unrestricted Jewish immigration. Obviously, the fewer Arabs there were in the country the more room there would be for Jewish immigrants. If the Arabs could be driven out of the land in the course of the fighting, the Jews would have their houses, their lands, whole villages and towns, without even having to purchase them. And this was exactly what happened.

Thus was created the problem of the Arab refugees – of nearly a million dispossessed people living in camps and caves on the fringe of their former homeland, and in many places in sight of it, hoping to be able to return, sustained by the Arab governments and the United Nations, but doomed to indefinite and unproductive exile in conditions of the utmost hardship. In the memorable words of the Labour Party resolution, they had been 'encouraged to move out as the Jews moved in'. And there they still are, proclaiming with the eloquence of tragedy the oft-repeated, but in this case blindly disregarded, truth that two wrongs do not make a right.

If there is something unheroic in the spectacle of a whole people turning away and fleeing from its country, instead of fighting for every homestead and every street, it should be remembered that those who fled were unarmed and un-organized civilians, and that the majority of them were ignorant peasants who did not realize what was happening, and had no answer to the sudden and murderous attack that was launched upon them but the seeking of refuge in one of the neighbouring Arab countries until the danger passed, as they imagined it would.

One after another the Arab states concluded an armistice with Israel in the course of 1949, and a United Nations Commission was set up to supervise the carrying out of the armistice terms and the maintenance of the armistice frontiers finally agreed upon. The United States, Britain, and France also issued a joint declaration guaranteeing the new frontiers against infringement from either side. What was left of Palestine to the Arabs was incorporated in the kingdom of Jordan (whose integrity was guaranteed by her treaty with Britain) and the high-sounding but illusory 'All-Palestine Government' headed by the Mufti in Cairo and recognized a few months earlier by Egypt and some of the other Arab states, ceased to exist.

While, however, military necessity compelled the Arab states to accept a cessation of hostilities, nothing could induce any of them to consider a permanent peace, or accord any kind of *de jure* recognition to Israel. For months the Arabic press persisted in referring to her as the 'alleged' or 'so-called' state of Israel, and even when this prefix was dropped in deference to immediate realities, the mentality that inspired it remained. The Arab countries organized a rigid economic, political, and social boycott of the Jews in Palestine. The Iraqi Government prohibited the sending of Iraq Petroleum Company oil to the pipe terminal at Haifa, and maintained this prohibition in the face of many representations amounting to pressure from Britain. Nor can there be any doubt that an Iraqi prime minister who yielded on this issue would have promptly lost his position, not to say his line, such was the intensity of public anger and indignation at the loss of Palestine. Similarly Egypt asserted a right to stop any ships going to Israel through the Suez Canal, if they were carrying cargoes of war material.

Thus ended – for the time being – one of the sorriest episodes in history – an episode which showed all the participants in it, including the victims, in a discreditable light. The Zionists had pursued a fevered vision which could only be fulfilled by the infliction of a grievous wrong on the Arabs. Britain had given continuous support to the fulfilment of this vision for thirty years, deluding and breaking faith with the Arabs repeatedly. America had used questionable methods prompted by questionable motives to get the partition scheme adopted by the United Nations. The United Nations itself had failed notoriously as an arbitrator, allowing the Israelis to break its resolutions with impunity. Above all, the Arabs, to use the words of a great but just friend of theirs in the West, had 'proved unworthy of their cause'. For to have a morally unassailable cause does not, by itself, ensure victory. And in spite of all the international influences that were massed up against them, the Arabs would have won the battle for Palestine had there not been something false or rotten in themselves.

7

This was the conclusion of the Arabs themselves. The shock of their defeat in Palestine – their greatest reverse since the loss of Spain – caused in them a new kind of awakening, quite different from that of the nineteenth-century cultural revival and from that of the political movements of al-Fatat and al-Ahd, which had finally culminated in the Arab Revolt of 1916.

That first awakening had been largely a romantic dream of self-glorification, a dream of the returning splendours of the Arab past. It was based on a great deal of the illusion and vanity encouraged by Arabic poetry and rhetoric. The process of self-inflation had been vastly stimulated by the ardours of nationalist resistance to Britain and France in the various Arab countries. Frustrated and for the most part powerless, the Arabs had sought compensation in a dream-world of self-conceit and bombast. For years this had been the tone of the press and of speeches at all public meetings in the Arab countries.

The loss of Palestine ended this dream in a general reaction of self-depreciation and criticism. For the first time in thirty-five years the Arabs (while still feeling intensely hostile to the West, and particularly to America now) turned away from blaming the British and the French for all their woes and began blaming themselves. A good deal of this self-blame had a Dostoievsky quality of helplessness and uselessness, but some of it was of constructive value. In particular a pamphlet headed *The Meaning of the Disaster*, by Dr Costi Zurayk, a distinguished historian and vice-president of the American University of Beirut, and a book entitled *The Lesson of Palestine*, by Musa Alami, a progressive Palestinian leader whose independence of mind had earned him the hostility of the Mufti in past days, analysed with a candour and courage hitherto unknown in public the weaknesses of the structure of Arab life, and suggested practical remedies. The weaknesses were not far to seek. Both writers found them in the poverty and ignorance of the vast majority of the Arab peoples, in the little-cared-for health and well-being of the masses, in the selfishness and cynicism of the big merchants and land-owners, in the inefficiency and corruption of the governments that grew out of, and reflected, this unhealthy state of society. As for the remedies, which were propounded at some length in Alami's book, they began with the thesis that the countries of the Fertile Crescent (Syria, Lebanon, Iraq, and Jordan, with what remained of Palestine) were separately too small to permit of the kind of development planning that could transform Arab life in fifteen or twenty years, not to mention the paramount fact that unless they came under a common government and had one army their chances of being able to resist further encroachments by the Zionists would remain poor. The basic remedy therefore was a union of all these countries. Thus Alami went further than Nuri Pasha es-Said had gone in his 1942 Arab union scheme, in that he proposed the inclusion of Iraq in the projected Arab state; but like Nuri Pasha he was anxious not to alienate either the Egyptians or the Lebanese Christians, so he emphasized that the Fertile Crescent union was not intended to supersede the Arab League, but would be a member of it together with Egypt and the other Arab states; and at the same time he proposed that within the union the Lebanon should have a guaranteed autonomy. Next, he outlined a programme of liberal-socialist reforms to be carried out within the framework of this union – revision of land tenure, increased taxation in the higher income-groups, education, health services, and a modest social insurance scheme for the people. From a population thus improved better armies could be recruited and more capable governments would arise.

This book proved to be one of the best sellers of modern Arabic literature, impression after impression of it being rapidly consumed throughout the countries of the Fertile Crescent. This was but one symptom of the widespread popular disillusionment over the Arab League and discontent with the existing conditions and political systems and parties of the various Arab countries. Prognostications of uprisings against the governments in power were rife, nor were they long in coming true.

The first country in which it happened was Syria, where the government of the National Bloc, that had for years represented the traditional nationalism, was overthrown in

March 1949 by a military *coup d'état*, the hero of which was Colonel Husni ez-Zaim. The immediate and specific causes were many, but the chief reason was the army's humiliation over its defeat in Palestine, and the prevalent feeling among army officers that they had been let down by the politicians. Furthermore, the army sensed, and by its action expressed, the people's general sentiment. The *coup d'état* was greeted with enthusiasm not only in Syria, but also in Lebanon and other Arab countries. After the Palestine catastrophe there was much talk that only an Atatürk could save the Arab world and regenerate it. People prayed and waited, and then came the news from Damascus and for a moment there was hope that the saviour had arrived: Zaim was going to be the Atatürk of Syria, of the Arab world!

Alas, he was not, though he saw himself in that role and did, during his short tenure of power, introduce a number of modernizing measures, including the political emancipation of women – a truly significant and daring step in such a conservative Muslim capital as Damascus. But Zaim had no coherent policy, no well-thought-out programme. In particular, he had no clear ideas on what Syria's relations with her Fertile Crescent neighbours should be. For, a few days after his seizure of power, he made statements which seemed to suggest a willingness to unite with Iraq, and exploratory visits were paid to Damascus by Nuri Pasha es-Said and the Regent, but nothing came of them; and a short time later Zaim was invited to visit Egypt and returned from Cairo definitely aligned with the Egyptian-Saudi Axis against the idea of any closer *rapprochement* with Iraq or Jordan.

Zaim was not a great leader, nor did his stature grow with the exercise of power. His position depended on the support of a clique of officers, and he was tactless enough to offend some of them, who naturally began to think, 'If Zaim did it, why not we?' There being no answer to discourage them, they proceeded to overthrow Zaim and execute him. Some time later, the author of this second *coup* was, in his turn, overthrown by a third, engineered by Colonel Shishakly.

Thus, what had happened in Iraq before the war was being repeated in Syria – the supersession of a weak and still rootless democracy by the army, without the emergence of a military figure big enough to impose himself on the army and the country and establish a stable dictatorship, such as Turkey had enjoyed.

Colonel Shishakly's regime, at one moment, seemed to have achieved a certain permanence and was doing good work, particularly in the domains of land reform and economic development by means of artificially irrigated cotton cultivation. Also, the regime was being successful in combating profiteering and corruption, and in introducing a number of reforms aiming at secularizing the state – in other words, liberating the government from the cramping influence of reactionary religious interference. One of the Colonel's reforms was to make it a punishable offence for anyone who was not a qualified doctor of Muslim law to wear the traditional robes of the Ulema, this being a common and easy way of obtaining a certain pseudo-religious authority among the people.

This promising regime, however, came to an end as soon as Colonel Shishakly restored parliamentary government under a new constitution promulgated in 1953. The old political parties, controlled by the landowners and big merchants, whose fears Shishakly had aroused, became active again and won over a rival section of the army which compelled Colonel Shishakly – now President of the Republic – to resign and leave the country.

The next victim of the Arab failure in Palestine (though in his case internal partisan intrigues played their part too) was King Abdullah of Jordan, who was assassinated in July 1951 as he was going, one Friday morning, to pray in the Old City of Jerusalem. His removal, however, was an act of single vengeance, aimed at the man himself, and carried out by a group of conspirators. The King's eldest son succeeded him, and later, when a mental affliction compelled him to abdicate, the succession passed on to his son. Here perhaps the British connexion (through the subsidy and the command of the Arab Legion by British officers) was a factor making for stability and peaceful continuity.

However, the passing away of King Abdullah coincided with a profound change in the character of his kingdom – a change which, had he lived, he might have found it difficult to adapt himself to at his advanced age, and with the set habits of an autocrat. Until the Arab disaster in Palestine, Transjordan (and then the Hashemite kingdom of Jordan) had been a small country of some four hundred thousand inhabitants, most of whom were nomads, so that a benevolent despotism, tempered by British advice, had not been difficult to maintain in it. With the incorporation in it of what remained to the Arabs of Palestine, the situation was entirely changed. A large proportion of the Palestine Arabs who thus became Jordanians were educated and politically conscious. Many of them had served under the British regime in Palestine and become experienced and responsible administrators. This new sophisticated population now predominated in Jordan, and clearly demanded a more democratic form of government than the old King had been used to. The docile and unreal Council, which in the past had merely recorded the decisions of the King, had now to become a real cabinet responsible to an elected chamber.

The most important revolution, however, was that which took place in Egypt in the summer of 1952. The Egyptian officers, like their comrades in Syria, had returned from the Palestine war deeply humiliated, and with a burning sense of grievance against the old politicians and the King. Their resentment was inflamed by the exposure of a great scandal concerning the purchasing and supplying of defective arms to the troops in Palestine by a number of unscrupulous profiteers, including some of the King's friends. At the same time, the King's own conduct, private and public, was becoming the subject of widespread criticism; nor was the reputation of the Wafd (in spite of its introducing certain progressive measures such as increased supertax and death duties, and free secondary education) much better since power had started slipping out of the hands of its ageing leader, Nahas Pasha, into those of his ambitious wife and her family. A growing middle-class conscience was becoming increasingly shocked at the condition of the people, the gulf between rich and poor, and the general corruption of the administration. There was much talk of the need for reform among the intelligentsia, which naturally included a fair proportion of officers. Even the masses, who had suffered in silence for centuries, were becoming audaciously vocal. In Cairo, porters, servants, taxi-drivers, and pedlars would utter audible imprecations, pointing to the palaces of the rich or to some large limousine conveying a Pasha's bulky form.

Matters came to an appalling head on 26 January 1952. As a result of a combination of factors – including the struggle between the King and the Wafd, the Wafd's encouragement of anti-British terrorism in the Canal zone after its unilateral abrogation of the treaty, and the resurgence of the Muslim Brotherhood together with other revolutionary reform groups – savage rioting broke out in Cairo, accompanied by large-scale incendiarism. Although the main attack was directed against British property and British individuals, Jews and foreigners in general suffered, particularly those who purveyed such features of the Western way of life as the Muslim Brotherhood disapproved of, e.g. bars, wine shops, cinemas, and the like. In some cases sumptuous buildings and cars were attacked regardless of whether they belonged to foreigners or Egyptians – that is to say, merely as a symbol of unjust and hated wealth. Order was only restored when the army was called in towards the close of day.

At the same time something extraordinary happened in one of the provinces. A rich Egyptian landowning family, spending a week-end in its country mansion, found itself surrounded by a veritable 'peasants' revolt' – the first for who knows how many centuries? Fellahin who had bowed in servility and borne oppression and exploitation for ages rose suddenly as a result of a small quarrel with their landlord's

estate manager and, receiving quick support from the surrounding villages, attacked the feudal country-house and its
inmates with murderous intent. They pillaged and burned in
a frenzy of released hatred until large police reinforcements
arrived by lorries from the ne arest town.

Meanwhile, a group of well-i ntentioned young officers,
remembering how easy it had been for the army to overthrow
the civil regimes in Syria and (before the war) in Iraq, were
maturing their plans for a *coup d'état*, which they knew would
have the support of the intelli gentsia and the masses, so unpopular had the King become, so compromised or ineffectual
were all the politicians. Also, t he officers' sense of power had
no doubt been enhanced by the calling in of the army to
restore order in Cairo on 26 January, and the fact that for a
few days the country was virtua lly under military rule.

At an apparently advanced stage in their planning, the
revolutionary officers approac hed General Neguib – a senior
and much liked and respected officer who had served with
distinction in Palestine and been severely wounded – with an
invitation to be the leader of their revolt. He agreed, and the
blow was struck in July 1952. At first the army tried to rule
indirectly, exercising power through civil agents and existing
constitutional forms. For a few days they even professed an
intention of keeping Farouk on the throne, since he had
accepted their government and agreed to the reforms they
proposed. But it was known that the first of these reforms was,
indeed, the removal of the King himself; and soon the usual
pattern of the revolution-by-stages was unfolding itself.
Farouk abdicated in favour of his infant son (the official
policy being still to preserve the monarchy) and was compelled to leave Egypt. A council of regency was set up, and a
civil cabinet headed by a minister of the *ancien régime*, in whom
the officers had confidence, continued to function as the
ostensible government of the country, though it was obvious
that real power lay with the military junta that had carried
out the *coup d'état* and now for med the Council of the Revolution. A few months later, however, the inevitable logical

steps followed. General Neguib became Prime Minister himself and, when the monarchy was abolished, President of the Republic, thus bringing to an end the dynasty of Mohammed Ali which had ruled Egypt for a century and a half.

The reforms introduced by the Revolutionary Government started with the abolition of all titles together with the monarchy – a measure which was more than an empty gesture in a country that had become title-ridden and in which Pashaships and Beyships symbolized the semi-feudal status of many of their holders and emphasized the rather servile condition of those who had none. Next, the new government addressed itself to the task of purging the administration of corruption and punishing ministers and other persons in high position who had amassed fortunes by irregular means. This was a labour of Hercules, and the Government succeeded in it to a remarkable degree. Another vigorous and successful campaign was waged, in the interests of the poorer classes, against the high cost of living.

Turning from these immediate needs to long-term social and economic projects, the Government enacted a new land-reform law, increased taxation on the higher incomes, and created a National Production Council charged with the task of exploring widely and energetically all possibilities of economic development as well as a Social Services Commission to plan for expansion and reform in the fields of education, public health, etc. New labour laws were passed authorizing the formation of national federations of unions and generally ensuring better conditions for the workers.

But perhaps more important than all this was the psychological effect of the new regime's character and policy – the birth of hope after years of despair or cynicism, the infusion of a spirit of idealism and public service into the government, the knowledge among the people that those in power were men of integrity seeking the public good and not the filling of their own pockets.

A conflict, however, soon appeared between General Neguib and Colonel Abd-el-Nasser, the effective leader of the group of younger officers who had planned the revolution. General Neguib became immensely popular with the people, and wanted his powers to be commensurate with his popularity; whereas the younger officers, apparently, had cast him mainly for the part of figurehead. Another difference was that General Neguib proposed an early return to constitutional government – a move which, if carried out, would have brought back to power the old parties and politicians and largely undone the achievements of the revolution. This conflict developed into an open crisis in February–March 1954, the final result of which was that General Neguib surrendered all his powers and titles and Colonel Abd-el-Nasser, a young man of thirty-six, became Prime Minister and the real head of the military junta. The project to restore parliamentary government was abandoned, and the Council of the Revolution proceeded with the accomplishment of its mission.

In the West, where the army officer class mainly represents the conservative elements of society, it may be thought strange that both in Syria and Egypt revolutionary governments should have been set up by the army to carry out programmes of social and economic reform in the interests of the under-privileged. But, as Charles Issawi points out in his *Egypt at Mid-Century*, in the Arab countries officers come mainly from the middle class and tend to be radical. Toynbee had drawn attention to the same fact with regard to Turkey as well as Egypt. The explanation is that in Oriental countries trying to assimilate Western civilization, the army is often the first institution to be modernized, thus becoming naturally a vehicle for the infiltration of Western reform ideas.

1952 saw also the overthrow of the Lebanese President under whom the country had won its independence, and who had been in power since 1943. While his overthrow cannot be traced back to the Palestine disaster in as direct a manner as the Syrian and Egyptian revolutions, it did, nevertheless, fundamentally express Arab discontent with the corruption of the *ancien régime*, which was in power everywhere when the

Palestine catastrophe occurred, and which symbolized the political and social rottenness that had cost the Arabs Palestine. Also, the examples of Syria and Egypt had no doubt pointed the way to the Lebanese.

The army in the Lebanon was still little more than a mere *gendarmerie* of a few thousand, and so did not hold the same important position in the life and politics of the land as did the armies of Syria and Egypt in their respective countries. The Lebanese so-called 'Rosewater' revolution was not the result of a *coup d'état* planned in secret by a group of officers; it was the result of a general strike expressing the widely felt discontent of the public. The President, however, held out against the mounting tide of popular anger until the commander-in-chief of the army told him that he must resign. But the Lebanese army had no intention whatever of taking over the government. It only intervened to bring about the dissolution of a regime that had become very corrupt and unpopular, and its replacement by a new set of civilian politicians who represented a coalition of reforming tendencies and were wanted by the people.

Only in Saudi Arabia and Iraq did the existing regimes survive the failure of the Arab League in Palestine and the resultant exposures of weakness and corruption. Saudi Arabia's structure as a medieval society ruled by a theocratic despotism remained little changed for the time being, despite the discovery of oil in its soil and the arrival of American technicians to extract it. There was still no middle-class nationalism in the country, no political consciousness of any consequence. A large proportion of the people continued to be nomads; and even the townsmen were very backward judged by Egyptian, Syrian, or Iraqi standards. Over the land the towering figure of Ibn Saud still held undisputed sway.

As for Iraq, the reasons why it retained its political stability despite the shock of defeat in Palestine are quite different from – even the reverse of – those that operated in Saudi Arabia. Iraq had had too much nationalism and too many changes of government brought about by army intervention in the inter-war period. The major intervention of the army, during the war (the Rashid Ali rebellion), had ended in ignominious failure, and the army had not yet recovered sufficient prestige to take it upon itself to challenge the Regent and the civilian politicians once more. Also, just before the Palestine war, the tranquillity of the country had been threatened by the nationalist outburst that greeted the signature of the Portsmouth Treaty. So that, partly by reaction to a tumultuous past and its lessons, the least stable of the Arab regimes was able to hold itself together after the Palestine defeat. But above all, perhaps, the regime was strengthened by the enormous increase in the country's revenue from oil in the years immediately following 1948, and by the wise and public-spirited manner in which this new wealth was being spent.

The Yemen had had nothing to do with the Palestine war, but even in that inaccessible and mystery-shrouded country the first stirrings of a desire for reform culminated in a violent *coup* in 1948. The old and autocratic Imam was murdered by a party which sought to establish a more liberal regime. But the Imam's eldest son succeeded in overthrowing this *coup d'état* government and installing himself in his father's place, from which he apparently proceeded to govern the country with the same absolutism and the same archaic methods that had characterized his father's rule; though the fact that he has not deemed it wise to appear publicly in his capital of Sanaa, since his accession, would seem to suggest the existence of a latent revolutionary threat to his position.

8

We must now, once more, turn to the Arab countries of North Africa, or the western Arab world.

The one clear gain which World War II brought to the Arabs here was the liberation of Libya from Italian rule and its establishment as a new Arab state.

It had been realized by Britain, even before the outbreak of war, that should hostilities with Italy ensue, the Arabs of Cyrenaica could play a useful part in helping the British forces in the Western Desert. Certain Libyan notables, who had been exiled by the Italians and were living in Cairo, approached the British authorities with offers of help against the potentially common enemy – a move reminiscent, on a smaller scale, of the overtures made in 1914 to Lord Kitchener in Cairo by Hussein and his son Abdullah. The negotiations were raised to a higher level when Sayed Idris es-Senussi, the religious leader of the Arabs of Cyrenaica (and the only obvious candidate for the headship of an Arab state in the country) was brought into them. A Western Arab force was raised from among the Libyans to serve with the British army operating from Egypt. But help came also from the entire Arab population when the British forces had to retreat from Cyrenaica. British troops, cut off and isolated by the Germans, were taken into shelter by the Arabs, given food, and helped back to their units across the desert.

In 1942 Mr Eden, as Foreign Secretary, declared that 'His Majesty's Government are determined that at the end of the war the Senussi in Cyrenaica will in no circumstances again fall under Italian domination.'

At the end of the war, however, certain complications arose with regard to Libya (which consists of Cyrenaica, Tripolitania, and the Fezzan) as a whole. Mr Eden's pledge had only mentioned Cyrenaica. In Tripolitania there was a large Italian population in the capital city, and from them came a demand for reunion with Italy, now no longer a Fascist state but a democracy whose good-will Britain and America were anxious to cultivate. Italy herself naturally supported the demand of the Tripolitanian Italians, and put forward a strong claim to this part of Libya. The French wanted the Fezzan, in the liberation of which Free French forces had taken part. Also, France was generally opposed to Libyan independence, being afraid of the impact it might have on her own Arab provinces in North Africa. Libya marched with Tunisia, so that if it became independent it would bring the frontiers of Arab freedom well within the western Arab world and make of Morocco, Algeria, and Tunisia continuous compartments with the chain of independent Arab states that stretched all the way through Egypt into Syria, Iraq, and the Peninsula.

For a moment, therefore, there was a danger that this small and poor Arab country of barely one million inhabitants, a large proportion of whom were nomadic, would suffer the fate of the eastern Arab world in 1919, or of Palestine in 1948, and be partitioned in order to satisfy rival claims that were preferred against its united independence. This danger was aggravated by the fact that the Arab parties in Libya were themselves at first in disagreement over certain matters, particularly the recognition of Sayed Idris es-Senussi as King of the whole country.

However, in the end agreement was reached both at the United Nations and inside the country itself, and Libya emerged at the end of 1951 as an independent federal kingdom under the Senussi. The country, however, was very short of trained men for its various services, and sorely needed help from abroad. This came from Britain (with whom the new state concluded a treaty of alliance) and from the Arab countries to the east, particularly Egypt.

As for French North Africa, the independence of Libya was only one of the many factors that stimulated in it the growth of the nationalist movements during and after the war. An earlier encouragement had come with the achievement of independence by Syria and Lebanon – two countries where France herself had ruled. Still another was the formation of the Arab League which, in its early days, had aroused great hopes throughout the western Arab world. Then there was the collapse of France and her coming under German domination – a fact which terminated her prestige in the eyes of the North Africans; there were the Anglo-American landings in North Africa and the campaign which not only destroyed the Axis forces in that theatre but definitely introduced Anglo-Saxon influences into what had been an exclusively French preserve; there were the comings and goings of Mr Churchill and President Roosevelt, the latter of whom had a personal interview with the Sultan of Morocco and showed himself sympathetic to Moroccan aspirations. Finally, there had been the Atlantic Charter and other war-time declarations promising in general a world in which peoples would be free and governments democratic; and the end of the war saw the appearance on the United Nations' platform not only of the Arab countries of the east, but also of the two new great states of India and Pakistan that were known to sympathize with all anti-colonial movements.

Throughout the war the Moroccans had behaved in a friendly manner towards the Allies and had sustained the principles for which the Allies professed to be fighting even when these were menaced by the French themselves under German dictation – as when the Sultan had refused to apply anti-semitic measures during the Vichy regime. The Moroccans therefore felt that their aspirations deserved recognition at the end of the war; but though their nationalist movement had for a quarter of a century demanded only 'reforms', it still found no adequate response from the French. Very few Moroccans had been given higher education or introduced into the more responsible posts of the administration. The native political institutions of the country had been left static and without power. Around the beautiful cities built by the French, hideous shanty towns – *bidonvilles* built with kerosene tins, with bits of wooden packing cases or with reeds, were springing up to house the native industrial population needed by the French manufacturers. Of the money spent on education and health services, the Moorish population received a piteous fraction, in proportion to its size, compared to what was spent on the French settlers' needs.

In 1944, the nationalists, despairing of reforms, adopted independence as their goal, and changed the party's name from the original *Action Marocaine* to *Istiqlal* – the Arabic word for independence. Thereupon the party's leader, al-Fasi, and

Secretary-General Belafrej, were arrested, and there was some bloodshed. Thus began a new chapter in the history of Morocco – a struggle between the Moroccan nationalists, increasingly supported by the Sultan Mohammed V, and the French, in which (at least until the advent of M. Mendès-France to power) any tendency towards liberalism by the Paris Government was defeated by the intransigence of the settlers and the French officials in Morocco, supported by a number of reactionary feudal leaders, such as el-Glawi, the Pasha of Marrakesh. In this struggle, the aim of the French authorities in Morocco has been to have a Franco-Moroccan state, enjoying a certain autonomy but controlled by France as part of the French Empire, and governed internally by a partnership in which the three hundred thousand French settlers would have as much power as the eight million Moroccans. The nationalists, on the other hand, want an independent Muslim Morocco, in which French settlers would have the right of resident foreigners. They welcome the continuance of French cultural, but not political, influence; nor are they satisfied with reforms which leave the political relationship unaltered while advancing a few Moroccans to positions of greater prestige.

It began to be evident, as far back as 1946, that the Sultan was determined to play a leading part in the struggle for his country's independence, and that he was not going to be deterred even by the danger of losing his throne. He was very active on the cultural side, encouraging in particular the establishment of schools in which instruction was offered in Arabic – a vital matter for the nationalist cause. And he gave a personal example himself by having all his sons and daughters given a thorough education in Arabic as well as in French.

On the political side he soon began to clash with the French authorities in Morocco, while the state visit he was invited to pay to France led to no result, the French Government rejecting his bold proposal to negotiate a new treaty to replace that of 1912.

In the winter of 1952–3 the nationalists scored a moral international success by getting the United Nations Assembly, for the first time, to take cognizance of their cause. Through the efforts of the Asian-Arab *bloc*, and against the opposition of France, the Assembly was persuaded to discuss the question of Moroccan independence. The French delegates, taking a leaf out of the Russian manual on U.N. procedure, absented themselves from the debate and the result was a non-committal resolution, since neither Britain nor the United States was prepared to take sides openly against France on this issue.

This fact encouraged the French reactionaries in Morocco itself. Using el-Glawi and his Berber tribesmen as their instrument, they staged a 'popular' movement demanding the deposition of the Sultan, and compelled the monarch to leave the country. Sacrificing his throne for the nationalist cause he had espoused, and bowing to superior force, Mohammed V was taken to Corsica; and another member of his family – an elderly and complaisant person – proclaimed Sultan in his place. Shortly afterwards an attempt was made to assassinate the new Sultan, and ever since then Morocco has been living on the edge of a volcano, with the nationalists conducting a campaign of terrorism and the French authorities resorting to repression on a mounting scale. The repressive measures that followed the deposition of the Sultan in 1953, together with the entire attitude of the settlers and the French officials in Morocco, elicited a strong protest from the conscience of liberal France, to which the well-known Catholic writer, M. François Mauriac, gave the most eloquent expression.

This Franco-Arab conflict in French Morocco has had a curious and somewhat ironical sequel in the Spanish zone. For some time General Franco, feeling the loneliness of an outcast in Europe, had been trying to cultivate friendly relations with the Arab League, based on the bitter resentment felt by the Arabs towards the Western Democracies on account of Palestine. The Arab states, for their part, had no reason to dislike Franco, and having had not only the Democracies but also Russia ranged against them over the Palestine issue, they also felt somewhat lonely in the world (outside Asia) and were glad to receive Franco's overtures. King Abdullah paid a visit to Spain and there were other friendly exchanges.

On the Spanish side this *rapprochement*, though no doubt fundamentally political and self-interested, reflected also a new trend in the thinking of Spanish scholars and historians – a trend harking back with some enthusiasm to the past centuries of Hispano-Arab civilization, and also to the friendly living together of Spaniards and Arabs in the various Christian and Muslim states of Spain, even while these states waged intermittent war with one another.

The constitutional position of Spain in Morocco was a peculiar one, depending, apart from considerations of history and geography, entirely on her treaty of 1904 with France, whereby she was to have the same position in the zone accorded to her (a slice of territory comprising one million of the total eight million inhabitants of Morocco) as France had in the rest of the country. With the Sultan himself Spain had no treaty, though the fundamental integrity of the country was constitutionally maintained by the presence in the Spanish zone of the Khalifa, towards whom the Spanish Resident-General occupied the same position as his French opposite number occupied towards the Sultan.

When the French deposed the Sultan they not only offended the Spaniards because they did so without consulting them, but also gave them a further opportunity to show sympathy with the Arabs. As a result of all these circumstances, a paradoxical situation has arisen in which the Fascist dictatorship of Spain is following in its zone a more liberal policy than the Democracy of the Fourth Republic is doing in French Morocco! This is not to say that the Spaniards are ready to grant independence to their zone immediately. But they do talk of a future when the Moroccan people (having been sufficiently trained and equipped) will govern themselves and be bound to Spain by the ties of friendship and memories of a common past. And they are not pursuing a policy aiming at co-sovereignty or co-citizenship between Moors and Spaniards.

In the government schools in the Spanish zone Arabic is the language of instruction (whenever qualified Arabic teachers are available) and an attempt is being made to produce Arabic text-books. In the French zone, on the other hand, French is the language of instruction and Arabic is only taught as a 'subject'. Similarly, in the Spanish zone the headmasters of the official schools are Moroccans, with Spanish 'assessors' to supervise the good running of the school at a distance; while in French Morocco the headmasters are Frenchmen, and the Moroccans no more than form teachers. If the Spanish zone is poor, its poverty (largely intrinsic and inevitable) afflicts both the Moroccans and the Spaniards; nothing is to be seen in it comparable to the gulf that divides the luxury of Rabat and Casablanca from the squalor of the Arab tin-can towns outside them.

Moving eastwards from Morocco, we find that the basic conflict between Arab nationalism and French colonization has reached roughly the same stage in Algeria and Tunisia as in Morocco, though local conditions and history give it in each territory its special character. Nevill Barbour, analysing the North African nationalist movement as a whole and in sections, finds that Algerian nationalism is marked by a particular bitterness and disillusionment. Not only has the number of French settlers here reached one million among eight million Arabs; but the policy of complete assimilation to France and of equality of citizenship between Frenchmen and Arabs has not been honestly carried out. The equality remains largely theoretical. In fact few Arabs can rise to the higher grades in government service; while education, health services, and general conditions of living among the Arab population remain far below those enjoyed by the French section. The Algerians feel that they have been cheated, that direct French rule has destroyed or prevented the growth of native Arab institutions without giving them worth-while compensation for that loss. For a long time French citizenship could only be acquired by a Muslim if he were prepared to renounce his personal status as such and accept the jurisdiction of the civil courts in matters relating to marriage, divorce, and inheritance – a galling condition which largely nullified the seeming generosity of the offer. On the cultural side, the French tried to spread their language among the whole population; but while a few educated Muslims learned to speak it really well, the masses acquired only a smattering of it. Meanwhile, the standard of Arabic – the mother-tongue of the people – sank very low. Alone among the Arab countries Algeria uses dialect, instead of the classical language, as its principal medium of broadcasting in Arabic.

In 1945 the hunger and discontent of the people, who had been promised much by Allied war-time propaganda and expected fulfilment as the war came to its end, led to a rising in which 88 Frenchmen were massacred and 150 wounded. The French authorities struck back with bombs, bullets, and bayonets, killing at least 1500 (though, according to some responsible estimates, the figure was nearer 8000) Arabs of both sexes and all ages.

In 1947 the Statute of Algeria promised many reforms, few of which, however, seem to have been carried out in practice to the full extent of what was offered and expected. Thus, though Muslims were theoretically made eligible for the highest administrative and judicial posts, the complaint is still made that they are not in fact appointed; while enlarged electoral rights are held by all Algerians to be of little value in view of the administration's manipulation of elections.

By the same statute Algerians were allowed to enter France without restriction. Thousands of them went there in search of employment and better conditions of living, only to find the distress they had known at home enhanced by expatriation.

Tunisia emerged from World War II with a more advanced Arab population and a more mature nationalist movement than either Algeria or Morocco. This easternmost of the three French territories of Arab North Africa (with a population of three million Arabs and two hundred thousand French settlers) had always been ahead of its two sisters. Unlike Morocco, it had never become an isolated state encased in an unbroken mould of medievalism until the twentieth century; on the contrary, being the nearest both to the eastern Arab world and to Europe, Tunisia had had, to a great extent, the best of both worlds: the standards of Arabic culture in it – of which the chief centre was the university-mosque of Zaitouna – had remained high, the country participating in the revival of letters that had started in Egypt and Lebanon in the latter half of the nineteenth century; while Western influences – first Italian and then French – had acted on it for a longer period and penetrated it more deeply than they had done Morocco or even Algeria, producing a highly advanced intelligentsia, strongly grounded in the double heritage of European and Arab civilization. Very symptomatic of this dual cultural affiliation is the fact that the feminist movement of Tunisia to-day is led by Bashira Murad, a daughter of a former Sheikh al-Islam, and that Habib Bourguiba, the leader of the Neo-Destour party, has both a native's mastery of Arabic in speech and writing and the politico-cultural equipment (not to mention a French wife) of the European.

The Tunisian leaders were greatly stimulated by the formation of the Arab League in 1945; and at first reposed great hopes in it, becoming very active at the Maghreb Office in Cairo which, as already mentioned, was founded as a means of liaison between the League and the western Arab world. The Palestine catastrophe, however, and the threatened dissolution of the League brought about a certain reorientation in the policy of the Neo-Destour men. Once more they tried to attain their aspirations through an understanding with France. Chief among these aspirations were the reaffirmation of Tunisian sovereignty in a manner that would invest with it the whole nation instead of keeping it confined to the Bey and his dynasty, the creation of a Tunisian Parliament and the exercise of autonomy in all internal matters. As for defence and foreign policy, the Tunisian leaders were mostly willing to leave them, for a considerable time, in the hands of France. It will be readily seen that these demands fell far short of the complete independence which had been achieved by Syria and Lebanon unconditionally, and by Egypt and Iraq subject to the retention on their territory of British military bases; that they were even less exacting than the demands of Morocco's Istiqlal movement, or those of the majority nationalist party in Algeria led by Messali Hajj.

In 1950 the French responded sufficiently to this new approach by the Tunisian leaders to allow Neo-Destour participation in the government, while the French Resident-General still supervised the actions of the Bey. Unfortunately this first step led not to further steps being taken in the same direction but to a new rupture between the Neo-Destour and the French. The latter claimed that instead of proving their competence in governance the Tunisian leaders used their opportunity to agitate for greater concessions. For their part, the Tunisians felt that the French were trying to take back with one hand what they had given with the other. The crucial issue came to be the French attempt to secure legal recognition of co-sovereignty between them and the Tunisians, which had long existed in practice but which the Tunisians were unwilling to concede in principle.

The breach came in 1951, and was followed by disorders, arrests, and an appeal by the Tunisians to the United Nations. Repression of the nationalists led to acts of terrorism and this, in its turn, provoked counter terrorism by the French settlers.

In both Morocco and Tunisia the years 1952–4 saw the pattern of the struggle between the nationalists and the French develop steadily along the lines of what one may call 'civil war' terrorism. The French settlers, personally afraid of the future and therefore far less liberal than the Paris government, showed an increased tendency to take matters into their own hands – not only by enforcing, with the help of the local officials, a policy of repression rather than reform, but also by organizing themselves into gangs to hit back at the Arabs with acts of unofficial violence. Nevill Barbour goes so far as to say that in Algeria the settlers (one to eight of the total population) might, if they felt that Metropolitan France was failing them, be tempted to follow the Whites in South Africa by setting up a government of their own based on European supremacy.

The deadlock in Tunisia was broken by the French Premier M. Mendès-France, in the summer of 1954. No sooner had he come to office than he proceeded to carry out his declared intention of adopting a 'realistic' policy in North Africa. His realism may have been encouraged by the Anglo-Egyptian Agreement, whereby Britain finally undertook to withdraw all her military forces from Egypt within twenty months, and which was bound to reinforce the nationalist cause throughout North Africa. However that may be, France abandoned all attempt to force co-sovereignty on Tunisia, announced that she would grant Tunisia autonomy in all internal matters, subject to certain conditions safeguarding the interests of the settlers, and agreed to the participation of the Neo-Destour in an All-Tunisian cabinet. In return the Neo-Destour agreed that foreign affairs and defence should remain in the hands of France.

Although, when the French Premier announced his 'realistic' policy he included Morocco in its scope, nothing has so far been done to carry out that policy in the second protectorate. The position here is much more difficult than in Tunisia. For one thing, the Moroccan nationalists demand complete independence, which French 'realism' is certainly not prepared to concede. For another, the deposition of the Sultan Mohammed V in 1953 and the installation of another member of his family on the throne has created a delicate dynastic question which does not seem to admit of an easy solution. Even though the present Sultan, Mohammed ben Arafa (tired of the hostility with which he feels himself to be surrounded), may be willing to abdicate, it is very doubtful whether the French will agree to the return of his predecessor. A new candidate may be proposed, possibly one of the sons of Mohammed V, but unless the nationalists agreed to such a solution, the situation would be no different from what it is to-day.

Lastly, the Moroccans are not as advanced in the techniques of modern administration as the Tunisians; and their country contains more turbulent elements. It is doubtful, therefore, whether they would be able to assume immediate control of all their internal affairs without a serious risk of relapse into anarchy. This is not only what the French say, but what a good many patriotic Moroccans think. The fact that France herself is largely responsible for the present technical and administrative backwardness of the Moroccans – after half a century of French rule – gives the nationalists a dialectical point but does not help to solve the present problem. What, therefore, can the solution be?

The most that can be hoped for is a radical and visible change in the objectives and orientation of French policy, and a willingness on the part of the nationalists to wait a while for the complete fulfilment of their aspirations. If immediate independence is impracticable, at least it can be prepared for in stages by a policy whose object would be independence and whose means would be more, better and quicker education and administrative training for the people of the country. But this demands the acceptance by the French of the principle of independence, and the acceptance by the Moroccans of a certain delay in attaining the substance of it.

CHAPTER SIX

INTO THE FUTURE

———

I

OUR survey of the Arabs throughout their history has now brought us to the present day. And here we observe a remarkable phenomenon which makes of the Arab achievement something greater, in one sense, than the achievement of either Greece or Rome. There is no 'Greek world' to-day, nor a 'Roman world'; but there is an 'Arab world'. The ancient Greeks, after spreading throughout the Mediterranean basin, shrank back eventually into their land of origin. Their language is no longer spoken except in Greece and the islands near it. Similarly, the Romans no longer exist as Romans. Their language is a dead language. But it is different with the Arabs. They still live as a universal society occupying the whole of North Africa and most of the Middle East; and in spite of certain differences of race and religion, they all (with very few exceptions) speak Arabic and call themselves Arabs. The writer, for example, though a Christian of the Lebanon, remembers the expressions 'children of the Arabs', 'son of Arabs', and 'daughter of Arabs' being used in his childhood among the Christians of Beirut to distinguish themselves from foreigners, from the 'Franj'.

The total population of the Arab world to-day is about sixty-five millions, and it is increasing rapidly. Like a swollen river it is also surging forward, changing as it plunges into the future, its waters having thawed after a long freeze. Through what regions is it now flowing? Whither is it going?

What are the obstacles in its way?

As the reader will have become aware by now, the chief feature of Arab life during the last hundred years has been its intermingling with the life of the West. Even while the Arab peoples were struggling for their freedom against Western imperialism they were, both consciously and unconsciously, absorbing influences from the West and establishing indissoluble contacts with the Europe from which they sought independence.

It is true that the struggle against imperialism increased for Muslims the difficulty of accepting Western civilization, already prejudiced in their eyes as the civilization of the Christian world: movements like that of the Muslim Brotherhood combined in a peculiarly powerful form the revolt against foreign political and military domination with reforming idealism and a fervent reassertion of Muslim values against the Western way of life. This movement spread chiefly among the urban lower middle classes, whose members had few opportunities of forming intellectual or spiritual contact with Europe and therefore merely felt her presence as a hostile power. On the other hand, the nationalist struggles themselves demanded the adoption of Western techniques and so the partial acceptance at least of the civilization that produced them. The Arab defeat in Palestine gave a glaring demonstration of the inadequacies of the traditional Arab way of life and strengthened the demand for modernization.

Thus, by and large, the Muslim Arabs of the towns (excluding those of Arabia itself) are to-day living as much under the influences of Western civilization with its essential secularism as under the influence of their past religious beliefs. Among the more highly educated minority the former influences predominate; and, as in the Christian world when it entered its own modern age, agnosticism is spreading, sometimes as a positive intellectual attitude, sometimes merely as libertarianism *vis-à-vis* religious observances in private life.

To drink alcohol and cease to pray five times a day or observe the fast of Ramadan may not be positive virtues, though it is arguable that they indicate a certain emancipation of mind which has its valuable side. But there is one respect in which the transformation of Arab-Muslim life that is taking place to-day is positively and undeniably good: namely, the emancipation of women, already mentioned, and the disappearance of polygamy.

As the Arab countries achieve real independence, as the character of the West changes in their eyes from the aggressive and domineering to the friendly and helpful, they are bound to become more receptive to Western influences, more willing to share fully in that world civilization which was born in Greece and Rome and Palestine, and which they themselves nurtured so assiduously and nourished so generously at one time.

The example of Turkey tends to confirm this belief. For the readiness with which the Turks took to Western civilization (despite their Islam and their holding the Caliphate for many centuries) was largely due to the fact that they were not, and had never been, under Western rule. When they decided to modernize their life after World War I (and after an initial defeat similar to that of the Arabs in Palestine) they had the proud psychology of an imperial race; not the inferiority complex of subject peoples. They did not have to bolster up their *amour propre* with a political xenophobia of the modern type or with the reaffirmation of an outmoded theocratic way of life. Western imperialism, on the other hand, has forced the Arabs to react in both these ways.

In the early days of the Arab revival the Christian communities in the Arab world – particularly the Lebanese and the Copts – embraced Western civilization (down to European Christian names for their children) with a receptive eagerness impossible for the Muslim Arab. Not only did the Lebanese and Copts find no difficulty in assimilating the cultural values of the West; they found in this identification with the advanced nations of Europe a psychological compensation for their inferior position as Christian minorities under Muslim suzerainty. The Europeans who came to Egypt and the Lebanon at that time used to find it easier to communicate with the Christians than with the Muslims; and there is no doubt that the Lebanese, in particular, have played a useful role as interpreters of Western civilization to the Muslim Arabs. But these differences have largely disappeared to-day. On the one hand, a large proportion of Muslim Arabs are as Westernized, or as ready to accept Western civilization, as the Copts or the Lebanese Christians. On the other, these last are far more closely identified with their Muslim fellow-countrymen and not so blindly pro-West as they were before.

With the Anglo-Egyptian and the Anglo-Iraqi questions finally settled now, the whole of the eastern Arab world (save for the bases in Jordan and the protectorates of Aden and the Persian Gulf) becomes free from European military occupation or political control. The altered attitude of Egypt towards Britain will cause a great difference in Arab feelings throughout the Middle East, since the influence of the Egyptian Press is predominant in the whole region and was in the past responsible for much of the hostility felt for Britain.

It is obvious, however, that the problem of the Arab world's political relationship with the West will not be completely solved until French North Africa too obtains its freedom. We have seen that in Tunisia and among a section of the Algerian people this freedom means to-day not complete independence and separation from France, but self-government within the French Union and subject to the continued direction by France of defence and foreign policy. The lessons of history, however, teach that sooner or later complete independence will be demanded and achieved by all the North African countries, who will want to have their own armed forces, their own foreign representation, and their own individual seats at the United Nations. Anything less than this complete sovereignty will seem to them humiliating as their self-confidence increases with the exercise of autonomy, as their intelligentsia grows in numbers and their resources develop. It will seem particularly humiliating in view of the full independence achieved by all their sister countries in the eastern Arab world. If the Arab League remains in existence, particularly if it develops in power and cohesion, the North African countries may wish to join it, which they could not do unless they had complete control of their foreign policy and armed forces.

But this brings us back to the fundamental question of the future of the Arab world. After settling their relations with Europe, the Arab countries will have to determine their relations with one another. What course are these relations likely to follow?

2

For some time after the Palestine disaster there was much talk and speculation as to whether the Arab League could survive, as to whether it was worth preserving. Its fate hung in the balance for several months while Egypt and Jordan fought out a press and radio battle of mutual recrimination. Particularly in Egypt (whose nationalism had run its own course until the formation of the Arab League) there was a strong revulsion of feeling against any further involvement in Arab affairs. Egypt had headed the move for the creation of the League in order to gain prestige. She had, instead, suffered a galling defeat and felt abandoned and betrayed by her allies. The cry naturally arose, 'Why did we join the Arab League? Why should we remain in it?' And a new school of political thought began to preach the thesis that Egypt's destiny did not lie in the Arab world but in Africa, along the Nile, in the direction of the Sudan.

However, Egypt did not withdraw from the League, the League did not disintegrate. In spite of all its weaknesses and failures; in spite of the fact that it has not been able either to save Palestine, or even to abolish customs, passports, or *visas* between its member states, the League still exists, now joined by Libya since its establishment as an independent state in 1952. The League Council meets from time to time and affords the Arab states an opportunity of discussing their common interests and presenting a united front to the world on certain issues of foreign policy. At the United Nations, the Arab states continue to be, together with the Iron Curtain countries and the South Americans, one of the recognized voting *blocs* of the Organization. In internal matters, the League encourages the adoption of common educational curricula and the strengthening of all cultural, social, and economic ties between its member states.

This mere continuing of the League in existence (even the Egypto-Iraqi dispute over the pact with Turkey in the early months of 1955 did not lead to the dissolution of the League though it has severely shaken its present structure) has a certain significance. It confirms that the coming together of the Arab states in some form of confederation answered a strongly felt aspiration, satisfied a need, however imperfectly. It shows that the statesmen of all the Arab countries are conscious of having created in the League at least a potentially effective instrument of common action – something which, even though largely useless at present, it would be a grave mistake to abandon.

Naturally, the question arises whether there is any immediate hope of drawing tighter the bonds of union between the various members or any group of them. And the answer is that, at least among the Fertile Crescent countries – Syria, Lebanon, Jordan, and Iraq, most of the conditions for a closer union exist, and may at any moment become effective enough to result in the creation of a federal state. Several of the obstacles in the way of such a consummation have been removed, while the others are not irremovable. One of the Syrians' two chief objections to union with Jordan was their personal opposition to King Abdullah, who is no more. Also, Egypt was, until some time ago, antagonistic to the creation of a Greater Syria or Fertile Crescent state, partly because she disliked King Abdullah and the Hashemite dynasty in general. Now, Farouk has disappeared from the scene as well as King Abdullah, so that in so far as Egypt's opposition was due to dynastic rivalries, it has ceased to have any *raison d'être*. These facts lend credence to a report from *The Times* correspondent in Cairo that Colonel Abd-el-Nasser has assured the Syrian Ambassador to Egypt that his government would not object to any project of closer union between themselves which the Fertile Crescent countries might wish to adopt.*

Three difficulties, however, remain in the way. First, there is the Syrian and Iraqi objection to accepting union with Jordan when this country is bound to Britain by a treaty which imposes certain restrictions on its sovereignty, such as the presence of British troops and bases on its soil, whereas Syria and Iraq themselves now enjoy unrestricted independence. Secondly, the Lebanese Christians are not in favour of the scheme and would have to be given a special position guaranteeing their autonomy in any closer Arab union. Thirdly, the fact that both Jordan and Iraq are monarchies (though their respective kings are cousins) makes any unification or even federation difficult – indeed impossible unless one of the two royal houses were to step down so that the federation should have either a president or *one* king at its head. There is no sign of anything of the kind happening in the near future, so that the first step towards Fertile Crescent unification – barring unforeseen developments – will have to be a limited one falling short of complete federation. But this certainly is one important direction in which Arab consolidation may and is expected to proceed.

Next, there are the possibilities of Egypto-Sudanese co-operation. It is almost certain now that the Sudan will opt for independence rather than union with Egypt, since even the National Unionist party that won the elections in 1953

* Since this paragraph was written, the Egypto-Iraqi dispute and Egypt's attempts to detach Syria from Iraq have altered the situation for the time being at least.

is now declaring for a sovereign Sudanese republic (with its separate President, Parliament and Army) associated with Egypt on a footing of equality. But whatever institutional form the relations between the two countries may take, there is no doubt that the future is going to bring increasing intercourse and co-operation between them. They have the Nile in common. The regulation of its flow and full exploitation of its waters depend upon the operation by a joint effort (that must also include Uganda and Abyssinia) of a number of dams in both countries, several of which still have to be built. And there must be agreement on how the new volume of water is to be shared. Again, the Sudan, with its eight or nine million inhabitants in one million (though largely desert) square miles, is underpopulated and could both benefit and help Egypt to solve her over-population problem by opening its northern regions to Egyptian immigration on a limited scale. Climatic and other conditions are very similar in the northern Sudan and Upper Egypt, and a few hundred thousand Egyptian peasants could be easily assimilated by the Sudanese people. Lastly, Egypt is the Sudan's highway to the outside world – to the other Arab countries, whether in the east or the west, and to Europe.

Prophets and visionaries may go beyond this and see in time a real federal Arab state comprising all the countries from Iraq and Yemen to Morocco – the United States of the Arab World. But even assuming that the processes of history are to be allowed to work themselves out without interference by the hydrogen bomb, it is impossible to say at this stage whether such a consummation will ever be achieved. Certainly many factors are making for it. Arabs in every country are discovering themselves and their fellow Arabs in other lands. If the fundamental cultural identity of the Arabs has been preserved for thirteen hundred years by the sameness of the written language in all Arab countries despite the evolution of different spoken dialects, these spoken dialects themselves are to-day being intermingled. The radio, films, gramophone records, and air travel are all tending to mix the Arab peoples together at the popular level. All the Arab capitals have their broadcasting stations. Egyptian films are seen in Khartoum and Damascus, in Baghdad and Beirut. Iraqis, Kuwaitis, and Hejazis (for whom the journey to Lebanon before World War I was almost unthinkable) now come to the Mountain regularly for their holidays, accomplishing the journey in a few hours. In each country the spreading of education on the one hand, and the modernizing of the classical language on the other, are narrowing the gap between written speech and spoken dialect; and as this continues to happen in the different countries, their slightly different forms of speech must inevitably approximate to one another. On the political side, the pressures and needs of the modern world are working strongly in favour of regional groupings. In separation the Arab countries, even if each of them develops its own potentialities to the full, will remain without a really effective voice in world affairs. United in a federation they could become a major power occupying one of the most important regions of the globe.

But in order to achieve such a union they would have to overcome the rivalries and disruptive tendencies that have been until now the bane of the Arab League; they would have to acquire the fundamental political virtue of subordinating the lesser to the greater loyalty; they would have to learn a kind of discipline which the Arab character has never shown itself capable of for any length of time.

3

In the meantime, and leaving aside such questions as the future of the Arab League, there is an even more fundamental question to consider, namely that of the human and economic problem and potentialities of the Arab countries singly. For even a complete union between them would not do much good unless its component parts were in a strong and healthy condition.

Mention has already been made of the tentative reforms introduced in Syria and Egypt during the last few years. A great deal more remains to be done, both here and in the other Arab countries. The basic needs are the reform of land tenure, the abolition of feudalism, the breaking up of the large estates, the creation of small and secure peasant holdings, and the freeing of the peasant from the clutches of the urban money-lender.

The problem of poverty is at its worst in Egypt. Here, over-population is assuming appalling proportions. Thirty years ago, the population of Egypt was only fourteen millions. To-day it is over twenty millions and increasing at the rate of a quarter million a year. Its density is 500 (most of whom earn their living by agriculture) per square kilometre, as compared with an over-all density of 283 in Belgium and 207 in the United Kingdom – the most heavily industrialized countries in Europe. The figure for France, with her large agricultural population, is only 76.

It is calculated that half the population of Egypt is economically redundant, in the sense that one-half of it could still produce the amount of wealth that is being produced to-day. No further increase in cultivated land can take place until more Nile water is made available by the new irrigation schemes now in process of execution. But even when the last drop of water has been squeezed out of the great river, the production of the land will not increase sufficiently so as to raise the standards of living of the whole population; its increase will be merely cancelled out by the new mouths that will by then be demanding food.

There are only three ways of raising the standard of living for the masses: industrialization, emigration, and birth control.

With regard to the last-mentioned means, it is encouraging to know that the Mufti (the chief interpreter of Muslim law) of Egypt has pronounced that there is no incompatibility between it and the tenets of Islam. As for emigration, the Sudan, as already pointed out, offers a limited outlet;

while Iraq, which has vast irrigable lands and a sparse population, could take even a larger number if she would. There is, however, no sign of any such move in the near future.

There remains industrialization. Already a considerable number of industries – mainly textile – have come into being in the cities of Egypt, and the country has a greater concentration of funds for investment and of industrial skills than any other in the Arab world. Moreover, Egypt and the other Arab countries could become economically complementary to a large extent (as Charles Issawi suggests) if they relied on her to supply them with certain industrial products, such as textiles, cement, glass, vegetable oils, soap, and matches. In return, Iraq and Syria could offer her wheat and barley; the Lebanon fruit and an ideal summer resort; the Sudan and Libya livestock, and so on. As it is, most of these countries are now developing their own small-scale industries regardless of what is happening in the others, with the result that there is a great deal of duplication and inefficiency. The realization that it was in the interest of all to check this tendency led to the holding of an Arab Economic Conference in Beirut in May 1953, at which a resolution was passed providing for tariff reductions, the initiation of certain joint projects, and the establishment of a Regional Economic Organization. Whether this attempt at co-ordination on the economic side will prove more effective than the attempt at co-ordination on the political side made in the Arab League remains to be seen.

Whatever decisions are taken under this scheme, however, will have to recognize the astonishingly successful development of Syrian industry. Before the war, Syria had almost no industry at all, except for handicrafts. To-day (and without any foreign financial assistance whatever) the country is more or less self-sufficing in cotton and silk textiles, sugar, cement, glass, vegetable oils, matches, and other such products. In some she even has an export surplus. This progress is all the more remarkable for the fact that it has been accompanied by tremendous agricultural expansion, of which a few figures should give some idea. Annual wheat production has risen from an average of 459,000 metric tons in the five years before the war to 850,000 in 1952, and 1,340,000 in 1953; barley from 290,000 to 467,000 and 474,000; rice from 3000 to 20,000 and 19,000; cotton from 5000 to 45,000 and 50,000.

In the Sudan, as in Egypt, the principal industry is cotton growing. The Gezira scheme – one of the finest things left by the British in the country – is a partnership between the government and the cultivators which provides the state treasury with the major portion of its revenue. It is also, in the triangle of land contained between the Blue Nile and the White Nile south of Khartoum, revolutionizing the life of the people, not only by giving the farmers unprecedented annual incomes (reaching in years of bumper crops and maximum prices £700 per tenant) but also providing them with a well-planned system of social services, on which 20 per cent of the annual profits is spent.

Agricultural expansion on a large scale is also taking place in Iraq, and there are various projects under consideration for harnessing the waters of the Jordan and Yarmuk rivers in such a way as to benefit all the surrounding countries. As these include Israel as well as Jordan and Syria, and as the Arabs will not have any direct dealings with the Israelis, the carrying out of any of these projects will present many difficulties, but something may be achieved by the effective internationalization of Lake Tiberias and the setting up of a United Nations authority to distribute the water stored in it.

Near Jericho, in the Jordan valley, a very promising pilot scheme for cultivating this hitherto waterless and dead land is being developed by Musa Alami, referred to earlier as the author of *The Lesson of Palestine*. Disregarding all foreign expert opinions (including those of United Nations' technicians) that there was no water in the sub-soil of the Jordan valley, and that in any case the land was too salty to be cultivable, Alami proceeded to prospect and bore until he struck water in ample quantities. He then desalted the land and successfully grew several tropical and sub-tropical crops. His project, run by the Arab Land Development Society, is centred on an orphanage for the children of Arab refugees from Palestine. It already has several thousand acres under cultivation and maintains, apart from the children of the orphanage, a large number of peasant families who come daily to work on the land. Alami's principal object, however, is to demonstrate how a large proportion of the Arab refugees can be profitably and permanently settled in the Jordan valley.

But the greatest economic transformation that is taking place in Arab life at present is due to the discovery and extraction of oil. The transformation is all the more revolutionary because for the most part oil is gushing out in desert lands (Saudi Arabia, Kuwait, Bahrein) where there is no water for cultivation, and where the local economy had remained extremely primitive and the people poor and backward until the extraction of oil began during the last quarter-century. A few of the figures given by Stephen Longrigg in his *Oil in the Middle East* will help to convey to the reader some idea of the magnitude and suddenness of this transformation. In 1938 the Arab countries and Persia together produced 15 million tons of oil, or 5·5 per cent of the world's supply of 270 millions. This output had risen by 1946 to 35·5 million tons, or 9·4 per cent of a world total of 381 million. In 1952 the Arab countries alone (Persian production being then suspended owing to the dispute between the Persian Government and the Anglo-Iranian Oil Company) were producing 104·5 million tons, or 17 per cent of the total world output of 605 millions.

The distribution of this prodigious amount among the Arab countries themselves was as follows: Saudi Arabia, 41 million tons; Kuwait, 37; Iraq, 18·5; Qatar, 3·2; Egypt, 2·4; and Bahrein, 1·5.

By April 1953 the *monthly* total output of the Arab countries had exceeded 10 million tons, thus promising an annual production of more than 120 millions; and experts expect a considerable increase on this figure in the near future.

Of the proved oil reserves of the whole world the Arab countries possess about one-half, or 6800 million tons, of which Bahrein has 40 million tons, Egypt 80, Iraq 1650, Kuwait 2500, Qatar 300, and Saudi Arabia 2250 millions.

There is something fabulous about these figures and what they mean – a story that might have come out of the *Arabian Nights* themselves, of the sudden, dazzling gift of a genie. Yet a little arithmetic will show that the gift is not permanent, but has something of the transitory magnificence of a dream. In fifty or a hundred years' time, even the Kuwait oilfield, which is the richest in the world, will be exhausted. Therefore it is imperative for the great oil-producing Arab countries to use their present revenues not only for the immediate raising of their people's standard of living, but also for the long-term development of other sources of wealth to replace oil.

The country where this is being most satisfactorily done at present is Iraq. This is only natural, since of the three principal oil-producing countries, whose receipts permit of large-scale spending on capital development (Saudi Arabia, Kuwait, and Iraq), Iraq is the most advanced socially and politically, and is the only one to have the organization of a modern state and an active public opinion and press.

From the beginning Iraq acted on the principle that oil revenues should be allotted to capital development rather than used to pay for current expenditure in the annual budget, though the principle was sometimes infringed in lean years. However, in 1950 a special Development Board was set up to administer the oil funds independently of the Government and its budget. Thus it was hoped not only to secure the autonomy of the capital development work financed by the oil revenues, but also to 'take it out of politics' and give it a continuity not dependent on electoral fortunes. The board was to consist of eight members, of whom only the Prime Minister and Minister of Finance were to be members of the Government. The other six members were to be non-official, salaried members appointed by Royal Decree, and to hold office for five years. Two of them were to be experts in Irrigation and Finance respectively; and it is to the credit of the government of the day that it defied anti-foreign prejudice sufficiently to appoint an Englishman as Secretary-General and Finance Expert of the Board and an American as its Irrigation Engineer.

At first it was decided that all oil royalties should be handed over to the Board, but a modification of 1952 reduced the figure to 70 per cent, leaving the remaining 30 per cent available to local authorities for spending on their own projects.

Until 1950, royalties were paid by the Iraq Petroleum Company at a fixed rate per ton; but an initiative taken in that year (and after the Anglo-Iranian Company's disaster in Persia) by the Arabian American Company that operated in Saudi Arabia – Aramco – was to alter the basis of the re-lationship between the local Arab governments and the foreign *concessionaire* companies throughout the region. Instead of a fixed rate per ton, Company and Government were now to share profits on a fifty-fifty basis. This new arrangement, together with the increased output achieved in recent years, means that Iraq's revenue from oil is to-day about fifty million pounds sterling per annum – a revenue that can abolish the endemic poverty of the country and transform its whole life. Apart from the sums that are being devoted to irrigation, communications, and town construc-tion, the Development Board is spending lavishly on schools and hospitals, as well as other forms of social service.

It is, however, the story of Kuwait that comes nearest to a fairy tale. For this country is a mere Sheikhdom consisting of one large city and a small hinterland of villages, whose aggregate population is about a quarter million. It is one of the many small Persian Gulf principalities in whose fate the British Government became interested during the last hun-dred years because of their proximity to India, and which were induced to enter into treaty relations with Britain, whereby they accepted her protection and agreed not to allow any other foreign power to gain a foothold in them. In each, Britain has a Resident who advises the ruling Sheikh on matters of general policy; but the administration is purely indigenous and Britain does not interfere in it directly.

Before the discovery of its oilfield, Kuwait lived a backward, medieval life by building ships for navigation in the Indian Ocean, and also on the proceeds of a decaying pearl-fishing industry. To-day, it has a revenue of more than fifty million pounds a year and the fantastic existence of someone who finds himself standing with a magic ring, magically dropped into his hands. The present Sheikh is an enlightened man and, suitably advised by the British Resident, is spending a large proportion of his revenue on modernizing Kuwait and providing it with all the social services it needs. Whole streets are being pulled down, house by house, and rebuilt. Hospitals and schools are going up. Hundreds of students are being sent to England, Egypt, and Lebanon for higher education.

But the system of government is still medieval and autocratic. The oil revenue is paid to the Sheikh and is, in theory, his property and the property of his family. It is obvious that this state of things cannot last very long, particularly as a considerable sum of the revenue is being spent on the higher education of Kuwaitis abroad. Already a modern politically minded intelligentsia is coming into being; the old foundations of government are being questioned, and a demand for democratization increasingly heard.

In Saudi Arabia, too, the government is in the hands of an archaic dynasty, and the oil revenue (also more than fifty million pounds a year now) is paid to the sons of Ibn Saud. No clear line of demarcation is drawn between the privy purse and the public funds, so that the money from oil is, in theory, and largely in practice as well, the King's personal revenue. What is more, the country being much larger than Kuwait and to a considerable extent still in the pastoral age, the growth of a modern democratic movement in it is not to be expected in the near future. In the absence of effective representative institutions and a vigilant public opinion and press, it is difficult to ensure the spending of the oil revenues in such a manner as to benefit the whole people. Criticisms are heard that a disproportionate share of them goes to meet the personal expenditure of the Royal House. Nevertheless, as the result of an enlightened policy on the part of the Arab American Oil Company and of friendly relations between it and the Government, much is being done to improve conditions in the country, e.g. by the supplying of piped water to towns, the building of airports, the establishment of a wireless network throughout the country, the initiation of experimental schemes in modern farming (and particularly of mechanized irrigation), the boring of artesian wells at many places which had never known water before, and the improvement of the harbour facilities at Jeddah.

On the demand of the Saudi Government, Aramco has shifted its entire headquarters from New York to Dahran in Arabia, and has appointed two Saudis to its board of directors.

But oil is bringing development and modernization to Arabia not only through the vast treasure it is placing in her hands for the purchase of these advantages. It is bringing them indirectly as well through the industrial processes and the various other services required in the extraction, refining, and exportation (whether by tanker or pipe-line) of oil. In the first place, a large local labour force has to be employed by the oil companies, and so become accustomed to the conditions of a new life. Secondly, as there are not enough skilled workers and technicians among the local population, many have to be brought over from the more advanced parts of the Arab world, such as Egypt, Syria, Lebanon, and Jordan – where, in particular, the Palestine Arab refugees have in recent years been available for such employment. Finally, there are the European and American engineers and higher executives establishing small colonies of Western life in the midst of what was mainly a medieval Muslim population until the oil companies came in. All these factors must contribute in varying degrees to the process of change that is taking place in Arabia; and the change must inevitably be in the direction of more contact with the outside world – a move in thought and body into the conditions of the twentieth century.

Even Arab countries in which oil has not been found are involved in the tremendous operations of refining it and carrying it to the outside world. Pipe-lines from Saudi Arabia and Iraq carry the crude product across Syria, Jordan, and Lebanon to the Mediterranean. Although the Haifa terminal has been closed since the Palestine war, there are three others now, one at Banias in Syria, and two in the Lebanon, at Sidon and Tripoli. Throughout its long desert journey the oil has to be propelled by pumping at certain stations, and the pipe-lines have to be maintained.

Since this vast new wealth of the Arabian Peninsula was revealed, a certain question has been forcing itself on the attention of statesmen and thinkers in the Arab world – namely, whether the oil revenues must continue to be spent entirely on the countries in which the oil is produced, or whether some means cannot be devised to spread the benefits wider, so that countries like Jordan, Lebanon, and Syria, which do not produce any oil, may receive some of them. The question has acquired particular force from the fantastic disproportion between the size of some of the oil-producing countries and the revenues they receive – a disproportion which reaches its most glaring point in Kuwait, where a city-state with not so large a population as Beirut or Damascus disposes of annual funds exceeding the total budgets of Syria and Lebanon put together, and is incomparably richer than Jordan which has had to absorb several hundred thousand refugees from Palestine.

If the oil-producing countries could be united in a federation with those in which there is no oil, the problem would be solved. But there is no prospect of any such federation in the near future, the levels of social, political, and cultural development in the two *blocs* of countries being too far apart to allow of a federal union, not to mention the rivalry between the different local dynasties and ruling groups.

It may, however, prove possible to achieve a compromise solution by the creation of an Arab development bank into which oil revenue surpluses could be paid for financing development schemes in Jordan, Syria, and Lebanon. The Arab League may help in the carrying out of such a project in conjunction with the oil companies and the governments of the United Kingdom and the United States. The accidents of geography and geology, the meaninglessness of frontiers drawn across the desert sand, the interests of a local ruling family here or there, should not stand in the way of the widest and most beneficial distribution of oil profits among the Arab peoples.

4

Together with economic development education is transforming the Arab countries. It is true, that apart from Lebanon, where nearly 80 per cent of the people can now read and write, illiteracy still prevails, rising from 75 per cent in Egypt to 86 in Iraq and over 90 per cent in Saudi Arabia. It is also true that in the countries that live mainly by agriculture the funds necessary to provide school places for all children cannot be made available. Yet the campaign against illiteracy is being vigorously pursued, particularly in Egypt, Syria, the Sudan, and Iraq.

In the countries where there is a large nomadic population, like Saudi Arabia, the Sudan, and Iraq, education presents serious difficulties. The experiment was tried in both Iraq and the Sudan of having mobile schools to accompany the tribe on its annual migrations, but the results were disappointing. Attendance was irregular, and the teacher tended to become the personal clerk of the sheikh of the tribe. Now, recourse is being had to another expedient: boarding houses are being attached to certain primary schools in the towns that lie in the heart of the tribal areas, and the tribesmen are being encouraged to leave their children behind them as boarders while they themselves move from place to place with the tribe. It is too early to say whether this experiment is going to be more successful than the last. The final answer with regard to nomads may be that the only way to educate them is to terminate their nomadism and change them into a settled agricultural population.

But the progress that is being achieved in the cities and villages is tremendous. Egypt affords the best example, for comparative figures over a long number of years, since she was the first of the Arab countries to obtain her independence and be in a position to formulate and carry out her educational policy. A few comparisons will tell the story vividly. Gaining her independence in 1922, Egypt passed a law in 1923 making education free and compulsory between the ages of seven and twelve. The total school population, which had been 324,000 in 1913, rose to 942,000 in 1933 and by 1951 stood at 1,900,000. In 1920, Egypt spent £E1,600,000 on education, or 4 per cent of the national budget. By 1951 she was spending £E29,000,000, or 13 per cent of the total budget. In 1913 government secondary schools had only 2500 pupils – all boys. In 1933 they had 15,000 pupils, of whom 1500 were girls; and in 1951 the numbers had risen to 122,000 pupils, including 19,000 girls. In 1913 the country had very few university students; in 1951 it had 41,000 at home and another 1400 Egyptians pursuing higher studies abroad.

The fact remains, however, that less than half Egypt's children have school places to-day. To deal with this situation the government has planned the building of 5000 more schools during the next twenty years.

In countries where so much leeway has to be made up, adult education is of great importance. Due recognition was given to this fact by the Egyptian Government in 1944, when a law was enacted making it obligatory for big landowners and employers to provide instruction for their workers. By 1950 the number of illiterates being taught had reached 300,000. In 1951, Unesco rendered a signal service to the cause of adult education in the Arab world when, as a result of its work in an Egyptian village, a simplified form of Arabic was devised which could be taught to an illiterate in six weeks instead of the six months previously required under the traditional system of teaching. In 1953 Unesco (which includes on its staff a distinguished Arab educationist from Iraq) and the Arab governments collaborated in starting a Fundamental Education Training Centre near Cairo to serve the whole Middle East. Also, since 1946, free cultural and vocational courses have been available at what is called 'the People's University', established in Cairo with branches in the provinces.

One could go on quoting figures and instances to illustrate the great forward surge of the education movement in the Arab world. In Iraq, for example, the number of primary school pupils has risen from 8000 in 1920 to 181,000 in 1950; of secondary school pupils from 100 to 22,700; and of post-secondary students, from 65 to 4860. In Syria, the number of children attending school (of both sexes) has been trebled in the last ten years. Most significant of all, perhaps, is that of about 5000 students in the Syrian state university in Damascus (which used to be a citadel of Muslim conservatism) over 800 are girls, and in many departments the majority of them are Muslim girls.

The number of universities which give a modern, secular education to-day in the Arab world is ten. Of these four are to be found in Egypt, three being state-sponsored, indigenous institutions and one American. Lebanon has three: one American, one French, and a new state university in the initial stages of formation. Syria has one state university, and Iraq is now establishing one. In the Sudan there is a university college which is to attain university status in 1956; at present it prepares its more advanced students for the B.A. and B.Sc. of London University. Mention has already been

made of the large number of Egyptians studying at universities or higher vocational training centres abroad. Iraq
comes next with a contingent of several hundred. In 1953
the Sudan had about one hundred students in Britain; and
Kuwait is now using a fair proportion of its new-found wealth
from oil to send many of its sons also to Britain for a modern
education at the higher levels. Tunisians, Algerians, and
Moroccans seek their university education in France; but
their case is different from that of the eastern Arabs since they
have no modern, secular universities in their own countries.

Here, several points engage the interest of the observer,
some with the challenge of disturbing questions.

The first is the criticism that quality is being sacrificed to
quantity in the educational development of some of the Arab
countries; that the products of the new education are mainly
imitative, lacking in initiative, interested not so much in
education itself as in the prospects of a government job which
may be expected to reward it; that an inferior 'liberal'
education attracts the majority of pupils (and their parents)
as against a good vocational training, because it carries a
higher social status with it and will lead to a lazy clerk's desk
instead of to a hard-worked craftsman's bench.

In each of these points there is a measure of truth; but even
the aggregate weight of them all put together is as naught in
the balance against the fact that literacy and modern knowledge, however imperfect, are replacing ignorance and super-
stition. When it is remembered that girls are increasingly
partaking of the advantages of this education it will be
realized what a profound transformation the process is
causing in the life of the Arab peoples; the education that is
being acquired will not only increase the sum total of knowledge and skill in the Arab lands, but will basically alter the
relations between the sexes and therefore the entire character
of both home and social life among the Muslim Arabs.

Secondly, there is the problem of the gulf which is inevitably being created between the recipients of the modern,
secular education, with its basis in Western civilization, and

those Muslim Arabs who are still receiving the traditional religious education (slightly modernized by the introduction of a few new subjects) at mosque schools, with their apex at the Cairo university of al-Azhar. This problem involves the deeper one of the entire attitude of the Muslim Arabs in the modern world. In a previous chapter the spread of secularism and agnosticism was mentioned. The secularists are merely those Muslims who, under modern Western influences, have lost their religious belief, even though they may not proclaim the fact publicly. But there are the 'modernists', who have not lost their faith, who are very anxious to retain it – or at least to retain the belief that they still believe. This, however, they are unable to do unless they can restate their faith in a manner reconcilable with present-day science and ways of thought. Their tendency is to reject everything in medieval Muslim theology which conflicts with their reason; to assert, by giving it a more subjective and metaphorical interpretation, that the Koran is in harmony with the most up-to-date theories of science and philosophy. Professor Gibb finds that this subjective selectivity is destroying the whole structure of Islamic theology and opening the way to moral chaos. But did not the Christian modernists do essentially the same thing when they were confronted with the conclusions of Copernicus, Galileo, Darwin? Did not the body of Christians in the modern world split into three main groups: those who lost their religious faith, both as an explanation of life and a basis for morality, and become 'secularists'; those who, because they wanted to retain the medieval essentials of their faith, remained for long hostile to much of the new knowledge, such as the theory of Evolution; and lastly those who went on trying to restate their old dogmas in a form acceptable to the modern mind until they vaporized them almost completely? The conflicts and confusions which are noticeable in the Arab world to-day as a result of the clash between modern Western education and Orthodox Muslim beliefs is inevitable and need not lead to a deeper rift in the Arab soul than it has caused in the soul of the Western world.

Of course, Western education itself is not reaching the Arab world in one form or idiom, as it reached India, for example (if we exclude the small Portuguese and French settlements). Its French, British, and American versions are all to be found in the Arab countries. True, North Africa receives it entirely in the French form; and at the opposite end Iraq, Kuwait, Jordan, and the Sudan have not known any French influence. But in Egypt, Lebanon, and Syria the Gallic and Anglo-Saxon elements are both strongly represented. In the Lebanon there is a marked cleavage between the French-educated section of the population, with its intense assimilation of French culture and the French language (even as the means of ordinary daily intercourse) and the products of the American University of Beirut. In the past (and particularly during the period of the Mandate) French education predominated; but with the termination of French political control and the emergence of America as the supreme world power – as a power, moreover, with direct interests in the Middle East such as oil and Point Four Projects, the emphasis now is on the American educational connection. There is also a project sponsored by the British Council for opening an English secondary school in Beirut on the lines of Victoria College.

This last-named school has been Britain's major educational contribution to the Arab countries. Both the parent foundation at Alexandria and its offspring in Cairo give an English public-school education not only to Egyptians and residents in Egypt but to an increasing number of boys from Iraq, Saudi Arabia, Kuwait, and the Sudan. Before the eclipse of Germany in World War I and the disappearance of Tsarist Russia, there were also a number of German and Russian schools in Lebanon and Palestine. The writer remembers that in his childhood there was in his village in Mount Lebanon a school known to the villagers as the 'Muscobiya'. From these schools some of the Lebanese went on to complete their education at the university level in Kiev, Moscow, or St Petersburg.

Although this multiplicity of form in which Western education is reaching the Arab world may create temporary confusions, there is nothing fundamentally harmful in it. On the contrary, it is introducing an enriching diversity into the Arab countries. There is a common soil into which all these foreign streams will eventually sink and be absorbed – and that is the culture created by the Arabic language.

The cultural output of the Arab world – if one excludes the press – is still meagre, whether in Arabic or foreign languages. Charles Issawi gives the number of new books published in Egypt (the largest and one of the two most advanced of the Arab countries) in 1948 as 548, of which 67 were translations. However, in all the fields of scholarship and research, students trained in Western method are being produced in increasing numbers, and are applying their techniques with skill and integrity to the problems of the Arab world itself.

In the domain of the fine arts, there is little yet apart from literature that deserves mention. A very few sculptors and painters (mainly Egyptian and French-inspired) have attained a certain international reputation. Modern Arabic music is still a characterless hybrid – very popular among the masses whether in films, gramophone records, broadcasts, or live performances; but lacking both the charm and sincerity of old folk-songs and the original and complex harmonies of the Western models it tries to imitate.

Words – and chiefly measured and rhyming words – are still the Arabs' principal medium of artistic expression. But it is noticeable that under Western influences new forms of literature are appearing, chiefly the short story and the novel, in which pictures of Arab life are presented with a new kind of realism.

5

We cannot conclude this survey without attempting some answer to two questions that challenge any observer of the contemporary Arab scene. The first is that of the future relations between the Arabs and the Jews of Israel; the second is that of the Arab orientation as between Communism and the West.

For the present the Arabs have had to accept their defeat in Palestine and the establishment of the Jewish state. There are those among them who talk glibly or think wishfully of a 'second round' in the near future that would destroy Israel and regain Palestine for the Arab world. But such talk and wishes are vain, and the majority of thinking Arabs recognize them as such. The Arab states have not acquired, and for many years are not likely to acquire, sufficient unity of purpose or military power to be able to reverse by force the decision of 1948 – even assuming that the Western Powers and the United Nations were to allow them to do so. As it is, the United States, Britain, and France have guaranteed the present frontiers between Israel and the Arab states, and there is a United Nations armistice commission in permanent session, supervising the integrity of these frontiers. Moreover British influence in Jordan (exerted through the treaty, the subsidy, and the presence of British officers in the Arab Legion) as well as American influence there and in Lebanon and Egypt (exerted through Point Four Aid) will be steadily used to prevent any armed attempt by the Arab states to regain Palestine.

What many Arabs do not feel sure of is whether all these international influences will be used equally effectively to prevent further Jewish encroachment on Arab territory, particularly in the direction of Jordan. There is some evidence that the Israelis were antagonistic to the resettlement of Arab refugees in the Jordan valley, and tried to use their international influence to have as many of the refugees as possible permanently absorbed by Lebanon and Syria. This evidence the Arabs interpret as indicating a secret Israeli intention of future expansion into the Jordan valley. Also, the Arabs argue that the present Israeli policy of encouraging unrestricted Jewish immigration into their state is bound to lead to such congestion and economic pressure on the land in Palestine as to create an explosive situation dangerous to all the surrounding countries – even if it was not itself another sign of Israeli expansionist intentions. It may be that the Arabs exaggerate the international power of the Zionists, but the essential point is that they *believe* it to be very great – great enough, perhaps, to enable the Israelis (if the Arab states were unable to defend themselves adequately) to snatch another piece of Arab territory – in Jordan or the Gaza region – with impunity.

The first thought of the Arab statesmen is therefore to increase their military strength so as to surround Israel with an unbreakable iron ring.

But what then? Assuming that a repetition of armed conflict between the Arabs and the Jews, on any large scale, can be prevented by international action or by the establishment, for the time being, of a nice military equilibrium between the two parties themselves, is there any hope that real peace and friendship will ensue? that Israel will be accepted by the Arabs and integrated in their region, economically, strategically, socially?

The only honest and realistic answer that can be made to this question for any foreseeable future is an emphatic 'No'. In Arab eyes the Israelis have perpetrated against the Arabs an evil as ugly as that perpetrated by the Nazis against the Jews. They are aggressors who have deprived a whole Arab people of its country, who have reduced this people – or the vast majority of it – to the condition of destitute refugees living in camps in the surrounding Arab countries. To the Arabs, Israel is an alien, hateful, and dangerous intrusion into the Arab world – the expression of a militant and fanatical nationalism which is incompatible with the existence and healthy development of the Arab community. To the Arabs, Palestine is and will remain an indisputably Arab land which has been wrongfully seized by foreign invaders. To accept these invaders, to make peace with them, to have intercourse with them, to co-operate with them economically or strategically is so repugnant to the deepest Arab feelings that it is impossible to imagine the Arab states doing any of these things. It is now six years since the Palestine war ended, but there is not the slightest sign that the Arabs are willing to conclude peace with Israel, to give her *de jure* recognition, or to have any dealings with her. There is no communication between Israel and the surrounding Arab states, no traffic, no trade except a certain amount of smuggling which continues despite the official and largely effective boycott. The Cairo-Haifa train runs no more; the thousands of Egyptians who used to travel every year through Palestine to the mountain resorts of Lebanon, now either fly or go by sea. On the Beirut-Haifa road the thousands of cars and lorries that used to make the journey in both directions, carrying passengers and goods, are no more to be seen. No foreign traveller can enter any of the Arab countries if he has a *visa* for Israel on his passport.

Israel is, of course, very desirous of a final settlement whereby the Arab states would make peace with her and accept her in the Middle East community of nations. She knows that she can only achieve reasonable standards of living for her congested territory through industrial development, and that this development will not be possible for her unless the Arab countries open their markets to her products.

The Western powers too would like to see peace concluded between Israel and her Arab neighbours, because as long as there is no peace there will be the danger of a flare-up threatening the security of the Middle East; because the Middle East defence organization, so dear to the framers of American strategy in particular, would be much easier to achieve if the Arabs and Israelis would co-operate in it; and perhaps not least because, when you have done a grievous wrong to someone, your conscience continues to trouble you as long as the victim of that wrong refuses to be reconciled to it.

But the logic of the situation and Israel's attitude to the question of the Arab refugees give the Arab states the justification they want for not making peace with her. They demand that the return of the refugees to Palestine and the restoration of their property to them should be a condition of any settlement – indeed, a condition which Israel should fulfil in advance of any settlement. The Israelis will not agree to this; and even if they would they probably could not agree to it since there is no longer room in Palestine (now filled with recently introduced immigrants) for its former people. The most that the Israelis have offered by way of contributing towards the solution of the Arab refugee problem has been some financial assistance (amounting to no more than a fraction of the value of Arab property in Palestine, which is estimated at about £500,000,000) to help in resettling the refugees in *other* Arab countries. This the Arabs have rejected.

And so the deadlock continues and the Arab states refuse to relax any of the restrictions they have adopted towards Israel, even at the risk of putting in jeopardy their own immediate interests. Thus, Iraq stopped the oil-flow to Haifa though she stood to incur heavy financial losses by doing so. Also, it was noteworthy during the Anglo-Egyptian negotiations of 1954, which actually culminated in a new agreement between the two countries, that Egypt refused to commit herself in any way to the easing of the embargo which she has so far maintained on the passage of ships through the Suez Canal bound for Israel. Britain had to conclude the agreement without obtaining any pro-Israeli concession from Egypt, and all that the British Foreign Secretary could say to the champions of the Zionist cause in the House of Commons was that he hoped that the establishment of a new and more friendly relationship between Britain and Egypt would help in improving matters for Israel.

The question may be asked, what do the Arabs hope to achieve by this policy of boycotting and isolating Israel? To this question there are two answers: one on the emotional and unreasoning level, at which, however, many human actions are decided; the other, on the level of calculated policy. The first is that the Arabs' attitude towards Israel is now one of implacable hate. By boycotting Israel, the Arabs satisfy to a certain extent their desire for revenge, their sense of outrage at what has been done to them. The second is a profound hope that in the course of time their refusal to have anything to do with Israel will cause the isolated state to wilt and perish. They know, as well as the Israelis themselves, that Israel cannot thrive unless she has access to Arab markets; that without this access she will continue to be a liability to the American Zionists, who are still having to pour subsidies into the country to keep it alive. They wonder how long the American Zionists will be willing to maintain Israel by subsidies. They hope that if they force on Israel a low standard of living by denying her their markets, the trend of migration will be reversed and Jews will tend to leave Israel instead of coming into it – as, indeed, was the case in the years immediately preceding the advent of the Nazis to power in Germany. They remember that the Latin kingdom of Jerusalem came to an end after enduring a hundred years. To them Israel is another such artificial creation – a forced plant that has no place in the Arab world, a stone that has been pushed up against the force of gravity some way along the slopes of the Arab mountain. The Arabs of the Middle East alone number over fifty millions; Israel, one million and a half. Keep her isolated and outside the indigenous community of the region and she will eventually disappear before the growing wealth, strength, and integration of the Arab countries. The imported plant with its roots in New York will die; the stone resisting the forces of gravity will crash down to the bottom of the valley.

Those who believe that this attitude of the Arabs can be altered, that real peace and co-operation can be brought about between Israel and the Arab countries are, on the evidence available at present and as far as it is possible to prognosticate, indulging in wishful fancies.

* * *

And now we come to the orientation of the Arab states as between Russia and the West, Communism and the Free World.

First, as to the internal evolution of social and political forces within the Arab countries – this evolution certainly does not seem to tend towards Communism, but rather towards the Western pattern. Such Communist movements or parties as have existed in Syria, Lebanon, Iraq, and Egypt in the last twenty or thirty years have made very little progress, though the conditions of poverty and social unrest in which Communism may be expected to thrive have not been lacking. For this there are many reasons: the suppression of Communist activities by the governments in power (whether of the traditional or recent military type), the absence of a large industrial proletariat and strong trade unions which the Communists could capture, the hostility of Islam to a materialist atheistic creed and way of life; and the strong, even anarchic, individualism of the Arab character. Then again, the Arab countries have grown up to political adolescence under the influence of Western ideas – democracy, nationalism, sovereignty, independence. Even while they were fighting Western imperialism, they were doing so with Western concepts and aiming at Western ideals. Representative institutions of the Western brand – no matter on how insecure a foundation – had been established in most of them. Their higher intelligentsia was almost entirely educated in the West or in Western or Western-inspired schools in the Middle East. Even when part of this intelligentsia fell under the spell of Communist ideas during and after the war, their principal source of inspiration was the intellectual Communism of the West, towards which no mean proportion of Western liberals had turned in despair during the inter-war period.

When revolutions came to the Arab countries, like those of Syria and Egypt, they were carried out not by the Communists but by the army inspired by nationalism and ideas of liberal and mildly socialist reform. Thus one may say that the internal political evolution of the more advanced Arab countries has been along the lines of a lame and stumbling democracy helped by military dictatorship. The ideal of some of the modernists among the Arabs is Turkey – a Westernized, secular democratic state. Nor is Communism, as far as one can see at present, and provided Russia is kept out of the Middle East, the alternative that would seize the field if Western democracy and reformist military dictatorship failed. The alternative would be the forces of revivalist, theocratic Islam as represented by the Muslim Brotherhood. It is true that Communists have infiltrated into the Brotherhood and helped to organize it, but the movement remains in inspiration and composition predominantly Islamic. In French North Africa the nationalists, even in the bitterest moments of their struggle with French imperialism, refused an alliance with the Communists.

If we turn from internal evolution to foreign policy and international alignment, we shall find the same leaning of the Arab countries towards the Western world. There was a time when the West stood for Imperialism in Arab eyes, when it was difficult for the Arabs to see Russia as a potential menace to their freedom, because they had never been under Russian or Communist rule, whereas they had been for many years under British or French rule. But that time is passing away. In the eastern Arab world it has passed away almost entirely. In the western Arab world it is beginning to pass away in Tunisia. As the Arab states become free from Western political control and military occupation, their alignment with the West is bound to be strengthened; for then the only threat to their new-won freedom could come from the East. Already, with the revision of the Anglo-Egyptian Treaty, a decisive step has been taken by Egypt (and, one may say, by the whole group of eastern Arab states of which she is the leader) away from the neutralist policy in which, a few years ago, these states professed to see their salvation in any clash that might occur between Russia and the West. Not only has Egypt now agreed to the reoccupation of the Suez Base by Britain in the event of an attack on any of the Arab states; she has also agreed that an attack on Turkey should give Britain this right of re-entry, and the leading spokesman of the Egyptian Government defended this concession by saying that an attack on Turkey would mean a world war, and that in such an eventuality, 'it would not be a bad thing for Egypt to have Britain at her side.'

This, surely, is the end of neutralism for Egypt while the treaty lasts – that is to say, for at least the next seven years. And as it was Egypt, because of her opposition to the British occupation, that sponsored the policy of neutralism most ardently among the Arab countries, it is only to be expected that these countries (Iraq, Syria, Jordan, and Lebanon in particular), who have always had doubts about the efficacy of neutralism, will now incline more openly to a policy of closer association with the West.*

For some time past the Arab countries have been receiving arms and economic assistance from Britain and America. The economic assistance is being given under the American Point Four policy of helping under-developed regions to develop their resources and improve their standards of living – which, in the long run, is the only answer to Communism in countries whose chief curse has been poverty and whose masses might respond to any creed that offered them the hope of a better life. With the settlement of all outstanding political differences between Britain and the Arab states of Egypt and Iraq, the way will be open for more aid from the West to the Arab countries and for more genuine co-operation between the two parties.

Already in the oil industry there are strong bonds of union between the West and the Arab world. In Iraq, in Saudi Arabia, and all along the Persian Gulf, as well as in Egypt, the extraction of oil is bringing Britain, the United States, France, and Holland on the one hand and the Arabs on the other into a partnership of the greatest mutual benefit. It may, without any false optimism, be hoped that the tragic lessons learned from the Persian imbroglio, both by the people of the country and the *concessionaire* company, will

* Iraq has, indeed, done so already; nor is Egypt's opposition to the Turco-Iraqi pact to be taken as an anti-Western move.

prevent any such catastrophe occurring elsewhere, and cause the partnership already established between the Arab countries and the West in this tremendous field to evolve along healthy lines.

A glance at the map will show the close geographical relationship which binds Europe and the Arab world together. Here, around the Mediterranean, it is not a question of 'East is East and West is West'. Here, in terms of global geography, is a small, central sea, around whose shores all the great seminal civilizations of antiquity and the Middle Ages have flourished and intermingled. From Spain to Morocco is but a step; and Malta, Sicily, Sardinia, and Corsica have always been stepping-stones between North Africa and Southern Europe. In the Middle Ages it was the Arabs that encroached upon Europe, crossing Gibraltar, occupying Spain for eight hundred years, pushing into France and, at the opposite side of the Continent, pressing against Byzantium. In modern times the tide flowed in the opposite direction. It was now the European nations that impinged upon the Arab world; and while nowhere did they assimilate the occupied territory as thoroughly, or hold it for as long, as the Arabs did Spain, the control they established was much more extensive than Arab rule ever became in Europe, for at its peak it embraced almost the entire Arab world both in North Africa and Asia Minor.

Just as the Arabs, however, had to leave Spain ultimately, so too the European nations have had (or are having) to leave the Arab countries. Is it too much to expect that the time has now come for the two systems – Europe and the Arab world – to share the Mediterranean basin in a state of friendly partnership, neither encroaching upon the other, each occupying the countries which have unalterably become its own through the long operation of history, but exchanging all the benefits of good neighbourliness across the sea which belongs to them both?

*A selection of
other Pelicans is given
on the remaining
few pages*

A SHORT HISTORY OF THE WORLD

H. G. Wells

A 5

This is meant, as the author says in his Preface, to be read straightforwardly almost as a novel is read. It gives in the most general way an account of our present knowledge of history, shorn of elaborations and complications. From it the reader should be able to get that general view of history which is so necessary a framework for the study of a particular period or the history of a particular country. Its special end is to meet the needs of the busy general reader, too driven to study the maps and time charts of that *Outline* in detail, who wishes to refresh and repair his faded or fragmentary conceptions of the great adventure of mankind. It is not an abstract or condensation of that former work. Within its aim the *Outline* admits of no further condensation. This is a much more generalized History, planned and written afresh. This edition gives the book in its completed form as revised by the author on the eve of his death in 1946. There are twenty sketch-maps by the famous cartographer J. F. Horrabin.

Not for sale in the U.S.A.

THE PREHISTORY OF EAST AFRICA

Sonia Cole

A 316

Probably more is known about the very earliest phases of man's existence in East Africa than in any other part of the world. The geological background, including evidence of past climates, provides a framework for the dating of man's skeletal remains and material cultures. From the time of the first pebble-industries, nearly a million years ago, the progress of human skill is here traced until stone tools were gradually replaced by iron, perhaps no more than a thousand years ago. This is the first book to treat the prehistory of East Africa as a whole.

THE ETRUSCANS

M. Pallottino

A 310

Before the Romans could establish their empire they had first to conquer and unify the other cities and peoples in Italy. The most powerful and highly civilized of these other peoples were the Etruscans. In this study Professor Pallottino discusses the origins, culture, religion, and language of this ancient and little known civilization which flourished so brilliantly 2,500 years ago.

This translation by J. A. Cremona of the third Italian edition contains maps and diagrams and an inset of 32 plates, showing some of the wonderful objects that have survived the neglect of succeeding generations.

ROME BEYOND THE IMPERIAL FRONTIERS

Sir Mortimer Wheeler

A 335

The Roman Empire extended from the Clyde to the Tigris, but far beyond these boundaries Roman goods penetrated through trade and 'drift'. The extent of this penetration is illustrated by the occurrence of wares from the same Italic factories in Britain on the one hand, and in southern India, 6,000 miles away, on the other. For the Indian material, the author's own excavations are in an important measure responsible, notably in the discovery of a Romano-Indian trading-station on the shores of the Bay of Bengal. To this trading-station Roman table-wares and wines were carried in large quantities by sea and land during the first century A.D.; while in Central Asia contacts of a comparable kind profoundly affected the development of an important school of art. In Africa, south of the Roman provinces, French and Italian exploration has revealed Roman relics in the depths of the Sahara, and in Europe, beyond the frontiers of the Rhine and Danube, rich deposits of Roman glass and metal-wares have long been known. The present book brings these far-flung discoveries up to date in a succinct and readable form, with the aid of many plates and maps.

'Sir Mortimer Wheeler gallantly professes indebtedness to his predecessors .. but his claim to have added occasionally to their material and to "give it perhaps a new actuality and a new perspective" is altogether too modest.'
— *The Times Literary Supplement*

THE PELICAN
HISTORY OF THE WORLD

It is often urged that world history is best written without the limitations of frontiers, that, for example, a history of the development of Western Europe has more historical validity than 'nationalist' histories of France, Germany, the Low Countries, and Britain. Nevertheless it is national character, national development, and national power, which incite the curiosity of most of us, and it is these things which seem to be behind most of the international problems with which we are faced to-day. Therefore, in preparing the plan of THE PELICAN HISTORY OF THE WORLD the Editor, J. E. Morpurgo, has decided that the old and familiar emphasis upon national history has meant sufficient to justify its continuance in this series.

Each volume is written by a specialist, and the emphasis given to such matters as trade, religion, politics, foreign relations, intellectual and social life, varies and must vary between volume and volume, but the interplay of nationalisms is as much part of national history as internal events, and it is hoped that THE PELICAN HISTORY OF THE WORLD will be both a series of national histories and, in the true sense, a history of the modern world.

VOLUMES NOW READY

A HISTORY OF MODERN CHINA by *Kenneth Scott Latourette* (A 302)

A HISTORY OF THE UNITED STATES; VOL 1: COLONIES TO NATION; VOL. 2: NATION TO WORLD POWER by *J. E. Morpurgo and Russel B. Nye, Professor at Michigan State College* (A 313, A 314)

IN PREPARATION

HISTORY OF MODERN FRANCE by *J. A. Cobban, Professor of French History, University College, London*

HISTORY OF SPAIN AND PORTUGAL by *W. C. Atkinson, Stevenson Professor of Spanish, Glasgow University*

THE GREEKS

H. D. F. Kitto

'The best introduction that I have ever read to Ancient Greece. The author's liveliness of mind and style has enabled him to make a mass of information appetizing and digestible.' – Raymond Mortimer in *The Sunday Times* (A 220)

THE ROMANS

R. H. Barrow

'He has succeeded in conveying to the modern reader what is best worth remembering about the qualities which make up the genius of the Roman people.' – *The Times Educational Supplement* (A 196)

THE HITTITES

O. R. Gurney

The story of the rediscovery of the historical Hittites, a great race of Asia Minor, as the result of recent excavation. It describes their history, society, law, code, religion, literature, arts, warfare, and language (A 259)

THE LEGACY OF THE ANCIENT WORLD

W. G. de Burgh

The story of the triple legacy of faith, freedom, and law, which came to us from Israel, Greece, and Rome, to make up the unity of Western civilized life. 2 vols. (A 284, A 285)

ELECTRICITY
Eric de Ville

This is the story of a strange source of power, the discovery of which has revolutionized the conditions in which men live. Who first realized the existence of electricity? Where does it come from? How can it be explained? These are some of the questions answered in this book, which tells the story from the earliest discoveries of Dr Gilbert, physician to Elizabeth I, to the most recent work on electronics (A 323)

INTRODUCTION TO TYPOGRAPHY
Oliver Simon

A handbook for those interested in book production, which deals with many of the typographic problems which normally arise in each stage of printing a book, from the half-title at the beginning right through to the index at the end. There are also chapters on Choosing a Type Face, The Printing of Plays, and The Printing of Poetry, Illustrations, Binding, etc. (A 288)*

PRELUDE TO MATHEMATICS
W. W. Sawyer

In *Mathematician's Delight*, one of the most popular Pelicans so far published, W. W. Sawyer described the traditional mathematics of the engineer and scientist. In this new book the emphasis is not on those branches of mathematics which have great practical utility, but on those which are exciting in themselves; mathematics which is strange, novel, apparently impossible; for instance, an arithmetic in which no number is bigger than four. These topics are preceded by an analysis of that enviable attribute 'the mathematical mind' (A 327)

Not for sale in the U.S.A.

MARGARET MEAD

Coming of Age in Samoa

A 127

During this century we have become steadily more conscious of the effect of a civilization upon the individuals within it. Psychologists have explained how the treatment received by a child during its formative years has a major influence on its character in later life. And anthropologists, by studying man in diverse settings, have supported this theory with practical evidence. In order to collect information of this kind, Dr Mead went to Samoa, a South Sea Island. She concentrated upon the girls and women of the community, speaking their language and living in the conditions in which they live.

Growing Up in New Guinea

A 117

On the island of Manus, Margaret Mead found an isolated community untouched by missionaries or foreign trade. Here she watched the children grow up – schooled as babies to the hazards of the sea, sure-footed, quick-handed, with perfect physical adjustment to life.

Starting with one small section of human society, the author goes on in the second part of her book to the larger aspects of educational and emotional problems in the 'civilized' world of to-day. Like *Coming of Age in Samoa*, it comments critically and provocatively on a number of vital problems of modern life.

Not for sale in the U.S.A. or Canada

Archaeological Books by

SIR LEONARD WOOLLEY

*

Ur of the Chaldees

A 27

An account of the excavations that have taken place in Ur over a number of years, and particularly the recent expeditions sponsored by the University Museum of Pennsylvania and the British Museum under the directorship of the author of this book.

Digging up the Past

A 4

In this book Sir Leonard Woolley explains in detail what archaeology is all about, describing the preliminary organization of a 'dig', the delicate processes of getting inside a site, and the subsequent analysis of the evidence which has been brought to light. The text is illustrated by a fine series of plates covering many of the processes, and the discoveries of archaeology in Ur, Italy, Palestine, Knossos, Egypt, and Scandinavia.

A Forgotten Kingdom

A 261

An important new book by Sir Leonard Woolley which was published for the first time as a Pelican early in 1953. It is a record of the results obtained from the excavation of two mounds, Atchana and Al Mina, in the Turkish Hatay, with 24 plates and numerous text figures.

WHAT HAPPENED IN HISTORY

Gordon Childe

A 108

'Professor V. Gordon Childe is one of the foremost pre-historians. He has travelled widely and has done much work of great importance to the specialist; he has, as it were, personally added many bricks to the edifice of pre-historic knowledge. But he has also long realized that prehistory and early history form a continuum, and that, by standing back and contemplating the whole, many general conclusions can be arrived at with regard to the rise and fall of civilizations ...

'For this reason a special welcome must be accorded to Professor Childe's fascinating little book now under re-view. In it he discusses the changes in material well-being and mental outlook which have taken place throughout the ages up to the break-up of the Roman Empire. He gives us a brief survey of what he describes as Palaeolithic and Mesolithic savagery, of Neolithic barbarism, of the rise of the Metal Age cultures, and so on until a climax was reached as a result of the Old World unity made possible by the exploits of Alexander the Great. Finally, there is a stimulating chapter with the author's views about the decline and fall of the ancient world ...

'This more than worth-while book contains many facts – the background material for the study; but it is primarily intended to stimulate thought and to help the reader to understand the general story of human development and, maybe, to draw lessons which will help when our own civilization, now in danger of collapse, is once again in process of reconstruction.' – M. C. Burkitt, in *Nature*.

THE ANCIENT WORLD

T. R. Glover

A 120

The civilization of the Western World was born many centuries ago on the shores of the Mediterranean, and in this survey of its origin Dr Glover has reconstructed the achievements and discoveries of the Greeks and Romans. He was a scholar of great distinction who knew his sources intimately, but he reinforces his book-knowledge of the Ancient World by many prolonged journeys in this historic region. What he has to tell us, therefore, of the growth and influence of these empires of antiquity is illuminated by his own vivid response to the environment where so much history was made.*

THE ARCHAEOLOGY OF PALESTINE

W. F. Albright

A 199

The tiny country on the Eastern Mediterranean coast which has played so outstanding a part in human history has yielded up in recent years so many of the secrets of its past that a popular summary of the results has long been overdue. Professor Albright, who has himself done so much to bring the treasures of its past to light, here tells the story of their gradual unearthing, of the building up of a connected picture of Palestine's history, and of the light thus thrown on human history in general and on the Old Testament story. An introductory chapter of the greatest interest tells how the archaeologist sets about his task.

* Not for sale in the U.S.A.

IRAN

R. Ghirshman

A 239

Midway between Mesopotamia and India, the meeting-ground of Semitic and Aryan influence, the cradle of a great religion which, in either of its modified forms of Mithraism or Manichaeism, might easily have become that of the Western world of to-day, Iran – Persia – has for three millennia been a meeting-place of peoples and a battleground of civilizations.

Its prehistory, now being uncovered by the efforts of Western and Russian scholars, has not hitherto been exhaustively and competently dealt with between the covers of a single volume in a way that will appeal to the general reader. Professor Ghirshman, who has spent many years in field research in Persia, here outlines its story from the earliest times until the great wars in which over centuries the Persian Empire tried its strength with Greece and Rome, leaving the issue undecided until its unique Iranian civilization was reshaped and transformed by the Islamic conquest.